Fat Tire Flyer

REPACK AND THE BIRTH OF MOUNTAIN BIKING

CHARLIE KELLY

VELO
press

Boulder, Colorado

3002 Sterling Circle, Suite 100
Boulder, Colorado 80301-2338 USA
(303) 440-0601 · Fax (303) 444-6788 · E-mail velopress@competitorgroup.com

Distributed in the United States and Canada by Ingram Publisher Services

A Cataloging-in-Publication record for this book is available from the Library of Congress.
ISBN 978-1-937715-16-8

For information on purchasing VeloPress books, please call (800) 811-4210, ext. 2138, or visit www.velopress.com.

This paper meets the requirements of ANSI/NISO Z39.48-1992 (Permanence of Paper).

Cover design by Voltage, Ltd.
Cover and author photos by Wende Cragg/Rolling Dinosaur Archive
Back cover photo by Jerry Riboli
Interior photograph credits on page 252
Photo retouching by Andy Castellano
Interior design by Vicki Hopewell

Text set in Titillium and Warnock

14 15 16 / 10 9 8 7 6 5 4 3 2 1

This work is dedicated to the memory of Professor John Finley Scott, my friend and mentor, who had the right ideas but at the wrong time. He was the first to believe that two unlikely candidates were on to something important. John introduced me to the concept of word processing, which turned out to be useful in composing this manuscript, and he had that double-decker bus, too.

contents

FOREWORD

Unlike other people central to the development of the mountain bike, Charlie Kelly has not spent his entire working life in the bike industry. But in the early days of the sport, pretty much everyone who rode a mountain bike either knew Charlie personally or knew of him. Charlie was one of the main instigators of the sport.

In 1976 Charlie organized the downhill time trial called Repack—the crucible of mountain biking. From towns all around the base of Mount Tamalpais, we rode to Repack to compete and share ideas, spurring the bike's evolution. In 1979 Charlie and his buddy Gary Fisher founded MountainBikes, launching the industry. The following year Charlie created *Fat Tire Flyer*, mountain biking's first magazine and for several years the voice of the movement.

Charlie is first to recognize that people had been riding dirt since the advent of bikes, but as this book shows, the lineage of the Olympic sport of mountain biking runs directly back to Repack.

I first met Charlie in the summer of 1972. I was just out of high school and was hitchhiking home to Marin after visiting friends a couple of hundred miles north. I'd been standing for a while with my thumb out on Highway 101 in Novato. Having been on the road all day, I no doubt looked more than a bit disheveled in the waning

light. But an early-'50s Chevy pickup pulled over, and the two guys in the cab offered me a ride. After brief introductions I learned that the passenger, Charlie Kelly, was, like me, a cyclist—a rarity in those days. He and the driver, Fred Wolf, were a hilarious pair, and for the next 20 miles they regaled me with stories. Charlie took the lead.

Riding along in that truck, I had no reason to think that this Charlie Kelly guy would have any influence on my life. But I met him again later that year. He was helping to organize an upstart Marin County road-racing club, Velo-Club Tamalpais (VCT), and we younger racers were joining up.

When our club meetings grew unwieldy, Charlie took a spin to the local library to learn how groups got things accomplished. At the following month's meeting we found ourselves operating under *Robert's Rules of Order*. To me it was an early indication that, as relaxed and entertaining as he was, Charlie had a knack for moving things forward. His ideas and work would achieve just the level of organization required to transform chaos into productive enterprise.

I quickly learned that Charlie was a man always with a plan, and that plan started with getting smart about a situation. His leadership qualities were born not out of any ego-driven need to lead but rather

Charlie Kelly recording notes with Joe Breeze looking on. Mineral King Valley, September 1978.

racers. Outsiders looked askance at the beat-up bikes, but we loved their soulful essence and the fact that they opened up new terrain for us, right out our back door. Our area's hilly, twisty paved roads made for scenic and challenging road-bike riding, but our off-road experience was an intensely distilled version. Our fat-tire bikes doubled our riding territory and tripled our fun.

What with all the fun, the old clunker bikes with their mild-steel frames were prone to breakage. Charlie, tall and one of the heavier riders, broke his fair share of frames and was seeking a better machine. As I had been designing and building road-racing frames since 1974, Charlie asked repeatedly if I'd make him a new bike for off-road riding. I was focused on racing and a cross-country tandem record attempt with Otis Guy—and of course in my spare time I was having a ball on my old fat-tire bikes. So I put off the challenge.

But Charlie made it happen. He persisted until, in 1977, he plunked down $300 of enticement and got me to commit. I had just patched up my '41 Schwinn yet again and knew it was time to shift gears. When word got out that I was drawing up a frame for Charlie, more orders rolled in. The resulting first 10 Breezers of 1977–1978 immediately changed people's perception of what a fat-tire bike could be—my own perception included.

Charlie Kelly and Gary Fisher saw the market. After a few years assembling old Schwinn-type clunkers for the eager riders of Marin, they founded a business in 1979 to sell brand-new fat-tire bikes with frames made by Tom Ritchey. Having been there to see their MountainBikes business start and grow, I'm in a good position to appreciate the blend of expertise, organization, persistence, and unfailing

from quiet, thorough study followed by a drive to contribute for the greater good. And always in his approach there's been humor, often subtle and often Twain-like.

Velo-Club Tamalpais grew and became our extended family. We trained 200 to 400 miles a week, intimately learning the roads in a 75-mile radius, and we got to know each other well. On training rides and trips to races, Charlie entertained us with stories, and I found myself in awe of his range of interests and knowledge.

In 1973 clubmate Marc Vendetti turned me on to fat-tire biking, which he'd done in high school in Larkspur. At Marc's suggestion I paid $5 for a 1941 Schwinn fatty, which I rode down Mount Tam and eventually to VCT meetings. Others in the club were doing the same, and these "clunkers" became the alter egos of our refined road humor that made that business work. Charlie usually describes it as seat-of-the-pants, and I have no doubt that he called upon every skill he had to keep it stitched together.

When Charlie founded *Fat Tire Flyer* in 1980, the sport was in good hands. He published it through much of the 1980s, inspiring the growing numbers of mountain bikers with his original angles and humor.

Charlie never let a good story languish, and he was a relentless chronicler of the sport. On our rides in faraway places such as the High Sierra he'd pull out his notepad at every break, no matter how windy or exposed the stopping point. On our annual treks over Pearl Pass from Crested Butte to Aspen, there he'd be at the Cumberland Basin campsite getting down his notes, leading Gary Fisher to comment in 1979, "Charlie Kelly, master of the metaphor." Later I learned that reporting was in Charlie's gene pool. His ancestors headed west long ago in covered wagons, and his grandmother, as a girl, kept a diary of their travels.

In mountain biking, Charlie found something he was really good at. Or several things: race promotion, starting a business, marketing, writing. And the sport needed someone like him, keen-eyed and adaptable, with wide-ranging talents that he could develop as needed. He and Gary were natural leaders, and they used their gifts to bring the sport to a wide audience.

When *Fat Tire Flyer* folded, Charlie made piano moving his full-time job. That's not too distant from his life as a rock-and-roll roadie, but it's a challenge few would take on. In the hills, narrow streets, and steep stairways of Northern California, moving pianos—includ-ing grand pianos—is far from straightforward. The job took all kinds of talent. Charlie designed his own equipment and worked at it for over 30 years.

But in those early years Charlie was integral to the fun of mountain biking. He'd phone around, and we'd be there: Repack racing, Appetite Seminars, Klunkerz Banquets, rides near and far. Velo-Club Tam's full-moon road rides soon took to the dirt and followed the moon a good ways across the sky—sometimes to moonset and sunrise. It was a glorious time, being with friends, spinning a few miles, kicking back in the tall grass and gazing skyward on summer nights, talking about anything and everything. This was our family of cycling, our bond strengthened by fat-tire adventures.

The bicycle held our wheel of friends tight. Few beyond our circle had any idea what joy these fat wheels could bring. We couldn't keep it to ourselves, nor did we want to.

—Joe Breeze

chapter 1

EPIPHANY

I wish I had been able to love bicycles and bicycling from the earliest days of my childhood, but it was not to be. I had a couple of bikes, but I didn't have as much fun on them as a kid should have, and it never occurred to me that I would ever have a passion for bicycles. I assumed I would outgrow bicycles when I grew up.

It took long enough to grow into them. I was one of the last kids in my grade to learn how to ride a bike. I didn't have one myself, and my parents were probably concerned that a kid who came home bleeding now and then—even though he didn't own a bike—would die on one if he had one. It was embarrassing not to be able to ride a two-wheeler when it was a skill all my friends took for granted. But how was I going to learn to ride when I didn't have a bike to practice on?

I don't know where Dick Kircher and Bobby Mushen ended up because I lost track of them after the third grade, but they started me on the

Not a bike rider yet, but you can see the gleam in my eye.

road to bicycling notoriety. Bobby had a 20-inch bike, and the two of them coached me until I could ride it. I never had training wheels or a parent running along holding me up. I just had two friends my age who told me in their own way what to do, and I learned in a couple of afternoons.

My first coasting experience was in a little red wagon when I was about 5. One of the older kids talked me into getting in and coasting down the hill. I got about 20 feet before it flipped, and I had to run home for first aid.

My next coasting experience was even more memorable. When I was in the first grade, my friend Tim down the street had a Flexy Flyer, made by the sled company but with rubber wheels instead of runners. The idea is that you lie prone and go very fast while leading with your face. Tim lived next to a small hill, and we were working our way up the sidewalk starting one square higher every time, then zooming around the corner. On my last run—ever—I came around the blind turn and hit a rock on the sidewalk, then a tree. I ran home bleeding from my head, and that afternoon I got my first stitches.

My downhill racing career peaked in 1954. I was in the fourth grade when the local Cub Scouts held their annual coaster derby on Throckmorton Avenue in front of Old Mill School. My father designed and built an ungainly but effective coaster out of a couple of tricycles, a cheese box, and my old booster seat. He knew enough about coasters to build a damping system into the steering to cut down on front-end oscillation, the bane of rope steering. He also had a machinist polish the ends of the axles to a mirror finish and added graphite to sewing-machine oil for lubricant.

After a couple of test runs in the Park School playground we went to the races. I wore a leather football helmet and won all my heats, and a few days before my ninth birthday I was coaster derby

The peak of my coaster derby career, assembled from a couple of tricycles, a cheese box, and—hidden inside—my father's truly sophisticated steering system.

champion of Mill Valley, with a trophy and my name and picture in the paper and everything. Maybe I didn't have a bike, but I sure had the best coaster.

I never drove it again. In fact, it never went another inch. Apprehensive of what the kids might do with a coaster and lots of hills nearby and considering my history of coming home damaged from less-formal coasting contests, my father disassembled it and put it away for my brother Jim's shot at the title the next year.

The coaster derby didn't take place the next year or the year after that. The coaster axles rusted in the

rafters, the trophy remained at our house instead of going to a new champion, and Jim got cheated out of seeing his name on it next to mine.

My parents were not about to buy me a bike, so I bought my first one myself. I found an ad in the local paper for a used bike, and I saw that the address was just a few blocks from our house. I walked over and for $5 I purchased my first bike. I was about 9 years old.

It was junk. I don't know what brand it was because it had no label, and it had already been painted once with green house paint. Even in the early '50s, $5 didn't buy you much of a used bike. The fork was bent, and I didn't realize until years later that this was the reason I could never ride no-hands the way all my friends could. It never occurred to me that a fork could be straightened. At random times while I was pedaling, the crank would spin freely for half a turn. If you happened to be standing up on a hill when that happened, it would wake you right up. I learned to ride defensively, waiting for the slack chain to strike without warning. Sometimes the coaster brake worked; sometimes the crank spun backward for half a turn before it engaged.

My friends had stopped laughing at me for not being able to ride a bike; now they laughed at the bike I was riding. But it was all I had or was going to get, and it served its purpose for a few years. I painted it, got new fenders for it out of the Sears catalog, and found that it would work better if I rebuilt the coaster brake now and then. I delivered papers from it with canvas bags hanging from the handlebars, but I would rather walk to school than be seen on it there.

My younger brother, Jim, had better luck with his first bike, which cost him $15, bought used from a neighbor. It was another no-name, painted orange. He got it during our Easter vacation, but he was at the time seriously lagging in his arithmetic at school, and he spent that week of freedom working on math instead of riding his first bike. His rode perfectly, and he had better bikes than mine until I was well into adulthood.

When I was about 12, Jim and I were permitted to spend money from our college-fund bank accounts on new bikes, which we purchased from Montgomery Ward for about $60. We got identical Hercules Hawthorne English lightweight three-speeds. Fast. Light. *New.* I was in heaven.

For about a week.

I was showing off the speed of my lightweight multiple-gear bike to a neighbor, Kevin Ward. Racing him down the street, I looked back to see how badly I was beating him, and I ran directly into the back of his father's 1955 Chevy, which was parked in its usual spot in front of the Ward house.

The car was undamaged, but my beautiful new three-speed racer was never again the same. I had bent the fork (shades of my first bike), and once again I was so unfamiliar with bike shops and their capabilities that it never occurred to me that the damage could be repaired. Rather than expose my stupidity to my parents, I shut up and lived with my damaged bike and rode Jim's whenever he let me. That first week on my three-speed represented most of the enjoyment I had on my two bicycles during my entire childhood. Having fun on a bicycle was put off for more than a decade, and until I reached the magic age of 16 and got a driver's license, I was either a pedestrian or a passenger on the top bar of Fred Wolf's Schwinn three-speed, which he had modified with high-rise handlebars.

Jim was not affected by my problems, and he treasured his own bike. Several years later he added a three-speed rear cluster and a derailleur to convert it to nine speeds. While in high school, he was cited by the California Highway Patrol for taking it across a freeway bridge, and my father successfully defended him in traffic court by pointing out that there was no other possible route connecting the two points he was traveling between. When I was 18 I borrowed Jim's bike to ride about 5 miles to see a girl I knew, and she was thoroughly impressed by the great distance I had covered on a bicycle on her behalf.

One of Jim's high school friends was an Irish kid whose family was living in the United States, and he had brought his bike with him. One day I came home from school, and I saw a strange bike parked in front of the house, a Raleigh 10-speed. It had five different cogs on the rear wheel and two in front. This was before Jim had added a derailleur to his own bike, and I was mystified by the arrangement. I saw immediately that the different sizes of cogs gave it multiple-gear capability, but I couldn't figure out how the chain moved from one to another. I asked Patrick how his bike worked, and he showed me the levers that shifted the gears. My only previous experience was with the internally shifted three-speed, so I moved the shift lever and looked down at the wheel to see how the chain would move. Patrick nearly fell down laughing as he explained that you had to be pedaling in order to shift the gears.

When my sister, Edith, went off to college during my senior year in high school in 1962, she spent about $100 on her new bike, a Schwinn

Varsity 10-speed with a girl's frame. Although I was impressed with the gearing, I couldn't believe how heavy the bike was.

In any case, between the ages of 18 and 23 I do not believe I stepped over a bike. As a teenager I had no apparent physical skills other than the ability to walk for a long time. I was one of the youngest and smallest members of my class, and my athletic ability was equivalent to that of boys a couple of years behind me in school. I was a slow runner, and I couldn't throw a ball very far or hit one with a bat. I never completed a single pull-up as a teenager, I couldn't climb the rope that hung from the ceiling of the gym, and I was the last chosen for any team. I liked to play basketball in spite of my limited ability, but my ankles were not designed for the sport, and I suffered a long series of sprains in pickup games.

Jim was a good swimmer and earned a letter on the swim team, but for me there was not even a remote chance of participating in a varsity sport. The only glimmer of hope took place in early 1963 during my senior year, when President John F. Kennedy stirred up a short-lived fad for 50-mile hikes by observing that an old marine standard was that troops should be able to complete a forced march of 50 miles in 20 hours. For about a

month it seemed that everyone was talking about 50-mile hikes.

Accordingly some 400 people walked out of the Redwood High School parking lot early on a February morning to see whether they could walk 50 miles in 20 hours or less. Of that crowd, 97 walked back into the parking lot much later. Jim and I were numbers 12 and 13 of the finishers and did our 50 miles in about 13 hours. It was the first time in my life that I had been better than most people at any physical activity. I wasn't fast, but toughness had to count for something. After my high school graduation and too late to do me any good in gym class, I grew 4 or 5 more inches, finally packed on some muscle, and somewhat to my surprise ended up a 6-foot-tall adult male.

After I had left high school behind and had a driver's license, I never expected to ride a bicycle again. When I attended Tamalpais High School, bicycles were so uncool that not a single student rode a bicycle to school, and the school had no facility for parking bicycles. After all, bikes were for kids, and you never saw a grown-up on one.

My education can best be described as indifferent. Although on standardized tests I scored in the top 1 percent of those taking such tests, my teachers faced the dilemma of assigning grades to

a kid who was likable and smart and who did well on tests, but who never turned in a lick of homework, a discipline then considered essential to higher learning. The result was a high school GPA just above C level and, after high school, living at home and attending College of Marin, a community junior college, rather than experiencing a university. I had not a clue as to what aspect of life I was studying for, but the alternative to going to school was compulsory military service. The draft.

By the time I hit 20 I had flunked out of even this unchallenging level of formal education, and I was conscripted into the U.S. Army, never to return to a college classroom. Two years later, in February 1968, I hit the civilian streets again, a free man unencumbered by the "draft problem" then being faced by my high school classmates as they finished college. Within a few months of leaving the army, I had joined some of my friends from College of Marin who had a rock band called the Sons of Champlin. They needed someone to handle equipment, someone physically robust who could drive a truck and who wouldn't be drafted, and I fit the bill. For most of the next nine years that would be my job.

When I got out of the army, my first order of business was to get some wheels under me. Four wheels, not two. With a motor. The thought of a bicycle did not cross my mind. Nobody rode a bicycle.

For $250 I bought a very used Peugeot 403 four-door sedan that lasted me almost a year before my Sons of Champlin friends drove it into the ground. Everyone in the band used my car, and even when I rode in it myself, I was often a passenger in the backseat. When it stopped for the last time somewhere in the San Geronimo Valley, I was not in it, and the driver walked away from it. I never saw my car again.

I was faced with a transportation problem. I didn't have much money to replace my car, so if I bought something used, whatever I got was sure to be a wreck. I had seen the writing on the wall and knew that the band would appropriate any working set of wheels. If I got another car, it was destined for the same fate as the previous one.

For a while I got around by hitchhiking, hardly an efficient or dependable means of transportation. If I was going to get a car, it made sense to put it off long enough to save up a little more money in the pursuit of something that would last a little longer than the Peugeot 403. Meanwhile, I still had places to go and no good way to get there. In the spring of 1969 a friend mentioned that someone

had left a bicycle at his house, and the bike had been in the basement ever since. If I wanted it, I could have it.

I had hit bottom. I needed a bicycle just to get around. Nobody rode a bike in those days, but I was forced to.

The bike was a Schwinn Varsity 10-speed, the boy's version of the same bike my sister had purchased when she went off to college. It was in terrible condition and very heavy. I oiled the chain, and at the age of 23 I took my first ride on a 10-speed, fiddling with the shifters to see what they did. One thing was certain. None of my friends would borrow my wheels.

My first ride was interesting. The bike was not in working condition, and I had zero cycling skills, but I had to get somewhere and that was how I was going to get there. When I hit a rough patch of pavement and couldn't operate the brakes effectively, I crashed and landed on my face. After gathering myself up, I rode toward my friend's house, where I had been sleeping on the couch in lieu of traditional housing, and on the way I was bitten by a dog. That was the only time in 40 years of cycling that I was bitten by a dog, but at the time all I could think was that it was one dog bite and one crash for one ride, a ratio that didn't look promising.

The bike was crap, but it was all I had, and I kept riding it around. I managed to fall off it a couple more times. I began to think that if bikes weren't any more fun than this, I would have to explore some other possibility. Shortly after getting it I went to a concert at the Family Dog on the Great Highway, where I ended up talking to a girl about how I was getting around on a bike, but my bike was crap. She told me that there was a 10-speed bike in her garage that her brother had left there. Since he didn't ride it, and it was in her way, she wouldn't mind if I exchanged my crappy bike for it. She told me it was a Peugeot, and weren't they supposed to be good bikes? I didn't know one way or the other, but I was familiar with the brand name from my erstwhile car. Over the years I would hear from a number of people with no cycling experience that Peugeots were supposed to be good bikes. I had heard the same about my car from people who hadn't owned one.

I took her up on her offer and exchanged the Schwinn for a Peugeot UO-8 that was not in much better condition than the Schwinn but was a marginally better bike. Marginally. This bike had sold new for just more than $100 in the late '60s; it was no longer new by the time I got it, but at least it worked, and for the next year and a half

I rode it everywhere I went. I had it equipped with the thickest and heaviest clincher tires, on steel rims, because I figured ruggedness was preferable to lightness. Somehow I figured out toe clips and straps, and I put them on the bike and learned how to use them.

In 1969 there were no bike paths or bike routes, and you didn't see a lot of people on bicycles, even in Marin County where they are now everywhere. Most of the riders you did see were kids, because adults did not embarrass themselves by being seen on a bicycle. As my rides took me around the county, I noticed a strange thing. Even though I was relatively inexperienced and was riding a cheap bike, among the few other adult riders I encountered I never seemed to see anyone who rode as fast as I did.

In a day of riding I might see a dozen or so other people actually riding their bikes to get somewhere. For the first time in my life I found a sport that I was actually good at, and since I didn't know any better, I assumed I had a cool bike and that I was fast on it. Neither of those was actually true.

When the Sons of Champlin disbanded in 1970—temporarily, it turned out—I started spending even more of my time on my bike. My first long ride was to Santa Rosa, where I spent the night at a friend's house and rode home the next day. The total one-way distance was less than 50 miles, an easy distance by current standards, but my friends were universally astonished that I could ride that far in a single day.

My second long ride was from Santa Cruz back to Marin County. Santa Cruz is on the coast south of San Francisco; I got a ride down with someone, spent the night, and rode home the next day on the coastal route, Highway 1, a distance approaching 100 miles.

No one was less prepared for a 100-mile ride than I was in 1970. I had brought very few clothes with me, since I didn't want to tote luggage all that way. I wore cutoff jeans instead of cycling shorts and ordinary light athletic shoes instead of cycling shoes with a stiffened sole. My bike was cheap and heavy. I didn't eat much breakfast and jumped on my bike early in the morning. On the way out of Santa Cruz I spotted a pair of pliers lying in the roadway, so I picked them up and later needed them to make a minor repair.

Highway 1 north of Santa Cruz is scenic and very hilly, and the settlements are far apart. That day I had my first experience with bonking. It hit me in a hurry, and I could barely keep the bike moving. Struggling up a long hill, I spotted in the gutter a shriveled-up orange that had no business being where it was. Very little in the way of food has looked as good to me since as that tiny orange did then. I pounced on it, and it was refreshing all out of proportion to the amount of energy it contained. It got me over that hill and into Half Moon Bay, where I could get something to eat.

I was surprised to find that it took less than seven hours to get home. By midafternoon I was in Marin County, where my friends would be shocked at the distance I had covered and the relatively short time it had taken.

I rode my cheap Peugeot through the summer and fall of 1970. I spent the summer of 1970 in Boulder, Colorado, a college town where there were plenty of bikes and I was not out of place as an adult rider. I regularly rode up Boulder Canyon to Four Mile Canyon Road and took the turnoff to a house where I spent the night now and then. This was a climb of 6 or 7 miles, and for the last time in my life I weighed less than 170 pounds. I always rode alone, and I had no idea how tough I was getting, because I had no one else to compare myself to.

After returning to Marin County in the fall of 1970, I had an epiphany. While riding across the College of Marin campus, I encountered another cyclist who was riding the most beautiful bicycle I had ever seen. I stopped the rider and demanded information about his bike, a Mondia painted in rainbow colors. The rider worked in a San Rafael bike shop called Wheels Unlimited, where these bikes were sold, and he patiently explained sew-up tires and Campagnolo components to me. I was stunned at how light his bike was and determined to get one like it. I had no idea how I would do this, since I was then only marginally employed as the sound man for a San Anselmo nightclub called the Lion's Share. The job didn't pay much, but it left my days open for riding.

In December of that year a chance opportunity led to my first good bike. An eccentric musician was putting together an avant-garde recording called *The Ghost Opera* by splicing together about 130 snippets collected from several recording sessions. He needed a studio with an eight-track recorder. I was living in a recording studio at the time, and the owner allowed me to handle the tedious task of engineering and splicing for this project in exchange for a cut of the studio rental.

The producer and I worked in the studio for 36 straight hours, and at $15 an hour my share of the studio rental came to more than $500. It was the most money I made in such a short period until

years afterward, and I immediately spent $200 on my new bike, a Peugeot PX-10. All I knew about this bike was that in spite of my experience with a cheap model, Peugeots were supposed to be good bikes according to everyone who had an opinion and didn't have a bike. Since I had already owned a car and another bike from the same company, I stuck with the brand name I knew.

It wasn't as though I had a lot of bikes to choose from. In 1970 there were two bikes on the market that sold for about $200 and were light and equipped with sew-up tires, the Mercier and the Peugeot PX-10. I knew that Wheels Unlimited sold Mondias, but they cost at least $100 more than a PX-10. There was a Peugeot dealer in Palo Alto, where my girlfriend lived, so I walked into Sugden and Lynch Cycles and chose a bike on display.

I made a poor choice, but I probably made the owners of the shop happy by taking a turkey off their hands. Since I have long legs, I thought I should get a bigger frame. Instead of a frame measuring in the neighborhood of 23 inches, I picked a 25-inch frame, far too big for me. Then of course I had to get the funny shorts and the special road-riding shoes with a slotted cleat.

In spite of being a bad fit, the PX-10 was brand-new, light, and far superior to my previous bike,

and it served me for six or seven months. My new bike had sew-up tires, which I had no experience with and had only seen on one other bike before I bought mine. Fortunately I rode for four months without a flat, until I had worn out my rear tire and decided to put on the one I had carried as a spare. I was lucky that I hadn't had to deal with my first sew-up change on the side of the road because it took me several hours and a trip to the bike shop for advice to accomplish it. For the next several years I had a love-hate relationship with sew-ups. You needed them if you wanted to go fast, but the expense and the hassle would have driven any but the most fanatical riders away from cycling. The best sew-ups were made from silk, pretty expensive stuff to use for a bike tire, and the expense made it a good idea to patch them if you could. Bikes, I found, were a lot of fun, but the delicate wheels and tires on the nicest bikes were a hassle.

The next summer, in 1971, I was riding my trusty, if too big, PX-10 when I met Gary Fisher, a meeting that soon changed the direction of both our lives.

SPIDEY

Gary Fisher and I were destined to meet, because two guys with such similar interests could not operate for long in Marin County without eventually encountering each other. The catalyst was a girl I have never seen since. In 1971 I was seeing Rose, a Grateful Dead fan, and she told me that she knew a guy she described as being just like me. She knew him as "Spider," and she said he was a hippie bicycle fanatic with hair even longer than mine, and he hung around with the Dead. She said if we ever got together we would have a lot in common. That turned out to be something of an understatement.

One afternoon I was riding through San Anselmo, and I spotted someone who could only be Spider, riding with another fellow. He had long, skinny arms and legs and blond hair down to the middle of his back. He looked like the kind of person who would be called Spider. I rode up and asked him whether he was Spider.

Gary Fisher after claiming
a Repack win in 1977.
Gary was always a fast rider,
whether on a road bike,
a clunker, or a mountain bike.

He corrected me. "I'm 'Spidey,'" he said. It turned out that another member of the Dead "Party Krew" already went by the name of Spider. "But my name is really Gary."

I told him about our mutual friend, Rose, who had suggested that we would hit it off, and Gary introduced his companion as Marmaduke. "But his real name is John Dawson." Apparently I was the only cyclist who used his given name.

Gary was riding a bike I had never heard of, with the label "Paragon" on the downtube, while his friend was on a Mondia like the one that had captured my attention a year earlier.

I asked where they were going, figuring that wherever it was, I would go with them. I had never been on a ride with two other guys on good bikes. I didn't even know two other guys with good bikes.

Gary said, "We're riding down to the Grateful Dead office in San Rafael. Marmaduke plays in a band with Jerry Garcia called the New Riders of the

Purple Sage, and their first album is about to come out. We're going to look at the album cover art." I told them that I was the Sons of Champlin roadie and that I had worked on a lot of shows with the Dead. I don't remember whether I was invited or if I invited myself, but 15 minutes after I met these two guys, we were all sitting in the third-floor conference room at the Dead offices at Fifth and Lincoln in San Rafael, looking at dozens of drawings and photographs thrown across the big conference table. Marmaduke introduced the New Riders' bass player Dave Torbert to Gary and me, and the four of us listened to the acetate copy of their yet-unreleased album and pawed through all the graphic material. I had heard of this band, but I had never heard its music, and the album surprised me by how good it was. Within a couple of months it was more of a hit than anything the Grateful Dead had released to that point and remains a classic recording of Jerry at his peak on pedal steel guitar.

Dave and Marmaduke asked Gary and me what we thought of the various photographs and drawings. Gary and I were looking at each other, and I'm sure he was thinking what I was thinking, which was, "Why do you guys care what we think? You barely know us, and it's your album." In any event, we discussed some photographs taken in the

house that Marmaduke and guitarist David Nelson shared in Kentfield. I had not yet seen the place but would later spend a lot of time there. There was a series of photographs, including one with Jerry flipping the bird, which was a joke since he was missing most of the middle finger of his right hand. Gary and I agreed that it was the best photo, and it became the back cover of the album.

Gary was also intrigued by a drawing with a cactus and the letters "NRPS" in clouds, by Alton Kelley. We agreed that it was a catchy image. It became the front cover and the long-standing logo for the band, which Gary and I would not realize until the album was released. I was stunned when I saw the album on the shelves a few weeks later with the cover art that I had personally offered my opinion on. I have no doubt that the artwork decision took place in that room and at that very sitting because that was the way things worked in the Dead office. Even though Gary and I should have had nothing to say about it, we represented the critical votes. After about half an hour the meeting was adjourned, many compliments were given about the album, and it was time to go on a bike ride.

As the three of us left the office, Jerry showed up. He was then about 30 years old and already putting on weight. Marmaduke, in contrast, was

tiny, no taller than 5 feet 6 inches tall and about 120 pounds. Marmaduke chirped in his deep singer's voice that we were headed out to ride around China Camp, a loop of maybe 12 miles. Jerry made it clear that bicycle riding was not in his own future and that we wouldn't be running into him out there. Twenty years later I would be going for a bike ride with his fellow Grateful Dead guitarist, Bob Weir.

That ride around China Camp was the first time Gary and I rode together. I had been living on my new Peugeot for months, and Gary was the first good, experienced cyclist I had ever had the opportunity to ride with. Marmaduke had the nicest bike, a brand-new, full-Campy, Swiss Mondia with a rainbow paint job, but it was clear immediately that he was not in the same league with Gary and me.

It's the nature of the sport. In a crowd of riders new to each other, you have to find out who has what. I had never ridden with any other fast riders, but it was instinctive. Gary and I dropped Marmaduke easily and then for the last time in my life, I dropped Gary.

Gary was stunned because he was a real racer and I was just a geek with no experience and a marginal bike. The difference was that Gary had been

Tour del Mar race poster, August 1966. The race was promoted by Tom Preuss and the Belmont Bicycle Club. Tom helped found our Velo-Club Tamalpais in 1972.

out of organized racing for a couple of years and had been concentrating on his light show and the Dead Party Krew at the expense of bicycling. I had been doing little else than riding my bike.

Gary, like me, was then engaged in being a disappointment to his parents. He was not interested in academics, but now and then he reluctantly attended art classes to keep a little parental stipend coming in. He had been a bike racer as a kid, one of the youngest racers to be seen in the '60s in Northern California, but his long hair and rebellious nature had gotten him expelled from the Northern California Cycling Association by its legendary director, Bob Tetzlaff. In those days there were strict international rules about what bicycle racers could look like. They had to wear black shorts and white socks, and hair down to here was not going to cut it.

In a way, bike racing was to blame for Gary's long hair. He had raced at the 1966 Tour del Mar, where promoter Tom Preuss had hired a couple of hippie bands, the Grateful Dead and the Quicksilver Messenger Service, to play the post-race party. Gary had met the Dead there and had been accepted immediately as a Party Krew member, though he was still a teenager. From that point on he was immersed in the hip culture, and it would be years before he cut his hair. The staid world of bicycle racing would not tolerate his new image, and Gary could not tolerate the restrictions, so Gary gave up racing.

After graduating from Redwood High School, where he excelled in photography and shop classes, Gary used those

Gary raced cyclocross before most of us even knew it existed.

skills to put together a light show called *The Lightest Show on Earth* and worked at a few concerts. He lived cheaply and simply and sometimes got money from his parents, who were not thrilled and implored him to get a life and go back to school. At that time, if you couldn't play music, a light show was an artistic vehicle that made you part of the show, and it must have looked like an interesting avenue of expression. As things turned out, light shows were not a good long-term career choice, and by the time I met Gary the writing was on the wall and the light show wasn't.

When we met in 1971, Gary was living in Mill Valley in a big redwood water tank that he had converted into housing. At least that is what I was told, because I never saw the place. Most of the time Gary was at Marmaduke's house, which was far more comfortable. Within a few weeks of our first meeting, the New Riders' album had come out and the band was hot, so it was touring, and Gary was house-sitting for Marmaduke and David Nelson in their big house on Kent Avenue. The house was conveniently located 15 feet from the main north-south bike route through Marin County, and I made a practice of stopping by every time I came past to pick up Gary for a ride. We were not yet good friends, but we had plenty in common, and

he knew a lot more about bikes than I did, so it was instructive for me to ride with him and talk bikes.

Marmaduke had decided that his Mondia was not cool enough, so he put in an order for a custom bike with Albert Eisentraut, a Berkeley resident who at the time was the dean of American framebuilding. I was becoming all too aware of the shortcomings of my own bike; it was far too big for me and cheaply equipped in comparison to the Campagnolo-equipped bikes Gary and Marmaduke rode. Gary and Marmaduke constantly pointed out that I needed to upgrade to a bike worthy of my ability.

Marmaduke's family was wealthy and lived in an enormous mansion near Palo Alto. He made frequent trips down there to see his psychiatrist, and on several of those occasions I threw my bike into the trunk of his BMW and then rode home to get some miles in. On one of those trips I encountered another rider, and we started talking bikes. It turned out that he had a Colnago that he wanted to sell, and after some negotiation I returned a week later and bought it.

Colnago! Awesome! Next to a legendary and unobtainable Cinelli, this was the coolest bike on the planet. All Campagnolo and a much better fit than my Peugeot. Now I was a real cyclist. I had

Gary was one of the youngest racers
in 1960s Northern California.

an Italian bike and the black, scratchy wool shorts with the chamois liner that turned into a plank every time you washed them, along with a growing collection of wool jerseys.

Sometime in 1972 I rode my bike to the Marin City Flea Market, looking for some furniture for the house I rented in San Anselmo. I found a table and chairs, but I had no way to get them to the house. I ran into Gary, and he had his van with him, so we put my furniture in it, and he said he would drop it off for me.

Several days went by. I was starting to think Gary had stolen my $25 table, but he finally showed up and helped me carry it into the two-bedroom cottage at 21 Humbolt Street. I had just lost my last roommate, who had moved out to live with his girlfriend. Gary looked around and observed that it was a pretty nice place. He asked who else lived there, and I told him I was fresh out of roommates. I invited him to share it with me, and in a few days he moved in. For the next decade we would be joined at the hip, first as roommates and later as business associates.

21 HUMBOLT

The house at 21 Humbolt quickly became bike central. Gary Fisher and I customized our living arrangement by putting bike hooks in the living room ceiling and using our bikes as a decorative room divider. By then Gary had replaced his aging Paragon with a Colnago almost identical to mine. Our back door overlooked the main bike route, and Gary had a military range finder, essentially a big telescope, that made it possible for us to identify riders approaching from a quarter-mile away. If we saw some of our growing circle of cycling friends approaching, we had time to run down to the street and delay them long enough for us to gather our own bikes and join them.

Gary and I were fairly typical '70s hippie bachelors, and the house wasn't the neatest place in the world. It had a spacious basement, perfect for storing our collection of bikes. We found a tarantula somewhere on the property and kept it in the

The house at 21 Humbolt quickly became bike central.

basement in a big jar half full of dirt. The spider built a nest, and we tossed in a doomed potato bug once in a while.

The low ceiling of the basement was a perfect height to mount a boxer's speed bag, and we had one, so we installed it. We had a set of Cinelli rollers, the loudest piece of exercise equipment ever built. They howled like a jet plane taking off when you really got going on them. We dragged a huge speaker down there and hooked it up to the stereo upstairs, but in order to hear the tunes over the sound of the rollers and the speed bag at the same time, you had to REALLY TURN IT UP LOUD. Everyone in the neighborhood knew when the bike guys were working out.

It suddenly seemed that everyone I knew outside the realm of music was a cyclist. My girlfriend took it up, and a hitchhiker I had met by chance when Fred Wolf and I picked him up turned out to be a kid named Joe Breeze, whose father was

a prominent local cyclist. As a high school kid Joe had ridden with his brother, Richard, all over California, venturing so far from home that local authorities called their parents to see whether they were running away. Our house was so perfectly situated that it became an unofficial clubhouse even before we had a club.

Gary had followed international bike racing since he had learned to read, and I began reading about the Europeans as well, the legendary riders such as Jacques Anquetil and the newest superstar, Eddy Merckx. Although not a writer, Gary knew so much about bikes that he was an adviser for a small publication based in San Rafael that until recently had been the Northern California Cycling Association newsletter but had changed its name to *Bicycling* and become a general magazine for the sport. Later, when the magazine was purchased by publishing giant Rodale Press and became a prominent national journal, he would follow it back to

the new headquarters in Emmaus, Pennsylvania, as a technical adviser.

The bike boom of the '70s was inches away for the rest of the United States, but it had already taken place in my neighborhood. We had great bikes and lots of time, and I didn't have a car, so when I wasn't working, bikes and riding were all I thought about. After Gary moved in I was no longer under any illusions about my cycling ability because Gary had regained his form, and his years of competition had taught him every trick in the book. No riders I knew could stay with Gary if he didn't want them to.

The way to get better was to race my bike, and now I wanted to do that. One small problem: Bicycle racing was burdened by more rules than baseball. In addition to wearing black shorts and white socks, you had to belong to a sanctioned club. I had the shorts and socks, but Marin County had one sanctioned club, the Marin Cyclists, and I didn't fit

The Velo-Club Tamalpais business card.
Kevin Haapala did the artwork.

the profile of a member. Joe's dad was a member, and so was Ed Christiansen, who owned the bike shop we frequented. Trouble was, these guys were old, and we were not. Even though there had been a few young riders, such as Marc Horwitz and Jerry Heidenreich, racing in Marin Cyclists jerseys, none of our young crowd could imagine sitting through an actual meeting run by the stuffy older riders.

By this time I knew about a dozen other relatively young riders, and my new friends had other friends who rode. It was a network linked by a common passion. Most of my cycling friends wanted to get into at least one bike race to see what it was like. Gary was the only member of our crowd who actually had done so. He was still a member of Endspurt, an established San Francisco club, so if he wanted to race he could meet the club requirement, if not the image requirement, but none of the rest of us could.

Tom Preuss, who had promoted the race a few years earlier where Gary had met the Grateful Dead, was living in Mill Valley, and Gary hooked us up with him as an older but hip cyclist who had experience with bike clubs. One evening in 1972 a dozen or so young riders met at his house and agreed that we wanted to be a club.

Although Tom called the meeting that led to the club, he never became a member. It spun

away from him immediately, and the power center shifted from his house in Mill Valley to 21 Humbolt in San Anselmo. We never went back to Tom's house because the meetings now took place at our house, and Tom didn't even show up after the third one. Since there was not yet a structure or agreed-upon officers meetings were anarchic, but people volunteered to fill temporary roles, and things got done.

Saying we wanted to be a club didn't make us one in the eyes of organized cycling. Our club had to be certified by the national body, and that meant we had to show some semblance of order and purpose, not just a list of names. We needed a president and at least a treasurer. We needed to figure out how someone got to be a member and how much the dues cost and when the meetings were. If we wanted to race our bicycles, that is.

None of us had any idea how to start a club of the sort that would pass muster, but I soon realized that I wouldn't get to race unless someone figured it out. I knew where the library was, and I went there. The librarian set me up with a slim volume called *The Clubwoman's Handbook*; the title didn't sound promising, but it covered the basic information necessary to start a club. We needed documents to send to the national governing body, such

April 1974 *Bike World* cover, featuring me, Steve Wilde, and Gil de la Roza flying down Paradise Drive.

April, 1974 • 75 cents

Bike Wo

IN THIS ISSUE...
On Climbing Hills
Women In Cycling
Food Supplements

as bylaws and a statement of purpose. I could write that stuff, and I had a typewriter, so I copied boilerplate right out of the book. It passed whatever official review it was intended for and did exactly what the instruction book had intended it to do, and we were on our way.

My few typed pages set out our officers and elections. Laurie Schmidke provided the name Velo-Club Tamalpais (Tam for short, or VCT). He had completed an application for national recognition and was just waiting for members and documents of the sort I had written. Just as the club got started, he moved out of the area without ever becoming a member. Our dozen or so original members along with a few pages of bylaws met the sanctioning requirement, and in 1972 the club was born.

VCT filled a need, and the youthful membership swelled. It wasn't long before the club meetings outgrew the living room of 21 Humbolt. I don't remember how we found out about the Robson-Harrington Mansion, which was an enormous, historic, and beautiful old house, one of the first built in the area, with acres of spectacular grounds and gardens. Inside the big house were several huge, wood-paneled rooms used for meetings and classes. It had been left to the city in a bequest, and its use was regulated by the Parks

Sprinting for third in the 1974 Fairfax Criterium.

Department. Residents of San Anselmo with legitimate reasons to hold meetings could reserve the conference room and use it for free as long as the place was respected and kept clean.

We applied, and because a bicycle club sounded like a legitimate recreational use and because Gary and I were residents of San Anselmo, we were accepted. Our time slot was strictly regulated, first by the yoga class that had the slot before ours and promptly at 10:00 p.m. by the old lady who lived upstairs and kept an eye on the place. No bike club ever had such a plush place to meet, courtesy of the Robson-Harringtons. Bless them, whoever they were.

One day a friend called and told me that a photographer needed bike riders for a photo shoot. I showed up with two other VCT members, Gil de la Roza and Stephen Wilde, and we followed a motorcycle with a photographer on it. In the spring of 1974 we ended up in full color on the cover of a long-departed bicycle magazine, *Bike World*. It was my first magazine cover and far from the last.

The season of 1974 was the year I finally raced my bike. I was 28 years old before I got to give it a try, and there was a lot to learn, and everybody else had already learned it. It turned out that bike racing is really hard. When you play a game of bas-

ketball, half the guys get to win. When you race bikes, you never get to win.

I came pretty close in an informal club race around a loop on a country road in San Rafael. After a dozen laps I had pulled away with another rider, and I knew I could take him anytime I wanted. As we turned the last corner, I saw a friend and mugged to show him how well I was doing. The other guy took advantage of my distraction to sprint and clean my clock.

As a beginner I was Category IV, the lowest at the time, and I was not able to qualify to move to the next level. I knew all the theory of drafting, and I could work in a paceline, and I knew that you were supposed to ride near the front. Nobody lets you do that, however. If you're not on a team, nobody will let you in, and you end up at the back of the peloton. And you can't win from there.

Teaming up was the way to go, and the Santa Rosa Criterium offered a tandem race. That's a different kind of teaming than being on a team, but VCT responded with two tandem bikes, one with Otis Guy and Joe aboard, the other piloted by Victor Pritzker with me as the stoker.

Tandems aren't really criterium bikes, and I didn't have anything to say about how fast we went. It was Victor's tandem, and he was driving. At the first tight turn a dozen huge bikes converged, and I closed my eyes. Wow. We made it.

Joe and Otis won it, as they would do many, many times. They cranked through the turns with their pedals bouncing the rear wheel off the pavement. Victor and I were third. The photo of the four of us shows an incredible amount of long hair.

The peak of my road-cycling career was probably the 1974 Fairfax Criterium, where my friend Phil Brown got a photo of me racing hard and a very excited spectator jumping in the air while I sprinted for 3rd place. With a couple of great photos of me racing my bike in the trophy case, I retired without ever winning anything and turned my efforts to promotion.

My job as a rock-band roadie was not conducive to road racing. Working for the band put me on the road for a week or two at a time, during which I would get in very little bike riding. Instead, I drove a truck a few thousand miles. When I got back on the bike, everyone else was faster, and I was slower. I wasn't about to give up the money gig for bike racing, which was not ever going to pay me very much. Not ever. So the bike racing suffered.

The next year I played on a bar league basketball team, and we won the league title.

VCT racers Joe Breeze, Otis Guy, me, and Victor Pritzker at the Rose Festival races in Santa Rosa, August 1974. Joe and Otis won the race on their Albert Eisentraut tandem, while Victor and I placed third on his Schwinn Paramount.

SINGLESPEEDS

My job as a roadie involved the use of a big truck, but I didn't bring it home. For personal transportation I traveled almost entirely by bike. Gary had a couple of vehicles, the first an old delivery van that he had used to drop off my table on the day when he decided to move in, and later a beat-up BMW, but most of the time he rode his bike too.

There is one obvious problem with having a Tour de France racing bike as your main transportation. A Tour de France rider is followed by mechanics who can change a wheel or trade a bike when the rider has a problem because the high performance of the bikes comes at the cost of much higher maintenance. A Tour de France rider doesn't buy his own tires either, and a sew-up tire could run as much as $25, about a day's pay at my level of employment. Changing a sew-up tire on the road was no fun, and patching one was ridicu-

Otis Guy's modified
1941 Schwinn Texas Special.

lous, but you had to do it if you wanted to get a few more miles out of a tire that cost a day's pay.

It wasn't that we didn't enjoy riding our racing bikes, but it didn't seem like a good idea to wear them out by riding at night and carrying cargo, and there was always the issue of securing something so expensive when you went into a store. You don't need a Ferrari to do the job of a pickup truck, and we needed the bicycle equivalent of a truck. Gary came up with the first stash of old bike frames, a collection he had acquired from an old bike shop. Because he had gone to Redwood High School in Larkspur, Gary knew some members of the Larkspur Canyon Gang, who were already using old bikes to shred Madrone Canyon in Larkspur. He knew the value of old one-speed frames, and he had three or four, along with a collection of wheels, handlebars, cranks, and chains that we used to assemble a couple of working one-speed, coaster brake bikes.

The great thing about the singlespeeds was that everything was made to the same standard; that is, the bottom brackets, stems, cranks, and rear wheels all had the same sizes and threads, so you could swap parts almost at random until you had enough of them to call the result a bicycle.

In other words, we were no different from every surfer, college kid, or town bike rider who finds the comfort, simplicity, and durability of a balloon-tire, coaster brake bike more attractive than riding something as impractical as a 10-speed, 21-pound racing bicycle with delicate wheels and tires and an awkward riding position. We were just the latest to figure out what millions of other people already knew. If you didn't have to ride very far, an old "clunker" bike made a lot more sense than a racing bike.

Gary and I were hardly the only clunker riders in VCT. For all the same practical reasons, other members started riding old one-speed bikes. We

always rode old ones because of course there was nothing then being manufactured resembling the purity of purpose and design of a stripped-down, 1930s, one-speed relieved of its tank, chain guard, and fenders. Nothing extra and everything bulletproof. Singlespeeds were at the far end of the cycling spectrum from racing bikes but just as much fun, and it seemed like everyone in VCT had one.

I had known Fred Wolf from the sixth grade on. He had toted me around on the top tube of his bike when we were kids with one bike and two people needing to travel. Now he lived on top of a hill at the very edge of Fairfax. He wasn't a cyclist in the way that Gary and I were, but like every other kid in Mill Valley he had ridden his bike on the railroad grade or the Pipeline Trail, and our newsboy bikes reminded him of those adventures. A trail led from near his house onto a vast tract of undeveloped land called Camp Tamarancho, owned by

This photo was taken in November 1977, but it illustrates so perfectly what we were striving for that I placed it here. Taken on Mount Tamalpais looking toward Tomales Bay, that's Howie Hammerman on a Shelby, Otis Guy on a Schwinn Excelsior, Chris McManus on a 1937 Excelsior that belonged to Joe Breeze, and Joe on his Breezer number 1 coated in primer.

the Boy Scouts. Although we did not yet realize it, from there trails and fire roads led into all parts of the area of Pine Mountain and beyond, into Mount Tamalpais State Park and the undeveloped vastness of the Marin Municipal Water District.

On an afternoon sometime around 1973, Fred invited Gary and me to throw our bikes into his pickup and come up the hill to his house. From there we would go see if we could ride them on the trail from his house to Tamarancho.

I had spent plenty of time at Camp Tamarancho while growing up, first in the '50s with my brother, Jim, as Cub Scouts attending summer day camp. We caught a chartered bus a few blocks from our house in Mill Valley that took us to Fairfax and up the poorly maintained Iron Springs Road to the camp. We spent our summer days swimming in the tiny artificial lake, braiding lanyards, and unknowingly giving our mother some peace and quiet. In the late afternoon, we rode the bus home.

After moving from Cub Scouts to Mill Valley Troop 1 of the Boy Scouts of America, I spent even more time at Tamarancho. Each Marin County Boy Scout troop had its own designated campground on the enormous tract, so Troop 1 would put all its gear into backpacks for the rugged 10-minute walk from the parking lot to the troop's regular camp-

site, where we would pitch tents and start earning various merit badges.

We played epic games of Capture the Flag against other troops, with hundreds of acres of forest to use for our team territory, sneaking through the woods and the tall grass on the hillsides to ambush our opponents.

Of all the undeveloped land in Marin County, I probably knew Tamarancho better than any other part, even though I hadn't been there in the 10 years since I had left the Boy Scouts. We had already hiked the half-mile trail from Fred's house to the edge of the camp for Frisbee games on the nearby hilltop, but hadn't really penetrated much farther into the areas I was so familiar with.

On that afternoon, our math wasn't good. There were three of us and two bikes. The solution was obvious. Someone had to run while the other two rode.

It wasn't a problem because we were all pretty tough, even if we didn't do a lot of running. After a while we would switch off, and a rider would become a runner.

We didn't go too far, probably no more than a couple of miles toward White's Hill and part of the way up it. The bikes were junk, and we had no trail-riding skills, so the designated runner had

no trouble keeping up as we negotiated the slightly uphill singletrack. Breaking out of the woods onto a fire road, the bikes rolled along a little faster, but it was still slightly uphill. Finally we came to a place where we would have to push the bikes a long way if we were to continue, and that seemed like far enough. When we turned around, the runner was at a disadvantage.

It turned out that even on these funky bikes, riding downhill was a lot more fun than running after your friends while they coasted away from you, laughing insanely. As soon as Gary could round up the parts, he built Fred a bike, and we started riding regularly up the trail from Fred's house to Tamarancho, pushing our bikes to the top of White's Hill for the ride down.

One-speed clunkers entered our lives and the lives of most of our friends and never left. Non-cyclists such as Fred and his neighbors, Larry and Wende Cragg, got the bug, partly because they lived so close to the trail where we had taken that first ride. They knew that Gary and I could find enough parts to set them up.

Joe Breeze came from Mill Valley to the club meetings, a little more of a ride than Gary and I had to make. Once Joe started arriving on his old Schwinn, the other members of VCT also started coming to meetings on old coaster brake bikes. After a while, the Marin clunker was the only kind of bike you would find parked outside the meetings, as Marc Vendetti, Otis Guy, Tim DuPertuis, Jerry Riboli, Chris Lang, Jerry Heidenreich, Peggy Madigan, and others joined the clunker set.

Fred had a BSA 441 Victor dirt motorcycle, and in 1973 I rode on the back of it while we explored a steep road climbing out of the back of Cascade Canyon in Fairfax. We followed fire roads for miles and eventually completed a loop that brought us back to our starting point. The next summer, Fred, Peggy, and I decided to follow the same route on our clunkers, starting with the push up a steep dirt road that would eventually be called Repack. It took us all day, most of it pushing the bikes. It was our first ride on what has become known to mountain bikers as the Pine Mountain Loop.

Now that so many people we knew were getting into clunkers, Gary and I started hitting the U & I Trading Post in San Anselmo, a junk shop where old bike parts could be found. We were beginning to encounter the problems associated with riding 40-year-old bikes. Stuff was rusted and bent and unreliable. Gary and I cleaned the U & I out of everything useful on our first sweep and then monitored it for any new arrivals.

Even though the Morrow coaster brake, with its split-sleeve brake shoe, was the gold standard of the era, I never had one, probably because the Larkspur Canyon Gang had cleaned out every local source years earlier. I made do with Musselman and Bendix rear hubs found in a 5-gallon bucket of coaster brakes at the U & I. The most common coaster brake brand was New Departure, which used a stack of internal discs for the braking, but its smooth action on level paved streets turned to no brake at all under severe downhill conditions, so we couldn't use them.

The era of pure coaster brake bikes was brief. Although the Larkspur riders had taken the art of coaster brake downhilling to its logical extreme with top-to-bottom fire-road runs on Mount Tam, that kind of riding required skills that were totally alien to road riders. Stopping was not an option, but since the front wheel did not have a brake, the bike would steer through almost anything. The object of the descent was largely to miss things and try to keep the bike on the road.

A rider freewheeling through a turn has his outside pedal down, but a coaster brake rider has the outside pedal at the rearmost position with all his weight on it and his inside foot on the ground to control the inevitable skid. This places the rider's weight considerably farther back on a coaster brake bike and requires a handlebar with a lot more rearward sweep.

If modifying our riding style had been enough to get by, we might have left the bikes the way they were. However, the additional challenge with coaster brakes was that 40-year-old bicycle technology was not manufactured for what we were attempting to do with our bikes, and the abuse was most evident in the rear hub. "Repack" earned its name as the hill that cooked a coaster brake to the point where a repack was necessary to renew the grease that had been burnt to smoke. As the rides got tougher, tearing down and rebuilding the brake became a regular event.

The limited stopping power and lack of durability meant that a coaster brake alone was not sufficient for our purposes. After the sole brake on the bike faded away in the middle of a descent, the rider's options quickly became limited. Front brakes were a must, and a new treasure hunt started. We rounded up a few drum front brakes from various sources, made by Union, Schwinn, and Sturmey Archer. We found that there was a commercial supplier called Worksman that made a cheap but easily available version for industrial tricycles used in warehouses. You could install caliper front

brakes, of course, but they didn't work very well on wet, chrome-plated steel rims. In order to wrap around the bigger tire, the arms on rim brakes for a clunker had to be much longer than on racing bikes. The brake arms would flex, and the slick rims didn't give much of a braking surface. The drum brakes we could get left a lot to be desired in terms of pure braking power, and they were heavier than any other system, but they were our best option at the time.

Starting in the '60s, Schwinn had made a series of 20-inch Stingray bikes called the Krate Series, which was discontinued in the '70s because of a safety issue. These Krates had a French-made Atom drum front brake that was almost perfect for our purposes, except that it was drilled with 28 holes instead of 36 for the spokes. No problem; we put 4 more holes in each flange and laced it right up. The Krates are incredibly collectible today, and we helped create a scarcity by scrapping a bunch of them just for the front hubs.

Interchangeability was straightforward in some cases, complicated or impossible in others. Gary showed me that a 26 × 2.125–inch tire fit onto a single-wall, 1.75-inch rim, which was much lighter than the double-wall, 2.125 rims that were common. On the other hand, a tire marked 26 × 1¾

was not the same as 26 × 1.75 and was useless for our purposes because it didn't fit any of the rims we used.

Knowing what we needed and having a job with a rock band that sent me to all parts of the country set me off on a national treasure hunt. I hit every old bike shop I could find, looking for the elusive coaster brakes and front brakes that I would often find thrown into crates near the back of the shop. Our appetite for usable frames was voracious, and I hit a few mother lodes along the way. The best was near Los Molinos in Tehama County, where one of my relatives alerted me to a farmyard a few miles up the road piled with old bikes. I went there and got a couple of frames, one of which served me well on Repack. I picked up a few girls' frames because they were an important source of forks, which were always bent on boys' bikes. Unfortunately I had limited cargo space in the band equipment truck and couldn't leave with everything I wanted.

When I came home with the booty, a few of my friends mounted an emergency expedition that cleaned the place out of everything good. Within days, they returned with a number of the bikes that became our very best clunkers.

chapter 5

MARIN COUNTY KLUNKERS

Gary and I had no reason ever to give up our house at 21 Humbolt, but after a couple of years the inevitable happened. In early 1975 the house was sold, and the new owner was moving in. Suddenly we had to scramble to find a new place. We found one a few houses up the street, at 32 Humbolt. When we moved all our stuff, we didn't even use a truck—we just took our time and never made an empty-handed trip as we trudged 50 yards up the hill.

The house at 32 Humbolt was a bigger place, and we found another roommate to split the rent, Charlie Wirtz. The house was not easily divided three ways. I scored the master bedroom, and the other two had no privacy from each other in two much smaller rooms.

Charlie was instrumental in our early clunker assemblies. When you are putting together a bike from a bunch of parts, there are always little things you need that you don't have lying around. Char-

The first time we saw clunkers with derailleurs was at the cyclocross race organized by VCT member Marc Horwitz.

lie worked at Cycle World, a bicycle shop in San Rafael we called "Psycho Ward." When Gary and I worked on a bike we would tell Charlie what we needed—spokes, cables, housing, whatever—and Charlie would use his shop discount and bring it home that evening.

From the beginning, 32 Humbolt was bike central. If the Robson-Harrington Mansion was the official clubhouse, our relocated household remained the unofficial one because it was open for business every day. We had lots more room to expand the bike operations. The longer we lived there, the more bike parts washed up on the porch, piling up in drifts on the corners of our small deck. Eventually dozens of old chainrings hung from nails along our eaves. Inside the house we used the room usually defined as the dining room as a workshop, with a workbench nailed into the wall. Road bikes hung from hooks in the ceiling. Clunkers lived outside on the covered deck.

We went to the dump and bought an electric washing-machine motor for $5 and hooked it up with a wire wheel and grinder, essential for cleaning off rust. The workbench was also equipped with a vise that doubled as an anvil and a wheel-building stand. Tools hung above it on nails driven into the wall. Next to the window stood the bike workstand. We even had a shoemaker's last, handy for nailing old-style slotted cleats onto your cycling shoes. If you had nothing to do, there were always a few sew-up tires you could patch.

One day we came home to disaster. My Colnago and one of Gary's road frames were gone, along with some cash for the rent. It was the worst thing I could imagine, and we put the word out about it.

That evening one of my friends spotted my bike's distinctive paint being scraped off it in a front yard and told us where to look. Gary and I barged into the house without knocking and demanded the bikes. After a few threats, the two frames were produced but not the gruppo. It took a few more threats to get an address where the rest of the loot could be found. Gary and I went there after midnight, walked into a darkened house, woke up a naked guy, and kicked him out of bed while his equally naked girlfriend cried and cowered under a blanket. In somewhat stern tones, we demanded the bike parts. Without attempting to dress and without asking which bike parts we might be inquiring about, he produced a crate of Campagnolo parts that we took with us. It turned out to be a somewhat larger collection than we had been relieved of. Later on, I made the guy pay me for my time and trouble in reassembling my bike.

In December 1974, Marc Horwitz organized a cyclocross event in Mill Valley on a patch of filled-in salt marsh that would eventually be developed but was then a jumble of dirt humps, mounds, and weeds. Cyclocross is a European winter sport

Alan Bonds's bike leaning against a fence on Mount Barnabe, circa 1977.

of cross-country bicycle racing. It's conducted on bikes that are similar to road racing bikes but specially designed to take the abuse. Competitors are expected to carry their bikes over some obstacles, and part of the discipline is dismounting, running with the bike, and remounting without losing time.

Peggy Madigan and I rode to the race on the black Schwinn tandem that had found a home on Humbolt Street. On his cyclocross bike, Gary raced in the event along with several other locals and the usual crowd of Bay Area cyclocross freaks. There were also a few guys I had never seen who showed up on fat-tire bikes with derailleur gears. Their bikes were not competitive on a cyclocross course because they were so heavy that picking them up and running with them was out of the question. These fat-tire riders were hardly hardcore cyclists and wouldn't have been competitive against that crowd on anything that required pedaling, so they were quickly lapped and out of the race, but not before the VCT members at the race who were also balloon-tire riders had noticed the bikes. After the race we tracked the riders down and talked to them about their bikes. In addition to their derailleur gearing, they had their shift levers mounted on the handlebar next to the grip, the first time any of us had seen thumb shifters.

We had met the Morrow Dirt Club from Cupertino, California, a town about 50 miles away. We wouldn't see them again for 20 years.

We had seen and used front drum brakes, but that was the first time I had seen a rear drum brake for a bicycle. A rear drum brake opened up the possibility of derailleur gearing, impossible with a coaster brake. I next saw a rear drum brake a few months later, in mid-1975. It was in a wooden box along with a ridiculous Sun tandem frame far too small for ordinary humans and a bunch of other random parts associated with the former tandem. Gary had found the pile of parts at the flea market and had bought it only for that rear hub, which was probably the heaviest bicycle hub I have ever handled. It was made of steel, and the drum itself was large-diameter with a matching high flange on the cluster side and a beefy braking mechanism.

Gary didn't waste any time lacing up a wheel. He ran out of the right size of spokes and bent a couple to fit because it was late and he didn't want to go to the bike shop for a couple of spokes. Getting the hub installed onto the frame turned out to be a challenge because the tandem axle specs were much wider than the coaster brake axle specs. Gary had to bend his bike's stays apart while maintaining frame straightness. He had found that the thumb shifters used by the Cupertino riders were made for five-speed touring bikes and had picked one up at Sunshine Bicycle Works, just down the street from our house. It wasn't an easy task because Gary was working in uncharted territory, but eventually after hours of fiddling, he had a working five-speed clunker.

The first test of Gary's bike would be a lap of the Pine Mountain Loop, the eventual route of the Thanksgiving Day ride that would take place that fall and every fall thereafter. We went out on what turned out to be a blazing hot day in May 1975. The profile of the ride consists of two long climbs, and on the second of those Gary was able to get on his bike while the rest of us pushed our one-speeds, whereupon he rode easily away from us on a bike much heavier than the ones we were pushing.

I had to have gears on my bike. I don't remember where I got my Atom drum brake; it came either from the Koski brothers at the Cove Bike Shop in Tiburon or from John Lewis at Mill Valley Cyclery. I had known the Koski family since the four siblings and I were kids. The three Koski brothers—Don, Dave, and Erik—worked as mechanics at what had been a bike and toy shop but was moving rapidly to bikes only, driven by the three brothers' interest. Unlike the usual arrangement at a bike shop, where the mechanic in the back room just does what the boss tells him, Don, Dave, and Erik had a major say in the direction of the shop. The Koski brothers represented the only members of the off-road crowd with any influence on purchasing, and they stocked up on all the stuff clunker riders needed, including drum rear hubs, as soon as there was a demand for them.

The Cove Bike Shop had become the bicycle motocross (BMX) center for Marin County, and it was an easy transition to stocking parts for the clunker riders. The Koski brothers would order anything we needed, and it wasn't long before they, along with Mill Valley Cyclery, were doing such brisk business in tandem rear hubs that the Atom brake company inquired as to why the demand for an esoteric part had suddenly exploded in a microscopic part of the bicycle market.

By 1976 Gary and I had gone through a few third roommates. About a year after we started converting our bikes to multiple gears, the latest roommate moved in. Alan Bonds, originally from Oklahoma and a recent transplant to Fairfax, had met members of the Larkspur Canyon Gang. We met Alan because of his interest in the bikes, and although he was not a road rider like Gary and me, he fit right into our fat-tire scene.

Alan had roots in the Midwest and an indelible Oklahoma accent, and he worked as a painter. His background with go-karts had given him an appreciation for mechanical detail, and before moving into 32 Humbolt he had learned some of the lore the Canyon Gang had accumulated. By that time five-speed conversions were fairly common in San Anselmo and Fairfax, and Alan understood at once what was going on. He never went through the coaster brake phase of entering the young sport. He built a five-speed immediately and joined the crew.

Alan's job as a painter gave him an edge on all the other builders. Alan could paint anything, from a house to a delicate airbrush image, and he made hand-cut stencils of the spear-point or ram's-head trim that graced the original prewar paperboy clunkers. Along with his attention to detail, this made him the master of the short-lived craft of clunker modification. Over the next couple of years at 32 Humbolt, Alan built more bikes for other people than anyone else. Although I built all of my own bikes, I had a good job that took me away from the house for extended periods, and other than building a few wheels, I never built bikes for anyone else. Gary helped some of our friends set up theirs and built a few, but Alan's work was in demand, and he made a dozen or so bikes for other riders, each one unique and beautiful.

Over the space of a few months in the living room at 32 Humbolt, the classic Marin County Klunker reached the peak of perfection available with that level of technology as Alan, Gary, and I polished our arcane craft.

The ideal Marin County Klunker started with a Motobike frame manufactured by Schwinn in the '30s. It was sold under several different brand names but was known to us primarily by one of those names, Excelsior, and so in our world, all frames of that design regardless of the actual brand name were referred to as Excelsiors. Gary's personal frame had a BF Goodrich head badge but was still an Excelsior. These frames were tough and elegant and had the high bottom bracket and handling characteristics necessary for our use. From all the junkyards we had scoured looking for the distinctive hipstays that identified the "Excelsior," we had acquired a decent collection of them.

The first job was to respace the rear dropouts, forcing them wider apart to accept the rear drum brake hub. We would cold set the stays—bend them, that is—by wedging a 2 × 4 between them and stepping on it carefully. In order to keep everything aligned so the bike wouldn't crab down the road after it was assembled, we stretched a string forward from one rear dropout up around the head tube and back to the other dropout and then measured side to side to keep the seat tube in the middle. As we applied pressure to the 2 × 4, the idea was to work evenly from both sides.

It was generally tough to install the rear wheel because we didn't open the stays any more than we had to, but on these bikes you didn't ever want to remove the wheel when you weren't in the shop anyway. The brake required an arm attached to the chainstay, in an arrangement similar to the arm on a coaster brake. In addition to the arm fixed to the chainstay, there were a couple of cables attached, and when the wheel was removed everything would have to be recalibrated and the cables reattached to the frame. After the wheel was locked into place on the drive side, you had to center the brake shoes by holding the brake lever down with a big rubber band while you tightened the other side and attached the brake arm to the chainstay. All of this made field repairs difficult, so if you got a flat, you'd fix it without removing the wheel by opening the tire bead and pulling out enough of the inner tube to patch it.

The next task was to find a drum brake and build the wheels. We favored lighter single-wall, 1.75-inch rims to the much heavier, 2.125-inch rims because a 2.125 tire could still be mounted on the narrower rim. Wheel-building is not rocket science, and we could all do it. The stand was there on the workbench bolted to the wall in the dining room.

Forks came off old girls' bikes, along with pedals and sometimes saddles, because girls didn't destroy their bikes like boys did, so the supply of parts was more plentiful. We always spruced up the forks with marginally effective fork braces, which were nothing more than rods that connected the dropouts to the top of the steerer.

Alan and Gary liked longhorn-style, swept-back bars, but I found the widest set of BMX bars probably ever made and used them on several of my bikes. Cheap handlebars were notorious for snapping off without warning, but the BMX bars had an extra brace that prevented breakage.

Old bikes were built as one-size-fits-all frames small enough for a kid. Adult riders needed extra-long seatposts. The small diameter and thick walls of the old Schwinn tubing dictated a small-diameter seatpost, which often bent at the seat clamp. Schwinn also built an indoor exerciser with a seatpost much longer than those made for bicycles, and you could buy one of those at the same shop. Even better was a piece of high-quality aluminum rod stock, because the seatpost and the seat cluster were vulnerable parts of the bike. Putting a long seatpost deep inside the seat tube helped reinforce that part of the frame. With big riders bouncing around at the upper end of an extended seatpost, bent seatposts were common, so having a tough one was preferable to trying to save weight.

At the end of the seatpost, a Brooks B-72 leather saddle was by far the most fashionable. We found them in junk bins or on cheap Raleigh three-speeds that were worth buying for $10 for the saddle alone.

At first we built our bikes as five-speeds, but we found that on rough downhills, when the derailleur flapped around, the chain would fly off the front ring. I added a front derailleur clamped in place as a chain guide to keep it on. If there is a derailleur and a shift lever already on the bike, then it doesn't take much more to put them to use. The double chainrings from a Schwinn Varsity crankset bolted right up to any set of one-piece cranks, so soon enough I was riding with 10 gears, a high range and a low range of 5 gears apiece.

My first set of shifters was a pair of cheap stem shifters from a Schwinn Varsity. I had seen thumb shifters, but they weren't as easy to come by as parts from a cheap and common junk bike, so I used something that came from the same bin as the crankset. At first I mounted the shifters in the traditional spot on the stem but almost immediately realized that the diameter of the stem was the same diameter as the handlebar, and I could put them out by the brake lever where a thumb shifter would be if I had one.

Since I had two shift levers, the upgrade to double chainrings was easy. I shifted both derailleurs with the right hand, front atop the handlebar and rear below.

With mountains of bike parts and plenty of time on our hands, we messed with bikes constantly at 32 Humbolt. Someone was always building a wheel, grinding some parts, or filing or bending or hammering, all to a Bob Marley soundtrack. Since so much of the balloon-tire stuff was interchangeable,

Fat Tire Flyer • Marin County Klunkers

On Pine Mountain Truck Road looking toward
Pine Mountain Saddle, March 1977. Left to right
are Vince Carlton, me, Alan Bonds, Benny Heinricks,
Jim Stern, and Howie Hammerman.

we tried all sorts of fork-and-wheel-size combinations, such as a 26-inch fork and front wheel on a 24-inch frame, which I broke in half immediately.

One evening Gary used an X-ACTO knife to whittle the closely set tread of our only useful tire, the Uniroyal Nobby, into something a little more aggressive. He created an open V-tread pattern with more bite, then weighed the shavings to see how many ounces he had taken off the tire.

I was intrigued by an elliptical chainring I had seen advertised in a bike magazine, and I ordered one from Roger Durham. I thought it might be useful at the low RPM of a grinding climb, but at higher speeds it was awkward. At that point, I tried using it as the inner chainring with an ordinary round ring as the outer. Unfortunately, I found that every time I switched, the other gear felt weird, no matter which one I was shifting to. Eventually I would get used to it, but then shifting back felt just as weird.

During this experimental phase, I broke at least one of every part on a bike—frame, handlebar, stem, fork, seatpost, saddle, axles, rims, chain, derailleur. Many of the parts were as ancient as the frames and not in the best condition. With every bike a collection of mismatched and used parts, nearly every big group ride involved some attention to a mechanical problem and often a creative repair.

We found an adaptor that BMX riders used to modify a 2-inch bottom bracket to take an alloy crankset from a modern road bike. After we discovered TA cranksets, with their marvelous adaptability of crank arm length and chainring size, I broke the crank arms regularly, and one of my discards was immortalized by Craig Mitchell in 1979 as the "Mr. Repack Trophy."

By the start of 1976, there were a dozen converted clunkers being used around Fairfax, most of them built at 32 Humbolt. In Marin County there were dozens more of the previous generation of stripped-down coaster brake bikes with added front brakes. Everyone who wanted to upgrade the older style bikes to the next generation knew that a visit to 32 Humbolt would be part of that process. Either Alan or Gary would be asked to build one, or the applicant would grill them for advice.

Getting another bike out the door was like helping someone give birth. Some jobs, such as cold setting, were easier with two people. It was usually Alan building the latest, but he had all the assistance he wanted, or even more than he could use, as each new bike took shape over a period of days. Since the "standard" was whatever parts could be rounded up, no two clunkers were ever exactly alike.

Craig Mitchell made this Mr. Repack Trophy
from a TA crank that I broke.

REPACK

In the year or so between Gary Fisher's first five-speed conversion and the summer of 1976, Marin County clunker technology had peaked. All the conversion problems were sorted out and parts supplies established. Now it seemed a new clunker hit the trails every day, and people we didn't even know were starting to build similar bikes.

It cost about $400 to put together a clunker, a tidy sum to invest in a 40-year-old bike. You could scrounge up a lot of it, but drum brakes weren't just lying around everywhere and had to be purchased new. If you couldn't build wheels, you had to pay someone who could. You needed BMX handlebars and motorcycle brake levers, derailleurs, shift levers, and cables. A one-piece steel crankset would work, but now that there were conversion kits available for the bottom bracket, alloy cranksets were the new standard.

A lot of the early rides had ended in mechanical disaster when experimental assemblies failed,

One of Gary's 1940s Schwinns at the far end of the klunker's evolutionary scale: derailleurs front and rear, a triple crank, and drum brakes. A great machine for its time, but heavy; this bike weighs about 46 pounds.

inspiring some creative field repairs. The universal toolkit devised by the Larkspur Canyon Gang was a pair of Vise-Grips clamped to the seatpost. When bolts had been rounded off to the point where a wrench had no grip, a Vise-Grip would get a purchase. When parts separated in the middle, the tool could often be used to clamp things together long enough to get off the hill.

Attrition served to standardize the design. Things that worked stayed; things that didn't were discarded. For example, Fred Wolf attempted to use an internal three-speed hub with derailleur gears to achieve a super-low gear with extra-long cranks. The first time he applied the torque with his 210 pounds and another 50 pounds of bike, the tiny planetary cogs inside the hub exploded into dust. Very fine dust. Internal gearing was not going to cut it.

After some experimentation with shift levers, the standard had become the thumb shifters made for five-speed bikes. Since they were only made for a rear shifter, they did not come in pairs and were only made for the right hand. In order to use one on the left side for the front derailleur, we had to flip it around backward.

I tried using plastic brake levers made for mopeds, but I found that they were too flexible. Like most of my friends, I started buying my brake levers from the local Honda motorcycle dealer, but these levers had their own weakness: If you hit them just right you could snap them off. Joe Breeze used Magura motorcycle levers from Germany, which were long enough for proper leverage and made of malleable alloy that could be straightened out after a shunt without breaking.

Old-style handlebars were not made for serious off-road use, and various forms of BMX bars became popular (although hardly universal). Alan Bonds and Gary still preferred more sweep than I did and used bars similar to the original equipment on the old bikes. Real BMX pedals were an improvement over cheap "rat-trap" pedals.

As I mentioned earlier, the only good surviving forks came from girls' frames, and they were not especially robust. I scored big-time one afternoon when I was hanging around a bike shop and an Ashtabula sales rep came in. He had with him an experimental fork made for the new "cruiser" class, 26-inch, BMX bikes. Its shape was similar to an old fork, but it had been reinforced and specially hardened, and I bought it from the guy on the spot instead of letting him leave it with the shop as a sample.

My main problem was frames, plural. "Excelsior" frames, whether actual Schwinn Excelsior or otherwise, were all anyone wanted, and the supply was not expanding. Quite the opposite—it shrank every time I finished off another bike, and I wasn't the only person using up multiple frames. Interestingly enough, I didn't break them in the hills; I wore them out on the streets. Apart from my road bike, my clunker was my main transportation, and I used it for all errands within a radius of 10 to 15 miles. I rode it all the time, and I rode it hard, but it wasn't built with high-quality steel tubing like my Italian bike. After a few months I would crack the bottom bracket loose from the rest of the frame, and it was time to go out and find another Excelsior. Nobody was giving them away any more, and all the obvious supplies had been mined out. Now I had to pay real money for one, as much as $100. Looking into the future with my history of destroyed frames, I could see an ongoing expense and the monstrous hassle of building a new bike every few months.

Whatever it might cost to get someone to build a frame for me out of good steel would probably be worth it in the long run. I talked to Joe and to Craig Mitchell, and Craig accepted the challenge. He was a metallurgist and an expert welder as well as a passionate cyclist who had already built several experimental recumbent bicycles. I was willing to pay for some experimental work, and he agreed to dupli-

Descending Repack at Champagne Knoll on the frame Craig Mitchell built for me.

cate the Excelsior geometry in chrome-moly steel tubing. Apart from the tubing material, the other big difference was that the tubes in Craig's frame were straight, not curved. The frame was finished in the fall of 1976, the first purpose-built, chrome-moly, off-road frame for a new generation of bicycles.

Craig had used all the old Schwinn standards, so I was able to move all the components over from my clunker, including my treasured Ashtabula reinforced fork and the ridiculously wide BMX handlebars that I then favored.

With a growing circle of clunker owners, by 1976 there were all sorts of informal group activities. Those of us who didn't have to report daily to a form of employment started taking group rides, often throwing the bikes into the back of Fred's pickup truck and taking them out to a new place to explore, such as Point Reyes National Seashore or Bolinas Ridge, which were inviting but a little remote to ride to from Fairfax. We pushed and pedaled to the top of Mount Barnabe and Pine Mountain and lesser peaks in between and explored every trail in the backcountry of Marin County, learning the lay of the land better than any but the rangers who patrolled it.

Before anyone thought to make rules about such things, we found every singletrack in the

Appetite Seminar,
Thanksgiving Day, 1975,
around Pine Mountain Loop.

Water District and kicked off the primary political aspect of mountain biking when we offended hikers and equestrians by our mere presence in places once used only for their activities.

The first "Appetite Seminar" had taken place on Thanksgiving Day, 1975, when a dozen or so riders took a lap of the Pine Mountain Loop, the idea being that a long ride would set us up for a big dinner. The finish of the seminar was an exhilarating run down Repack, and the ride served as an introduction to it for the participants. Although the idea was spontaneous, we repeated it the following year. The Appetite Seminar is now the longest-running annual mountain bike event in the world and has become a Bay Area holiday tradition for upwards of a thousand mountain bikers.

Even with the new gearing, the bikes were still impossibly heavy, and pushing the bike efficiently was as much of an art as riding it. Sometimes pushing was faster even in areas where riding was possible. Trudging for half an hour up a steep hill beside a 50-pound clunker was not what most people consider fun, but we didn't mind. It wasn't any harder than trying to stay with the flying peloton in a road bike race, and even the trudging turned into a slow-motion speed contest as a couple of grim, sweaty riders tried to match each other stride

for stride at 2 miles an hour. The reward for these efforts was standing on the peak, then shredding the dirt road back down.

As the group rides grew, perhaps a dozen clunker riders would push off a peak after picnicking at the top and recovering from the trudge it took to get there. This was the rush we had been working for all day, and we wanted all of it. Two or three riders are manageable on a fire road, but the groups were now bigger. "Dicing" on the downhill started to be a problem when everyone was equally competitive but not equal in size. It became obvious that you didn't want to try to pass one of the bigger riders, who would ride you off a cliff to preserve his lead in a "race" that hadn't really been declared. Pure downhill was fun, but fighting another rider for the fast line through the turn was a distraction. Eating dust and not being able to see the road was a bummer and so was having another guy stick his elbow in your ear. Everyone liked to see the road with no one in front and all options open, but on any given ride only one rider seemed to.

The long rides and slow walks up hills gave us plenty of time to discuss every possible subject to death. We must have discussed the idea of holding a downhill race for hours over a period of weeks before it all came together at the top of Repack

Image

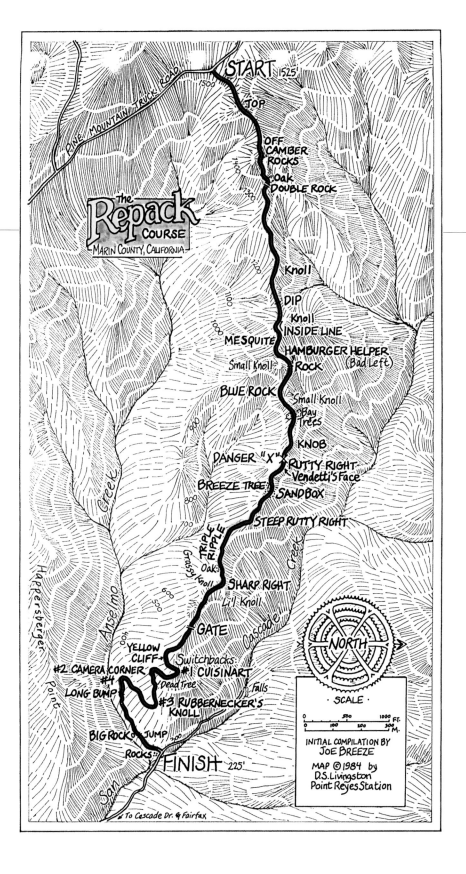

The map in the image contains the following labels:

The Repack Course — Marin County, California

START 1525
TOP 1500
OFF CAMBER ROCKS 1400
Oak DOUBLE ROCK 1300
Knoll
DIP
Knoll
INSIDE LINE
MESQUITE
Small Knoll
HAMBURGER HELPER ROCK (Bad Left)
BLUE ROCK
Small Knoll
Bay Trees
KNOB
DANGER "X"
RUTTY RIGHT Vendetti's Face
BREEZE TREE
SANDBOX
STEEP RUTTY RIGHT
TRIPLE RIPPLE
Oak
Grassy Knoll
SHARP RIGHT
Li'l Knoll
GATE
YELLOW CLIFF
Switchbacks:
#2 CAMERA CORNER
#1 CUISINART
Dead Tree
#4 LONG BUMP
Falls
#3 RUBBERNECKER'S KNOLL
BIG ROCK JUMP
ROCKS!!
FINISH 225'
To Cascade Dr. & Fairfax
PINE MOUNTAIN TRUCK ROAD
Happersberger Point
Anselmo Creek
Cascade Creek
San...
NORTH
SCALE
0 500 1000 FT.
0 100 200 300 M.
INITIAL COMPILATION BY JOE BREEZE
MAP © 1984 by D.S. Livingston Point Reyes Station

Footer

This map of Repack was compiled by Joe Breeze and drawn by Dewey Livingston.

on the morning of October 21, 1976. Not many sports can trace their birth to such a specific time, date, and location. As that date approached, and we discussed what we wanted to do, our perspective was different. We figured that we would settle one nagging question: Who among us was actually the fastest downhill rider? The once-and-for-all aspect was clear: Why would we ever want to go to all this trouble again to settle something that we settled to everyone's satisfaction on October 21?

If the race was downhill, Repack was the obvious place to hold it because it was the most challenging hill we knew, and it was in a perfect location just outside of Fairfax. It was well outside of the popular hiking routes and was virtually unknown to anyone at the time who didn't ride on it, so we could be reasonably sure that we wouldn't meet the local chapter of the Sierra Club on a Sunday hike. The average grade is about 14 percent, but parts are much steeper. The road winds along the top of a ridge separating two drainages that meet at the bottom. Because it twists so much, sightlines are more limited than speed, so the rider has to continually accelerate into the unknown around the next bend.

The descent is 1,300 feet of elevation over 2 miles, and the only limit to how fast you can go

Fat Tire Flyer • Repack

left page number
46

ch6

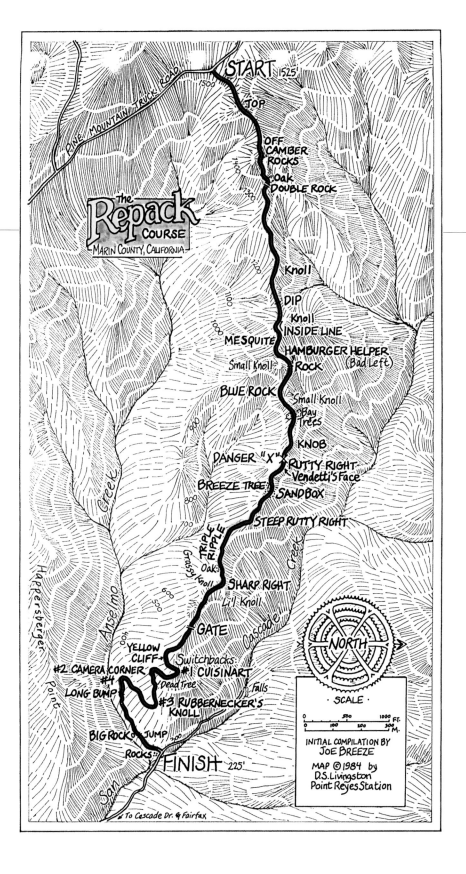

This map of Repack was compiled by Joe Breeze and drawn by Dewey Livingston.

on the morning of October 21, 1976. Not many sports can trace their birth to such a specific time, date, and location. As that date approached, and we discussed what we wanted to do, our perspective was different. We figured that we would settle one nagging question: Who among us was actually the fastest downhill rider? The once-and-for-all aspect was clear: Why would we ever want to go to all this trouble again to settle something that we settled to everyone's satisfaction on October 21?

If the race was downhill, Repack was the obvious place to hold it because it was the most challenging hill we knew, and it was in a perfect location just outside of Fairfax. It was well outside of the popular hiking routes and was virtually unknown to anyone at the time who didn't ride on it, so we could be reasonably sure that we wouldn't meet the local chapter of the Sierra Club on a Sunday hike. The average grade is about 14 percent, but parts are much steeper. The road winds along the top of a ridge separating two drainages that meet at the bottom. Because it twists so much, sightlines are more limited than speed, so the rider has to continually accelerate into the unknown around the next bend.

The descent is 1,300 feet of elevation over 2 miles, and the only limit to how fast you can go was how fast you want to go. There are huge ruts, deep ditches, hard switchback turns, and loose surfaces on off-camber turns to skid you over the edge. Sounds like . . . fun.

We gave our trails names that didn't appear on official maps. The "Broken Hand" trail was named in early 1976 when I went down in a turn and broke a bone in my hand, my first fracture, at the age of 30. The "Lost Lens" trail had claimed an expensive camera lens from Larry Cragg. Repack itself, of course, was named after our first few coaster brake rides down it, when the tortured brake gave up all lubrication in the form of smoke pouring out of the hub. After the brake had been smoked, it howled in pain with every application, and the only remedy was to tear it down, clean it out, and "repack" it with as much high-temperature brake grease as could be crammed into the mechanism.

The first time I saw Repack was around 1973, long before it earned that name, when Fred and I poached a new fire road on his motorcycle. We could drag the motorcycle under or around the gates that guarded Repack, and we kept going because we wanted to know where the road went. The two of us together weighed more than 400 pounds, but the little single-cylinder thumper chugged us up the steep hill. We then followed the road around Pine Mountain Loop, the first time I had seen that also. By the fall of 1976 we had been down Repack enough times that we had named it for what it did to our bikes.

It was obvious from the beginning that the race had to be an individual time trial, a "race of truth" in which no rider could affect another rider's result. In all but the biggest stage races, road time trials are generally run as "out and back," and the finish timer is the same clock that started the riders. But we didn't have that luxury. Our start and finish were nearly 2 miles apart, and there would be no communication possible between the two locations.

The clocks we found for our first event were a windup alarm clock with a sweep second hand and Fred's old navy chronometer, which he used as a wall clock. The latter item was essentially a pocket watch on steroids. It weighed a pound or so, and its round face was 4 inches across. The sweep second hand traveled about one-quarter inch per second.

On October 21, 1976, about a half-dozen riders (the actual number and names are lost to history) threw bikes into the back of Fred's truck and hauled them up Bolinas Road to the Pine Mountain Truck Road. We pedaled and trudged the mile or so across the flank of Pine Mountain, keeping to the right toward Woodacre Ridge at the fork where the truck road continues to the top of Pine Mountain. After another quarter-mile uphill over watermelon-size cobbles that got everyone off their bikes, we reached another fork where Repack took off downhill at a right angle to the ridgetop road we were on.

A big rock next to the road made a convenient marker, so we scratched a line in the dirt next to it and made up a list of start times. The first rider would leave at an agreed time and then others at 2-minute intervals. Someone jumped on his bike and carried the list and the alarm clock to the bottom, where Fred's wife, Emma, waited after bringing the truck back down the mountain.

Now that the clocks were set and running, suddenly Repack became a completely different animal.

A PASSION FOR RACING

Repack is steep, but we had conquered it on cruder equipment than those gathered at the top were riding on that fall day in 1976. The entire crew was now equipped with the latest converted clunkers, and my custom frame from Craig Mitchell would be ready very soon.

As far as I know, this was the first downhill, off-road time trial ever held, and we found that there was a lot to think about. Racing Repack wasn't like riding down a mountain in the company of other people; this was riding solo with no sound or distraction except crunching tires. Competition changed everything, and an amusing hobby turned into a passion for racing Repack.

With a judicious degree of caution, anyone could get from the top to the bottom, and we counted on that. We needed to synchronize timers and send a clock down from the top with a reasonable assurance that, with a 10-minute head start,

Left foot down through Camera Corner on Repack, toward the tail end of 1976. I've got the wide BMX bars I liked on this postwar Schwinn. Also note the fork braces and front drum brake.

a nonracing rider could get it to the finish line without crashing and still have time to set up the finish line. We chose a big rock where the two creeks came together to mark a finish line as permanently as the rock at the top marked the start.

Partway down Repack there was a gate across the course marking the boundary between Marin County Open Space and the Marin Municipal Water District. A couple of years earlier, after county fire crews had put out a blaze in Tamarancho, Larry Cragg, who lived a short walk from the fire site, had found a set of keys dropped by the firefighters. The keys opened gates on fire roads for such emergencies, and the key to the Repack gate was on the ring.

After we started the clocks, the finish timer, who was carrying the clock down the hill, would unlock the gate and swing it open. He would also check for anyone coming up the hill and warn them about what was about to come down, although after a while the people who were there knew what was coming down. After the race was over, whoever started the last rider would bring the starting clock down the hill and close the gate on the way. When I raced, I started all riders except myself and then started last with one person to assist with my start and then bring the clock down.

As soon as we turned on the clock, Repack pumped more adrenaline through my system than anything I had ever tried, including vertical skating. It was the race of truth, and the test was not only of strength and skill but also courage and preparation. The short sightlines on the course complicated the matter because the bike would handle the hill at speeds at which you couldn't see around blind turns. If you wanted to beat everyone else, you had to take chances and ride continually into the unseen. Taking those chances was a rush like nothing any of us had ever experienced.

There is no record of who carried the timer down or who handled the starting on the first Repack, but Fred's wife, Emma, counted in time with the second hand of the clock as riders crossed the finish. Someone else wrote the results on a yellow legal pad. We did the elementary math, subtracting the starting time from the finish time, and there was no argument that the rider who had completed the course in the shortest time was Alan Bonds.

According to the original proposition, this should have settled our arguments, but academic theory didn't stand up to inevitable reality. The initial event had been such an incredible rush that we wanted more of it. To Alan's disappointment, he

was forced to defend his championship less than a week after being crowned. It's the nature of sport, as we were just finding out. No title is permanent. People who don't hold it want a shot at it.

Everyone except Alan had a reason why the first race was not truly representative of the way things were. Someone's chain fell off. Some other rider skidded out. Tires were soft. Besides, that was an insane rush, wasn't it? Want to do it again? It wasn't that Alan's win was tainted, it was that racing is the only way you can achieve that feeling, and it becomes a goal in itself.

Five days later a crew went back to the top, and the second event took place. This time I brought a notebook instead of the yellow legal pad from the first race. The results from the second race onward were recorded in this and another notebook still in my files, the earliest written records of this form of racing.

The list of starters for the second race was "Fred, Allan [sic], Bob, Ariel, Wende, Bob Peterson, Jr., Stern, Jim." The results are written in Emma's hand. I acted as the starter, so I didn't have a time. "Bob" is Bob Burrowes, "Ariel" is Alan's dog, "Wende" is Wende Cragg, "Jr." is Fred's dog, "Stern" is Jim Stern, and "Jim" is Jim Adler. The two dogs were timed because they could fly down the hill,

Tuesday. October 26, 1976

2. # Name	Start	Finish time	E.T.
Fred	9:25	▮9:30:19	5.19
Allan	9:29	9:32:19	5:19
Bob	9:29	9:33:50	4:50
Arial	9:27	9:34:30	7:30
Wendy	9:31	9:36:43	5:43
Bob Peterson	9:33	9:39:24	6:24
Jr.	9:27	9:40:49	13:49
Steve	9:40	9:47:53	7:53
Jim	9:	9:54:30	

3. Saturday. October 30. 1976

Name	Start	Finish	E.T.
Bob Burroughs	▮9:40	▮9:45.08	5:08
Allen Bonds	9:42	9:47.34	5.34
Tim DuPertuis	▮9:44	9:49:43	5.43
Kenny Fuetsch	9:46	9:51:52	5.52
Jerry Riboli	9:48	9:53:41	5.41
George Newman	9:50	9:55:17	5.17
Joe Breeze	9:52	9:56:56	4:56
Wendy Gregg	9:54	▮	
Ian Stewart	9:56	10:01:49	5:49
Fred Wolf	9:58	10:03:08	5:08
John	10:00	10:07:30	7:30

1st	Joe	4:56	
2nd	Bob & Fred	5:08	Tie
4th	George	5:17	
5th	Allen	5:34	
6th	Jerry	5:41	
7th	Tim	5:43	
8th	Ian	5:49	
9th	Kenny	5:52	

Top: Repack log book entry for Race 2, October 26, 1976.

Bottom: Repack log book entry for Race 3, October 30, 1976.

and the owners wanted them to race each other. The dogs went on all the rides with us anyway, and they didn't have a problem with that.

Bob Burrowes, a San Francisco firefighter who lived in San Anselmo near the 21 Humbolt house, won the second event in 4:50. His bike was a yellow 1950s Schwinn frame with the standard clunker upgrade built by Gary Fisher. Every bike in the race had either come from our Humbolt digs or had stopped there in the process of being built because that was the only place where the art was practiced.

Bob had a background in riding motorcycles, and he customarily wore a hockey helmet when racing at Repack. That made him the only member of the original crew to worry about brain damage.

Four days after the second race the title was up for grabs again. This time the original crew was joined by four members of Velo-Club Tamalpais (VCT), Joe Breeze, Jerry Riboli, Tim DuPertuis, and Kenny Fuetsch. The Larkspur Canyon Gang was represented too, in the persons of George Newman and Ian Stewart.

This third event witnessed something of a step backward in bicycle technology, because George and Joe were both still coaster brake riders. George already had a reputation as the craziest of the Canyon Gang, getting in literally hundreds of top-to-bottom runs of Mount Tam in a single year, which he had tallied on

The Repack digital stopwatches, with bottle caps taped over the reset buttons.

a water tank every time he passed. Joe was a first-rate road racer and one of the best riders in VCT, and he and Otis Guy both clung to the old-school coaster brake technology, with the one concession to Repack being the addition of a front brake.

On his throwback equipment, Joe came up from Mill Valley and beat the locals on their own turf with a first run of 4:56.

After four races, the crude timing system was getting old, but I was having a lot of fun organizing the events. I decided to go all in, or at least a little further in. I went to a sporting goods store to see what an actual stopwatch might cost, expecting to get a round timer with a sweep hand. The clerk showed me the latest in timing technology, a digital timer accurate to hundredths of a second with a LED-illuminated readout. You could take split times while the timer continued to run, exactly what we needed. They were $70. I talked to Fred, and each of us put up the price of a timer.

Having made the investment, I was committed to using the clocks. That meant putting on some races. The only drawback to the timers that we could see was the prominent reset switch. If it got tripped and cleared the running time, the race would be over. To prevent such a disaster, I taped a bottle cap over the troublesome button on

each timer. We would start the two clocks together at the starting line and then send one down with the finish timer. At precisely 10 minutes on the clocks, we'd send the first rider off.

I was learning about starting. The finish time is only as accurate as the start time, so it was essential to send riders off properly. We didn't have a gate we could drop, and I found that every rider tried to leave early. The only way to prevent that was to hold the bike by the rear tire and only let go when the clock read all zeros and I yelled "Go!" If the rider tried to surge before I let go, he or she fell across the handlebars and lost more time than would have been gained by an early start.

All through the fall of 1976 there were Repack races. The fifth race was held on November 20, just a month after the first, but the trend as shown by the entry list was obvious. Gary showed up for the first time and turned in a blistering 4:50 for 3rd place behind coaster brake riders George and Joe. Now in addition to Larkspur Canyon Gang, from just a few miles away, the list included participants from all the way across the bay in Berkeley in the form of some loose-knit riders who called themselves the Berkeley Trailers Union. At this race, I finally took my new Craig Mitchell bike down the course, but I recorded a disappointing

George Newman on his Colson at the Repack 4 start line on November 13, 1976. Jim Stern holds the start list and one of the predigital timing clocks, a navy chronometer in a wooden case.

time. I took a few precautions against crashing, wearing heavy gloves, my old army boots, and a pair of kneepads I used in skate parks. As a final form of safety equipment, I elected to wear a huge firefighter's jacket, but at Repack speeds the flapping canvas slowed me down so much I didn't need safety equipment.

It became clear that memorizing the course was key because if you could visualize what you were about to ride into, you could maximize your speed. If you couldn't see it, you had to remember it, and it is indicative of our newfound passion that we spent a good part of that fall working on that. Joe drew a map that included the sequence of named turns as a mnemonic device. One day several of us accompanied Larry as he walked down the course and took a photograph every 50 feet. When the resulting two hundred or so slides were shown in succession, the slide show was a freeze-frame version of a ride.

With the recording systems established, all anyone needed to put on a race was the pair of timers. I had to go on the road for a week or so with the band, and I left the clocks with some of the Repack racers. The only race of the entire series that I missed was the one on December 5, when Gary set the course record of 4:22.

Wende Cragg (far left) and me (knit cap) at the bottom of Repack, race 4. Emma Wolf is recording the finish times with an alarm clock.

Above: Art Black on the upper reaches of Repack.
This photo is from October 1978.

Opposite: Me rounding Repack's Switchback #1,
circa December 1976.

1976 was a drought year, and the normal winter rains came late and barely at all. With dry weather we raced every chance we got until the end of December, a total of nine races. On December 12 the course must have been blazingly fast, because I got under the mystical 5-minute barrier for the first time, while Otis and Joe both rode inside the 4:30 mark. With so many races under our belts, we were beginning to understand better what it took to go fast and started trying to find ways to shave a second off nearly 2 miles.

Disappointed with my performance on the Craig Mitchell frame, I had switched back to my old, red Excelsior, and that was what I was riding in the last race of the season in late December when I suffered my worst crash ever. I went over the bars at speed on the first sharp drop. I was wearing the kneepads and elbow pads I used when I was skateboarding, and they protected the bendy parts, but I was so stunned that I couldn't assess whether I was injured or not. I didn't want to move initially because I was afraid I would hear bones grinding, but I knew that if I lay on the road for more than a couple of minutes one of my dear friends would ride over me.

When I finally gathered myself, I got back on the bike and completed my slowest-ever timed run. Most of my injuries were superficial, but I had injured my right hand. When I aggravated the injury again playing basketball a few months later, I ended up with a cast and then a mildly deformed right thumb that makes it impossible to this day for me to properly grip a bowling ball.

After the last December race of 1976, I left with the band for a recording session in Colorado at Caribou Ranch that would keep me out of town for several weeks. Racing was over until the spring.

chapter 8

THE MOST IMPORTANT BICYCLE OF THE 20TH CENTURY

By the time racing resumed in the spring of 1977, we'd had three months to think about Repack. Since I had the timers, I was the guy who needed to agree as to which day was race day. I also had the notebook with all prior results and the phone numbers of the participants. That made me the de facto promoter.

After a small warm-up race for a half-dozen friends, I put on an Easter race, and for the first time I offered prizes. By this time the news of the races was all over the bike shops. Each race seemed to destroy a significant amount of tortured old metal, and the assault on the bike shops by the clunker riders after a race had not gone unnoticed. I made the rounds of the shops and leaned on the owners. The Koskis' Cove Bike Shop kicked in a drum brake and freewheel for the first prize—clunker gold— and Alan Bonds took them home.

This was the only race after we got the digital clocks in which the results weren't recorded to the

Breezer number 6, built for Wende Cragg. Joe's flawless work is evident in every detail: perfect brazing, beautifully finished stay caps, reinforced seat collar. The nickel plating was the toughest finish I've ever seen on a bike.

Excelsior shirt group photo after Repack, April 1977. Alan Bonds silk-screened and air-brushed these T-shirts with the old 1930s and 1940s Schwinn Excelsior headbadge logo. Left to right: Alan Bonds, Benny Heinricks, Ross Parkerson, Jim Stern, and me.

second decimal place. The person who had previously served as the finish timer was not available, and the substitute timer noted only whole seconds, not thinking to capture the hundredths of a second for each rider. The result was a tie for second between Bob Burrowes and Joe Breeze, one second behind Alan's time of 4:39. Unless the riders had actually finished at the same hundredth, the tie could have been avoided by noting the decimal.

One day in early 1977, while I was on the road with the band, I was trapped in a motel in San Diego waiting for other people to get ready to leave with me. I spent the time writing a story in a spiral notebook about the nine downhill races we had put on during the previous fall. When I got home I typed it up with the vague thought of selling it, although I didn't know how one did that.

The Sons of Champlin called it quits that summer, and after nine years working with the group, I was out of a job. Fred Wolf and I bought the band's truck and used it to start a small moving company. Since I was no longer spending my summer touring, I finally got to ride all I wanted.

Also in 1977 Gary Fisher moved out of the house at 32 Humbolt to take over Fred's vacated cottage strategically located in the heart of Fairfax behind Celoni's Bar. Gary spent a lot of time on

Joe slideways aboard Otis Guy's state-of-the-art, fully modified 1942 Schwinn Excelsior on Repack's Switchback #1, September or October 1977.

Up at 4 a.m. to ride to the top of Mount Barnabe in west Marin for sunrise, coffee, and doughnuts. At the top on October 27, 1977, are Joe Breeze, Vince Carlton, Fred Wolf, Gary Fisher, me, and Eric Fletcher.

FRED WOLF (FAIRFAX)   WENDE CRAGG (FA.)   MARK LINDLOW (FA.)   ROB STEWART STUART (LARK.)   CHRIS LANG (F.A.)   JIM PRESTON   STEWART IAN STEWART (LARK.)   CHARLEY KELL

This 16-rider panorama from the summer of 1977 was shot next to Central Field (now Contratti Park) in downtown Fairfax by Jerry Riboli using an 8 × 10 camera. The riders are getting ready for Alan Bonds's Enduro, with a final leg down Repack.

the road that year, traveling to Europe with cycling coach Mike Neel to act as a road bike mechanic on a racing team Mike was managing. Alan and I didn't replace the third roommate, and Alan now had more space in the house.

One afternoon I was riding my clunker on San Anselmo Avenue and encountered Joe, also on his clunker. We stopped to talk, and a subject bubbled to the surface again. In the past year I had asked

Joe a few times whether he would build an off-road frame for me, and he had been too busy. This time I asked what it would take to talk him into it. Without much thought Joe came up with a vague number, $200 or $300. I took $300 out of my wallet on the spot and told him I was ready to do business, and was there anything I could do to help?

Joe was, along with Gary, one of the elite racers in VCT. A second-generation cyclist, he was

also a second-generation machinist. His father, Bill Breeze, had been a machinist for race cars in the '50s at his Sports Car Center in Sausalito and maintained an interest in bicycles all his life. Bill died in 1980 of a cerebral aneurysm.

Joe had been using his father's machine tools for his own bike projects since 1974, when he began building road frames. Joe had learned framebuilding from Albert Eisentraut, a legendary Bay Area builder. Joe had built road bikes for other members of the club, including fellow Repack racers Marc Vendetti and Otis Guy. The work was so meticulous that if anyone could build the kind of bike I wanted, Joe was the guy. He was also one of the best downhill racers, and he knew what it would take to build my "secret weapon" for Repack. Joe accepted my money. He said he would have to think about the project, and I let him, because Joe is the kind of person who always fulfills his obligations after he accepts them.

Joe's plan at first was to build my bike and possibly one for himself, but it didn't take long for the word to get around. Before long he had many more orders and decided to build 10 frames instead of 2. Fred and Otis wanted bikes, Wende and Larry Cragg wanted bikes, and several others were clamoring at the door.

Exiting Repack's Camera Corner with dust flying aboard my fully modified Excelsior.

Top: Rob Stewart in front, Roy Rivers at the back, and me in the middle approaching Pine Mountain Saddle during the Enduro. Alan Bonds's dog Ariel brings up the rear.

Middle: Trudging uphill was a big part of klunking because the bikes were so heavy.

Bottom: Handups were evidently allowed in the Enduro, because Gary offered me a water bottle as I got close to the top of the hill.

The biggest event of 1977 for most of the clunker crowd was the Enduro. Alan wanted to try his hand at race promotion. It would have been difficult for Alan to promote a Repack race independently of me since I owned the timers, and he wanted something that was his alone, so he thought in another direction. He wanted to do a cross-country race, an Enduro, as he called it, from his Midwest background.

On a September afternoon Alan and I laid out a course for his race, with ribbons on trees marking turns and trails. An early season rain caught us unprepared, but we had a mission, and it didn't rain for very long. We started on the Pine Mountain Truck Road and rode past Repack, then cut along a trail we had discovered a few years earlier that had once led to a hidden pot plantation. The erstwhile farm had been abandoned long before we ever found the faint trail, which led past a perfectly rectangular clearing that had once been surrounded by barbed wire. Completing a loop on the flank of Pine Mountain, we dropped down a steep singletrack to the service road below Alpine Dam, then climbed back up the Old Vee Trail to the Pine Mountain Road and hurtled down Repack to the finish.

Alan rounded up a crew of competitors, including several Repack participants and a couple of Larkspur riders. Before we threw the bikes into Fred's truck to take them up the hill, Jerry Riboli asked whether he could take a photo of us. Jerry would later become a professional photographer, and he already had a large-format camera. We lined up in a Fairfax parking lot for what has become one of the most iconic photographs in

64
ch8

Joe on Breezer number 1 on Repack, late 1977. This turn, called Big Dipper, leads into the first of four switchbacks not far from the finish line.

the history of bicycling and certainly in the history of mountain biking—16 fat-tire riders, most equipped with the pinnacle of Marin clunker technology. In the middle, Gary laughs while he balances on Joe and me.

Gary gave a lot of us a break by sitting out the Enduro. He was so much better than everyone else, it would hardly be fair if he raced. Joe should have been more competitive than he turned out to be. He had borrowed a multiple-gear converted clunker for the race. He said, "Unfortunately, the bike was not in tip-top shape, and I fumbled through the gears for the whole race. I think it was Jim Stern who at the top of Repack intoned (as if a TV newscaster), 'A classic example of too much time on the trail and not enough time in the shop.'"

In the same way that carrying your bike is a big part of cyclocross, pushing your rig is huge in clunking. You do a lot of trudging, and proper technique is important for gaining time at slow speeds. In Alan's Enduro I could feel that no one could touch me. Three of us broke away on a long push, and as we approached the road that we had started from, I kept pace with Robert Stewart and Roy Rivers, building a big gap on the next pushers. Gary was waiting near where we passed our starting point, and he handed me a water bottle with

Fat Tire Flyer · The Most Important Bicycle of the 20th Century

Joe posing with Breezer number 1 at the bottom of Repack, October 1977, after winning the race on the bike's maiden voyage. This was the first purpose-built chrome-moly mountain bike frame assembled with all-new components. The paint is red primer.

one hand while he snapped photos of the three of us trudging with the other. One of his photos later ran in the first issue of *Outside* magazine in 1979. As we crested the hill, Roy and Robert faded because they were coaster brake riders, and I had gears. For the very first time in my life I hit the front of a bike race knowing that I owned everyone else in it. I was well clear and adding to my advantage when I missed a course marker, sailed past a turn, and strayed off a course that I had helped mark just a few days earlier.

Alan didn't miss the turn. He thought he was losing to me until he got to the finish at the bottom of Repack. He was stunned to find that I hadn't showed up and that he had won his own race. When I did finally show up about 20 minutes behind the winner, I was not a very good sport about my own mistake, which everyone else seemed to think was funny since I had done the trail marking with Alan. I didn't have anything to complain about, but that didn't stop me. Gary taped my embarrassing outburst for endless later amusement.

On October 2 we were back at Repack. I had a good day, going just under 5 minutes and finishing 5th in the field. I finished 5th in the next race as well, with the same four riders ahead of me: Joe, Alan, Fred, and Bob Burrowes. Although the

results are undated, there were two races between the October 2 event and the finale on December 4. I had a couple of good runs that fall, including getting under 4:50 for the first time.

But that fall season changed everything because Joe showed up on his own shiny, new bike and won with it on his first try.

Joe was riding the first bike to be completed of the 10 he was then building. Since I had given him the first order, I was next in line, but my bike was still months in the future. Although the bikes he sold had forks from a BMX supplier, for his own bike he had styled the fork after the old-school bikes, with a pair of '30s-style fork braces added to a fork with standard, tapered blades. Unpainted, the frame was the color of red-oxide primer right off the shop floor, and Joe smoked the field at Repack on the most important bicycle of the 20th century. It was the first modern mountain bike, built from the ground up with all-new components.

That fall I got a call from a writer who wanted to know if I was the guy who did the downhill races on the old bikes. I 'fessed up, and he said he wanted to write about our bikes for the magazine called *Co-Evolution Quarterly*, published in Sausalito by Stewart Brand of *Whole Earth Catalog* fame. Accordingly a few of us met with Richard Nilsen

and his friend Mike Castelli, who took the photos for the article. Richard grilled us, and Mike took pictures. The photo session was what you might expect—a few trail-riding shots, a shot of me riding my bike down a flight of stairs, and a shot of a poorly chosen "typical" Marin clunker. There was also a shot of Joe's new experimental bike.

We asked Richard when we could see the article. He hoped that if he sold it, we would see it in the spring issue.

THE DIRT BICYCLE COMES OF AGE

Joe Breeze finished my bike in early 1978. I had been all over Joe for it as soon as his own bike was finished, but the frames had to be sent to the nickel plater as a group, and that meant he had to finish all nine before he could start assembling mine. Joe had settled on a final price for the bike, and I gave him the balance of $450 I owed on the total of $750 for what is now one of the most collectible bikes of its time.

Joe had painted his own frame blue, but all the rest would be bead blasted and then plated. The nickel plating was by far the toughest finish I have ever seen on a bicycle. None of the plated bikes ever showed signs of wear, and the distinctive silver finish and the unusual design turned heads.

Joe had added a pair of "twin laterals," tubes that braced the frame from the head tube to the rear axle. They made for a frame that was overengineered but would never fail. The fork was made by Cook Brothers and was similar to a commercially

Posing with my new
Breezer number 2, circa 1978.

available BMX fork but made to Joe's spec to fit the bigger wheels.

Joe was building most of the other nine frames into complete bikes, but I wanted mine sooner, so he delivered it partially assembled with bottom bracket, headset, and brakes. As my bike took shape I needed a set of wheels, and it was going to take a while to get the Phil Wood hubs that I wanted, so to get started I took what the bike shop had, a set of Durham bolt-on hubs. I used chromed steel rims because they were the only kind on the market at the time. Aluminum rims in the 26-inch size were still two years away.

My finished bike was lighter than a clunker but still wasn't that light, coming in at more than 38 pounds with the steel rims and Uniroyal Nobby tires. The Dia-Compe cantilever brakes were the weakest aspect because the slick, chrome-plated sides of the rims give them very little purchase in wet conditions. Joe supplied the bike with Magura

Left: Wende Cragg's Breezer number 6.

Middle: Close-up of Wende's drivetrain. A number of the first Breezers had double chainrings, not triples.

Right: Wende's bike also had Phil Wood hubs and a custom-made Cook Brothers fork.

motorcycle brake levers, available from Motorcycles Unlimited in Corte Madera. The enormous levers provided as much mechanical advantage as you could get, but on a wet day the brakes still worked poorly or not at all. The only other braking option would have been drum brakes, and that choice had its own drawbacks. Nothing on the market was made to do what we wanted our bikes to do, so Joe had to choose a lesser evil and put cantilever bosses on the frame.

Joe delivered the rest of the bikes over a period of a month or so, and now a good part of the Fairfax crowd was equipped with the gleaming new fat-tire bikes with the distinctive extra diagonal tubes. They were hard to ignore. I took mine to the Nevada City Classic, a long-running annual bike race in that Gold Rush town that lines the course 10 deep with spectators. When I cruised easily in my low gears over curbs and grass that would have stopped any of the fancy road bikes, people noticed. In a crowd of road bike fanatics, even the hardest core of them couldn't help looking twice at the beautiful workmanship on a bike with all those gears and . . . fat tires?

When the spring issue of *Co-Evolution Quarterly* came out, there we were, in an article titled "Clunker Bikes: The Dirt Bicycle Comes of Age." It was the first published recognition of the multigear, fat-tire movement, and it featured photos both of a converted clunker and of Joe's first fat-tire bike. While we were doing the interviews for the article, the writer, Richard Nilsen, had mentioned that he knew about some people in Colorado who used bikes in much the same fashion.

Apparently we were not the only people to stumble across what now looked pretty obvious, because in his sidebar Richard listed the events for these "clunker" bikes. He mentioned the Repack races and also a place in Colorado called Crested Butte, where there was a big annual fat-tire race, or ride, or something. To us the description of riding in Crested Butte suggested kindred souls. We were not alone in the universe.

Richard described the bikes used in Crested Butte: "The technology is not as advanced as in California; single-gear, coaster brake, balloon-tire, 26-inch Schwinns are what most all clunker riders use here."

Richard also described the event in Crested Butte:

The main event each year is the Crested Butte–Aspen–Pearl Pass Clunker Bike Race. This 40-mile, two-day overnight race leaves Crested Butte, climbs over 12,700-foot Pearl Pass, and descends into Aspen. The downhill thrills are earned after pushing your bike up much of a trail that follows a stream bed and crosses interminable scree slopes. Out-of-town contestants are most welcome, and heavy duty spokes and rims and a helmet are recommended.

The race takes place in early September. The first one was held in 1976. Last year's race had to be cancelled, ironically, due to the drought. Many of the racers belong to the local fire crew, and were out of town fighting forest fires during the month. Plans continue, however, for a race this year. For information contact the Grubstake Saloon . . . Crested Butte, CO 81224.

The summer of 1978 marked the end of the household at 32 Humbolt. The landlord had raised the rent just about the time a vacancy opened up a few blocks away at a house shared by other VCT members, so Alan Bonds and I moved out. I moved

---

CLUNKER BIKE RACES

California

The Repack Downhill Clunker Race takes place about once a month, weather permitting, usually on Sunday mornings. Currently from 10 to 20 racers compete on the mountainside course just outside of Fairfax, California, a small town about 20 miles north of San Francisco. Race dates are announced by telephoning previous competitors. Newcomers and racers from outside Marin County are encouraged to compete. Contact Alan Bonds or Charlie Kelly at 32 Humbolt St., San Anselmo, CA 94960. Telephone (415) 454-4359.

Colorado

Clunker biking in Colorado is centered in the small mountain resort town of Crested Butte, high in the Rocky Mountains south of Aspen. Balloon-tired bicycles are popular because there aren't many paved roads in town. There isn't even much dirt, but there are plenty of rocks. The technology is not as advanced as in California; single-gear, coaster-brake balloon-tired 26-inch Schwinns are what most all clunker bikers use here.

With last winter's drought and no snow, things began to pale in this ski town, and so some bike races helped to alleviate the boredom. There was a beer slalom through the back alleys of town, with beer stops en route. There were sprints down the main street, and a distance jumping contest on pavement off a 2-foot high ramp. The record was 27 feet.

But the main event each year is the Crested Butte-Aspen-Pearl Pass Clunker Bike Race. This 40-mile, two-day overnight race leaves Crested Butte, climbs over 12,700-foot Pearl Pass, and descends into Aspen. The downhill thrills are earned after pushing your bike up much of a trail that follows a stream bed and crosses interminable scree slopes. Out-of-town contestants are most welcome, and heavy duty spokes and rims and a helmet are recommended.

The race takes place in early September. The first one was held in 1976. Last year's race had to be cancelled, ironically, due to the drought. Many of the racers belong to the local fire crew, and were out of town fighting forest fires during the month. Plans continue, however, for a race this year. For information, contact The Grubstake Saloon, Box 229, Crested Butte, CO 81224.

---

into a huge, old house at 1320 San Anselmo Avenue with two other cyclists, an artist named Pete Barrett and a bike racer named Kent Bostick. This was my fourth rental residence in 10 years within a 100-yard radius. The house was one of the oldest in the area, which explained the plumbing and wiring. It had pear trees in the yard and a tiny fountain and fishpond with four sculpted dragons peering into the water.

Kent had an advanced degree in geology and worked at a large engineering firm in San Francisco. He rode his bike the 25 or so miles each way every day for his only training between weekends. In winter he raced the pro slalom ski circuit around Lake Tahoe under an assumed name, Winston Harper. He never won anything because the locals skied every day while Winston—I mean Kent—could only get up there on weekends to train. I went with him a few times and found that skiing with Kent meant you went down through some

The clunker article in *Co-Evolution Quarterly* included a sidebar with the first mention we'd seen of a similar movement in Crested Butte, Colorado.

Above: Wende and me riding our Breezers on the trail carved into the cliffs below Monarch Lakes, Mineral King, September 1978, in a photo taken by Joe Breeze. Sawtooth Peak is in the distance.

Opposite: Joe (on the right) and me in Mineral King Valley at 10,000 feet, on a 30-mile loop through the backcountry in California's southern Sierra, Sequoia National Forest (later incorporated into Sequoia National Park), September 1978. We're looking back down to the valley floor—and yes, we know how lucky we are.

places you wouldn't have picked otherwise. Kent later made the Olympic cycling team several times and won the national road championship at the age of 35. That was in the future, though. In our eyes, Kent was the star of VCT, and he also taught me how to play "Rock and Roll, Hoochie Koo" on the guitar.

"Chicago" Pete was a transplant from the Midwest, a Vietnam vet, and an early member of VCT. If you wanted a special T-shirt, Pete could airbrush something on it freehand for you, and long before I moved into the house with him, I owned a few of his hand-drawn shirts celebrating skateboarding and cycling. He had a huge slot-car track that circled his room above his drawing board. He drew piles of cartoon panels featuring unlikely characters, and his artwork adorned much of the house.

Joe's family had a cabin in Mineral King, now included in Sequoia National Park, and on September 6, 1978, Joe, Wende Cragg, and I drove up there in Wende's sagging sedan with our three

bikes perched on a carrier. We spent six days riding trails through areas that became off-limits to mountain bikers the instant any rules were made about such things. In addition to riding, we hiked, fished, and made a great vacation out of the trip. We encountered a few people along the miles of trails, a couple of hikers and a couple of men on horses leading a train of pack animals, and they expressed surprise that anyone could get a bike where these obviously were. The few people we saw didn't seem outraged at our presence. At least two were very happy to have met us.

On one ride we met a couple of deer hunters who had rigged a one-wheel litter to haul out their game. A bicycle wheel under the middle supported the load, and the two men had handles at each end to propel and steer it up and down the steep, narrow, switchback trail. Hours later, on our return trip, we met them again, and they had a flat tire on their rig. We provided them with a bicycle pump to get them moving again, probably the only bike pump to be found within 30 miles.

On our last day Joe mapped out a ride that turned out to be far too ambitious, as a storm had turned trails into bogs. We finished long after dark after struggling through the woods without lights. No longer riding, we dragged our bikes the last

Opposite: Wende and me in Farewell Gap above Mineral King Valley at 10,587 feet, September 1978.

5 miles down narrow trails we had never seen before and couldn't see then because it was so dark. We were out of food and well past hitting the wall. It was one of those epic rides that was relived for years to come.

At the time there weren't any rules about bicycle access, and we rode to some incredible places on that trip. Joe took a photograph of Wende and me riding on a trail above Mineral King and submitted it to a *Bicycling* magazine photo contest. Joe's photo won him the $25 third-place prize.

Gary Fisher was now working regularly for *Bicycling* and spent much of the summer at the company headquarters in Pennsylvania. He was still riding his old Excelsior and had taken it with him to amaze the more conservative eastern *Bicycling* magazine staff.

With responsibilities to the band a thing of the past, I was free to travel anywhere and do anything. Richard's *Co-Evolution Quarterly* article had tipped us off to an annual race of some kind in Crested Butte, so one day I made the long-distance call to the place the article had given as the headquarters for the event. I found myself speaking to Duane Reading at the Grubstake Saloon.

Above: Wende follows me around a right-hand bend on Sawtooth Pass Trail on our way down from Monarch Lakes. That's Empire Mountain in the distance. Joe's photo took the third place prize in *Bicycling*; the other two must have been truly spectacular to outdo this one.

chapter 10

CRESTED BUTTE

Duane Reading and I had a conversation, but I'm not sure we understood each other. We lived in different worlds, with different contexts for the same words, and we probably talked right past each other and heard what we wanted to hear. Duane told me that the "event" had only happened once, when some of the boys from Crested Butte held a traveling party over two days to Aspen. It wasn't a contest, although when I pressed him, Duane admitted that people liked to race a bit on the descent into Aspen. I misunderstood the informal nature of the challenge to be a formal one with rules and the like, but in any event I got the impression that the ride was on and the date was set.

Based on the phone call, a few of us decided we wanted to take our gleaming new bikes to their event. After all, the article had said that out-of-town riders were welcome. We talked to Richard Nilsen, whose article had inspired us and who had

a place in Colorado where we could spend the night on the way. He was up for it and would meet us in Colorado.

First order of business was for Joe Breeze to get a driver's license. Despite being the son of a race car driver, Joe, now 26, had never bothered to start driving, since he went everywhere on a bike. Now he had to share the driving on a trip of nearly 1,000 miles each way. Joe had no trouble learning the mechanical skill of driving, so he took the test and joined the masses behind the wheel at last.

Leaving from California were Joe, Wende Cragg, Mike Castelli, who had taken the photos for the *Co-Evolution Quarterly* article, and myself. We traveled in two vehicles, a rented sedan and Mike's pickup, which carried our bikes. Mike didn't have a custom bike, but since Wende was now on a "Breezer," Mike was riding Wende's green Excelsior clunker with the beautiful Alan Bonds paint

job. Gary Fisher was done with his gig at *Bicycling* and had his bike with him, so he would fly in from Pennsylvania to join us.

We took a couple of days for the drive, camping in Nevada and staying with Richard in Hotchkiss, Colorado, before pulling into Crested Butte on a crystal-clear September afternoon. Richard followed us in his own vehicle. The trusty upright touring bike that he planned to use was not exactly to our taste, but it was the only bike he had. We strolled into the Grubstake and asked for Duane.

We were a bit of a surprise. No one had expected us to really drive out from California for a silly, local, one-time event. It was like going halfway across the country for an Easter egg hunt.

But there we were. And look at those bikes. We might as well have landed a Lear Jet on Elk Avenue.

The Crested Butte to Aspen Clunker Tour had been a subject of discussion, but it had been two years since the only iteration, and no one was step-

ping up to make it happen now. It was easy to talk it up on the phone to the guy writing a story for a magazine, but then the people from California inconveniently arrived.

We had driven a long way on a thin premise, but we were there, and the town did not want us to stand there in vain. The ride was on. Duane immediately had us in the broadcasting booth of the town radio station, where we were interviewed at length for an audience numbering in the dozens. It was clear that our arrival was the most interesting thing to happen in town that afternoon.

There weren't many flights into the tiny town of Crested Butte, so tracking Gary's arrival was easy. The four of us rode our bikes out to the tiny airstrip a few miles out of town, and Gary's twin-engine, four-seat, commercial airliner landed in the thin air of almost 9,000 feet. Gary and his bike unfolded themselves out the small door. He had been forced to totally dismantle the bike to get it

Line-up in Pearl Pass (elevation 12,700 feet) during the Third Annual (but second actual) Crested Butte to Aspen Pearl Pass Klunker Tour, September 1978. Left to right (with bike in parentheses): Wende Cragg, Fairfax, CA (1978 Breezer); Neil Murdoch, Crested Butte, CO ('50s Schwinn); Richard Neilsen, Hotchkiss, CO ('60s Schwinn); Charlie Kelly, San Anselmo, CA (1978 Breezer); Joe Breeze, Mill Valley, CA (1977 Breezer); Jim Cloud, Crested Butte, CO ('50s Schwinn); Bob Starr, Crested Butte, CO ('50s Schwinn); Richard Ullery, Crested Butte, CO ('50s Schwinn); Gary Fisher, San Anselmo, CA (1938 Schwinn); Archie Archiletta, Crested Butte, CO ('50s Schwinn); Chris Carroll, Crested Butte, CO ('50s Schwinn); Albert Maunz, Crested Butte, CO ('50s Schwinn); Michael Castelli, Point Reyes, CA ('30s Schwinn).

into the little plane, and now he had to reassemble it on the gravel airstrip before we could leave. His drum brake clunker required a lot of reconnection and calibration before it was ready to ride, then we all stormed back into town.

We had no plan for a place to stay, and Duane felt responsible for our presence, so we ended up crashed all over his house and in a tent in the backyard. I have no idea whether this created tension inside the household, but it created a crowd in the bathroom and probably confused the dog about whose territory the backyard was.

The afternoon we arrived, Duane took us in the back of a coughing, tubercular wreck of a pickup truck up Washington Gulch to a pass high above town he called "The Ride to Die." It killed the pickup to get us there, but we had our bikes, and it was downhill all the way back to Crested Butte. The entire trip would have been worth it to us just for the chance to ride these glacial valleys on this crisp fall day, past beaver dams and golden aspens. We had never ridden in territory like this, and we were just getting started.

We were shocked to find that there were only a couple of bikes in Crested Butte remotely comparable to ours. They were owned by the bike shop guy, Neil Murdoch, and his friend Chris Carroll, but

Crested Butte's collection of bikes
was quite different from ours.

both were recent arrivals in town and not part of the group that had ridden into Aspen two years earlier.

The original crowd had been fellows from the forest firefighting crews, blue-collar guys similar to the miners who had established the settlement. In a town a half-mile long from one end to the other with only one paved street, everyone rode town bikes similar to the old one-speeds that Gary and I had first ventured out on. There was nothing any more sophisticated about these bikes than you would find in a Southern California beach village, although the inviting terrain outside of town had led a few of the locals to explore the wonders of coasting.

As we learned, the origins of the first ride unfolded like this: On a fall day in 1976, the town had been invaded from Aspen on the far side of Pearl Pass by a horde of cross-country motorcyclists who all stopped in at the same time for a beer at the Grubstake and wrecked the afternoon for the locals who had been drinking there quietly.

Afterward, a Crested Butte local suggested that they eclipse the Aspen riders by taking their town bikes over Pearl Pass to the bar at the Jerome Hotel in Aspen, where they could line them up outside like the motorcyclists had done at the Grubstake.

The ride was on. As I understood it, they took two days, with a campout, and hauled a lot of the bikes in vehicles at least partway if not all the way to the top of Pearl Pass, at 12,700 feet. Then they rode into Aspen for their drinks at the Jerome. Whether anyone at the Jerome noticed is a matter of conjecture.

The next year, 1977, there had been no ride, and it is unlikely that the ride in 1978 would have taken place if six people with fancy bikes hadn't showed up from out of town asking about it. But now it was on, and no one was ready. Between rides in the hills Gary, Joe, and I took over what passed for a bike shop. It was just the house where Neil Murdoch lived, and we worked in what would ordinarily be a bedroom.

The three of us had by then accumulated years of experience with everything the local riders were dealing with. We saw right away that some of their bikes were junk that wouldn't have survived a single run on Repack. They weren't onto any of the Morrow brake or Excelsior frame lore that we took for granted as a starting point. Crested Butte is small and isolated, and there weren't all kinds of old bikes lying around to be mined for prime specimens. The bikes we were working on had almost all come from a single raid on a faraway Denver dump and a truckload of old bikes that now represented the town supply. The bikes didn't have any competitive purpose like ours did, and there was no reason to refine them. Crested Butte town bikes were ridden at stately speeds. It didn't matter that some of them had high-rise, Stingray bars for the style factor, but for off-road riding, the bars were ridiculous. The same was true of the coaster brakes made for gentle slopes. And few if any had front brakes.

Roommates Chris and Neil were aware of the latest technology but hadn't pedaled many strokes toward it. Chris had a Phil Wood tandem drum rear brake that he planned to use, a piece of jewelry next to the industrial Atom hubs in the town's clunker supply. As we scrounged around to help get their bikes ready, though, we realized that his hub not only represented the apogee of improved technology but also was the sole representative. Simply put, there was no supply of better parts to upgrade the local equipment. Instead, we worked with what was there. Joe, Gary, and I built wheels, tore down and reassembled hubs and bottom brackets, and did what we could to make the wreckage serviceable. None of us, however, would have ridden such lame bikes to the corner and back.

On the day of the ride, the Crested Butte crew showed up mostly hung over. All of 14 riders started, and 13 later made it to the top of Pearl Pass and into Aspen for drinks at the Jerome.

It's 18 miles from Crested Butte to the campsite, with about 2,000 feet of elevation gained. With all day to make that distance, it's an easy ride. The mountains in Marin County are dwarfed by those we were riding in Colorado, and the scenery was everything anyone could ask for in a vacation. The California riders were having more fun than the hung-over locals. We crossed the creek repeatedly as we worked our way up the valley.

A few miles out of town, one of the Crested Butte riders had a flat tire. The disappointed rider looked on while we helped him out. In its subsequent coverage of the event, the September 29 *Crested Butte Pilot* observed the difference between Crested Butte and California: "The California boys immediately jackknifed into action. Tools selected after years of experience glimmered in the sunlight as the intrepid Californians removed the wheel, replaced the tube, tuned the spokes, remounted the wheel, slacked the cones a tad, adjusted the chain, and had Archie's bike back on the road in 35 seconds flat!"

A good 15 of us, including the supply-truck drivers, camped out at 11,000 feet on a night with no moon and starlight bright enough to play Frisbee by. We drank peppermint schnapps and ate steaks cooked on a campfire and talked and joked very late and generally had one of the greatest nights of all of our lives. At least so far.

In the morning we had pancakes and coffee and started the trudge over Pearl Pass. The road gets very steep, to the point where four-wheel drive might not be enough for some vehicles. Coming from sea level, we Californians found that at 12,000 feet we could barely keep our bikes moving on a slope that didn't look at all steep, and at walking speeds the forward advantage shifted back to the tough locals. A couple of hours later, 13 people with a strange assortment of bicycles stood on top of Pearl Pass under a threatening sky, posing for another iconic photo in the annals of mountain biking.

As with every other occasion when a group leaves the top of a hill, the descent turned into a race. The descent from Pearl Pass is brutal, 7 miles of steep downhill with softball-size rocks on top of watermelon- to bathtub-size rocks. The Breezer riders didn't suffer from the braking problems that afflicted the coaster brake equipment of the Crested Butte riders, but the stiff front end sent a lot of shock right through the rider to the point where it became hard to hang on with two fingers and operate the brakes effectively at the same time. The coaster brake riders could hold the bars tighter, but now and then they had to stop at the stream next to the road and throw some cold water onto the brakes to cool them down. The last two-thirds of the descent were paved, and the high gears on our bikes let us pull away easily from the coaster brake riders.

We regrouped at the edge of Aspen to put balloons on the fork blades. The idea was to simulate the arrival of the motorcycle riders whose presence in Crested Butte two years earlier had led to what we were doing. I suspect that the Aspen residents who paid any attention at all to the noisy bike parade didn't connect what they were seeing and hearing to any such thing.

There was enough money left over from our "entry" fees to keep us drinking for a couple of hours, and while we abused our welcome in the bar with our rowdy attitude and the sidewalks of Aspen with our bikes, Gary had an epiphany. A couple of kids recognized that his Excelsior was a cool bike, sort of a BMX on steroids, and yelled to him to do a wheelie. Gary attempted to oblige and snapped off his handlebar. It didn't escape him that this was just after the wild descent of Pearl Pass, when that might have been deucedly inconvenient.

The Excelsior was toast. Gary knew he needed a new bike. Fortunately, he was done with it for the moment, and he threw it on the truck with the others for the two-hour ride back to Crested Butte.

chapter 11

GETTING ORGANIZED

When I returned from Colorado that fall, the road trips to Mineral King and Crested Butte had kicked my enthusiasm for our bikes even higher than when the main idea had been to race them. They were fun to do anything on. Having no other career plans before that summer beyond working for the Sons of Champlin, I was in uncharted personal territory after that gig ended. Without a rock band dictating my personal schedule, I found freedom to travel and organize events, and I was discovering that I had a knack for getting a lot of people in one place to do stuff. After assuming the role of promoter for the Repack races, I was becoming the de facto leader, or at least a major planner, for everything the loose-knit clunker crowd did as a group.

I had met Denise Caramagno in Fairfax before leaving town for Crested Butte, and shortly after I returned she moved into the house I shared with

Repack poster by Pete Barrett for October 29, 1978. The original art is now in the collection of the Smithsonian Institution.

Kent Bostick and Pete Barrett. She brought with her a puppy named Amelia that became my dog for the next decade and a half.

Since our rental house at 1320 San Anselmo Avenue had been passed along through members of Velo-Club Tamalpais (VCT), it remained bicycle central, conveniently located on the main bike route through town.

It had been a while since the last race, and all the new Breezer owners were leaning on me. They hardly needed to. I had gone to a lot of trouble to get a bike built for racing at Repack, I had owned the bike for months, and I hadn't raced it because there hadn't been any races. I chose a date of October 29. This time I turned some of my energy toward promoting it more creatively than just calling everyone on my phone list.

I had Pete draw a poster for the event, the first of his many artistic contributions to the growing movement. A pen-and-ink drawing was cheap to reproduce on a photocopier, and Pete was right there in the same house. It was too easy not to do. His depiction of a rider leaving the bottom of the frame and riding straight down captured the spirit of the race and was the first advertising of any kind for what would eventually be called a "mountain bike" event. His cartoon bike was a diamond-frame, fat-tire bike with a derailleur, also the first advertising image of this type of bike.

The poster had a purpose other than advertising. It was never a problem rounding up people to race, but by that fall I started to realize that Repack was something special and that I should make sure I documented my involvement. A poster with my name and a date would do that. The poster also established a tradition of posters for future events.

Since it was a given that only four or five riders were competing for the overall win, I created separate categories for novices and experts, with separate prize lists. From previous results, I identified riders who had finished in less than 5 minutes and made them experts. There weren't that many, a dozen or so. New riders and those who had never crossed that barrier were novices.

Even though prizes were given out, there were no entry fees for the Repack races I put on. I felt that if I took money it would make me more responsi-

ble to the riders than I already was. If I didn't take money, no one could possibly complain about being ripped off no matter what happened, even if the timing system failed. At least they would have had a ride on Repack where they could go as fast as they wanted, and that was worth something.

Pete's poster went up in bike shops and coffeehouses. It was a head-turner artistically and a head-scratcher otherwise. It advertised an event and a date, but not a race venue, all by design. If you wanted to race, you called me. If you had no idea what the poster was about, you weren't anyone I cared about, and you weren't likely to call me. If you didn't know what or where Repack was, the poster wouldn't lead you there. The bicycle underground and anyone who worked in a bike shop understood its message clearly, but it wasn't something that would draw official notice to our dangerous, competitive activities on public lands. Like Edgar Allan Poe's purloined letter, the promotion of Repack was hidden in plain sight.

Our house stood in San Anselmo, but it was close to the border with Fairfax, so we did most of our business in Fairfax. Fairfax is a small town with two types of people, the kind who leave town to make money somewhere else and the kind who don't. We were the second kind, piling our

bikes in front of the coffeehouses while we discussed the events of the day, then taking off on rides. We were hard to ignore. Since the start of Repack racing two years earlier, the crazy downhill race and the highly visible clunker riders were well-known in Fairfax. People had seen the pink, stakebed, 1951 Chevy truck grinding up Bolinas Road packed with funky bikes and funkier riders and seen the howling, muddy celebrants returning to town sometime later.

With the posters going up and enough people in the know about Repack, there was a new trend to the race: spectators. People had heard about it, and now there was a chance to watch it. Spouses and significant others came out for support. It's a short hike from Cascade Drive to Repack and then you can walk uphill to one of the prime corners. Now we had people hiking to the best vantage points to check out this crazy race. It was the best free show in town.

One of the spectators was a Tiburon resident who lived near the Cove Bike Shop and had been invited by the Koski brothers. He was a recently retired national champion motorcycle racer named Mert Lawwill, and he checked out the races with his associate Terry Knight. Don Koski had fabricated a fat-tire bike-frame mockup from electrical conduit and wanted Mert to produce it for Cove in his motorcycle research-and-development shop. This race was the first opportunity for the Koskis to show Mert what it would be used for.

On race day, I sorted the entries by previous performance based on the records I had kept. First-time riders started first, then novices with a previous run in order of their times, slowest riders first. After that the expert riders, once again in order of their fastest times, fastest riders last. Sorting them this way made sure that the spectators a mile below would get a good show because theoretically the riders would improve and the speeds would go up as the race went on. At the starting line, the crowd of riders waiting to leave was noisy at first. Nervous riders riding their first race were hyperactive, but as the number of waiting riders went down, the level of experience went up. By the time the start crowd had thinned to six or seven riders, nobody was talking at all.

Like the race itself, the mood at the top of Repack can't be duplicated in any other way. The dwindling number of riders who were left at the top all knew each other, and all had made multiple timed runs. The competitiveness among them precluded any chatter. We lived for the 5 minutes of intensity, and like all athletes, the riders had per-

sonal rituals they went through while they focused on what they were about to do. These rituals didn't include conversation with rivals.

The stopwatch in my hand allowed me to time the riders' start from the line where I held the clock to the crest that marks the high point of the course. Taking splits of riders revealed that a fast hole shot was worth 2 or 3 seconds in the first 150 yards over an average start. This advantage explains why the three top times were held by road racers who could accelerate uphill over that distance on the sandy surface. It also showed that even though Bob Burrowes had a slow start, he rode the lower part of the course faster than the other riders.

In that first race of 1978, Joe Breeze on his Breezer nipped Gary Fisher riding his repaired Excelsior to notch another win for modern machinery. Joe went on to take a hat trick, winning all three of the races held in 1978. His bike was something else, and he was unbeatable on it. Nothing got the attention of the clunker crowd like success, and Gary's Excelsior frame was falling apart. He was already looking around for someone to build a custom frame for him.

In previous years, the Appetite Seminar had been informally organized, but now I added it to Repack as another clunker activity that would

include people I didn't know. For the end of November 1978, I promoted an all-clunker Thanksgiving weekend with a poster and a contact telephone number for both the Appetite Seminar and the next Repack race, a few days later. Pete drew up a poster that advertised both events, one at each end and reversed from each other. After the Appetite Seminar the poster would be rotated 180 degrees to become the next Repack poster. On Thanksgiving Day, I led the small group around Pine Mountain Loop, and for the next few years the Appetite Seminar was an annual promotion with its own Pete Barrett poster.

That winter, Joe and I took a stab at cyclocross on our Breezer bikes. It had been only a few years since we were inspired by the Morrow Dirt Club making the same mistake with their first-generation clunkers. The annual Tilden Park Cyclocross was the venue, and we did not change any minds with our performances. On a course made for light bikes, the extra ruggedness of our heavy-duty bikes did not make up for the difference in weight. Alloy rims and light tires were the future of mountain biking, but they had not yet arrived. On dry pavement, the cyclocross bikes were much faster, and they were considerably lighter to carry over the barriers than our 38-pound bikes. I was unable to

Pete's combination poster for the fourth annual Appetite Seminar Thanksgiving Day ride and the following Repack race, 1978.

finish after I caught my bike's somewhat delicate TA chainring on an obstacle and bent it enough to disable the bike. We did get to celebrate a victory, though, because the winner, Joe Ryan, was a member of VCT and was wearing the same jersey that Joe and I wore.

By the end of 1978, the social circuit around our burgeoning clunker movement had grown to several dozen avid Repack racers and clunker riders. It seemed like time for a party, and as the race promoter I also became the party planner. I reserved a good role for myself as master of ceremonies. The theme would be a faux awards ceremony called the Clunker Awards.

Since Wende Cragg was a fabric artist, I persuaded her to make the actual awards, mock "gold medals" with ribbons. She labored mightily for a week, far harder than she expected to, and harder than I would have ever dared ask of her, and turned out works of art, quilted gold medals with a four-cross, spoked wheel embroidered in the center.

The entire membership of VCT and everyone who raced at Repack wanted to be at the party, which was going to be the social event of the season for the bike set. The Fairfax Women's Club would be the venue. I ordered prime ribs from the Deer Park Villa, a few blocks away, and hun-

1978 Klunker Award made by Wende Cragg. I received this at the first Klunker Banquet Awards in 1978 for being the "Best Organizer" and having the "Most Metal/Mental Breakdowns."

dreds of oysters from Tomales Bay. I made a floor plan and rented the tables and chairs. I had to sit somewhere, and more people wanted to join me at my table than I could accommodate. Everyone, it seemed, promised to bring a fine bottle of wine.

Then one week before the big night, two long-time VCT members who had already bought their tickets, Tracy Hite and Eric Fletcher, were killed in an automobile accident. Despite the tragedy that struck our hearts, the dinner was too close to cancel; instead, we took a moment during the evening to toast our absent friends.

This was my first try at putting together a big party, and I didn't want to delegate much of it to anyone else and be let down. Next to Wende's yeoman work making the awards, what I needed to do wasn't rocket science, and I was sure everything was under control. By the chosen evening I had everything humming, and with an hour to go before guests started arriving, I was doing my last errand of picking up charcoal to grill the oysters, when the roll-up door on my truck came down on my hand, virtually severing a fingertip. It was still there but dangling and bleeding.

That certainly changed everything.

A nearby store clerk called 911, and a police car was the first to arrive. I jumped into the front seat spurting blood and told the startled officer that we should go to the hospital pretty soon, and I didn't need an ambulance. He got me there quickly, with a siren and lights, skidding on the rain-slick streets and calling ahead to alert the ER that we were coming in. At the ER I jumped out and ran past the crew running the other way with the stretcher to get me out of the police car. I had things to do, and I wasn't waiting.

Seventy people were about to show up for a party, food was already being cooked, and the tables, chairs, and rented china were in the truck that had injured me, parked where I had left it in front of a hardware store. I had a date for the evening who was looking forward to sitting at the head table, and she might want to know where I was. I needed to mobilize people, and I needed a phone to do that.

I also wanted to keep that fingertip. I had conflicting priorities.

The ER staff understandably tried to calm me down, thinking that my crazed demands for a phone were the result of shock. Finally I convinced someone that I had important business to conduct, and while a physician sewed the tip back onto the middle finger of my left hand, I made calls on a wall phone in the ER with my right.

My date picked me up from the hospital, and by the time I arrived at the Women's Club my friends had rounded up the rented supplies and organized the party. Even though I was late and had a huge bandage on my finger, I was able to change into my black-tie outfit and assume my duties as master of ceremonies. The doctor had told me that I had to keep my hand elevated if I wanted his work to be worthwhile, so while standing at the podium addressing the crowd, I flipped them an enormous white bird for the entire evening. Knowing that there would be great bottles of wine at the party, I didn't take any pain medication. I didn't want to combine pills with alcohol and give an incoherent presentation, and I preferred to drink the wine. If anything, the pain kept me alert!

The awards themselves were arbitrary. I had made up a list of people who were important to the clunker scene, then figured out the awards to give them based on all the racing we had done over the previous two years. Some awards were tongue-in-cheek. Alan Bonds picked up one for owning the fastest dog on Repack. Jerry Heidenreich picked up the "Best Dressed" award for racing in a tuxedo. Other awards honored real accomplishments. Gary's was for "Fastest Time" and Joe's for "Most Wins." As each recipient stepped up to receive his or her award, a slide would be shown on a screen behind the podium.

Gary was in Pennsylvania during the awards, but we gave him the number for the pay phone at the Women's Club, and he called in to accept his award.

I didn't choose a category for an award for myself, but I got one nonetheless. Wende and the others figured out what honor I deserved, and it was a surprise to me when I handed the rest out and then came to my own. My Clunker Award had two designations, "Best Organizer" and "Most Mental/Metal Breakdowns." The latter title celebrated the constant destruction of my riding equipment before I got the Breezer as well as my now infamous tirade after losing Alan's Enduro race through my own stupidity.

One local rider known to be more talk than walk was honored with the "No Show" award for never actually competing at Repack. When his name was announced the screen went white because there was no slide of him in the projector. Of course there was no actual award either, and the party in question hadn't shown up at the dinner to not receive his nonaward. It was the perfect conclusion to an evening that could have gone all wrong but turned out fine in the end.

I also received an early Christmas gift that December from an unexpected source. Gary had taken my story about the Repack race with him to *Bicycling* magazine, and he told me that they were going to run it in the January 1979 issue. It was a story that I had written more than a year earlier, at a time when only a dozen or so races had taken place. It was the first story I ever wrote, and I sold it for $225 without even submitting it to anyone. All I had done was to give Gary a copy. In the piece, I attempted to describe what the race was like. My panting prose from 1977 captured it then as well as I could ever do now:

What is it like to ride this course? As the rider before you leaves, you have two minutes to prepare yourself. For a surprising number of entrants this means a fast trip to the bushes for emergency urination. Wheeling up to the line with a minute to go you find your breathing a little strained, fast, and loud in your ears. "Thirty seconds." Squeeze brake levers to make sure they are adjusted for maximum grab. "Fifteen." You check for the eighth time to make sure you are in the right gear. "Ten." Up onto the pedals as the starter holds the rear wheel. "Five." The world shrinks and becomes twelve feet wide, stretched out in front of you. Conscious effort is required to hold back from an early start. "GO!" The wheel is released and the bike shoots forward as if propelled by a tightly wound spring.

The first 150 yards are level with a soft surface and then a slight uphill. It is imperative to ride this section as fast as possible since there is a two- or three-second difference between a fast rider and a slow one here.

Over the rise and into the first downhill and you are already gasping from the initial effort. No time to let up though, for this section is straight and even though it is steep you are still standing on your highest gear.

Blind left turn onto the steepest section, covered with ruts and loose rocks. Watch that little

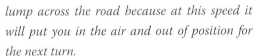

The Repack sign didn't last long before it was stolen, but it legitimized our name for the Cascade Canyon Fire Road. The road was even identified as "Repack" on official maps for several years.

lump across the road because at this speed it will put you in the air and out of position for the next turn.

Now the road becomes a series of blind corners which all seem to look the same as you approach. This section favors the experienced Repack rider who can remember which corners to brake for and which ones can be taken wide open. Since Repack is in more or less a straight line at the top, most of the corners can be taken at full speed, which is a thrilling prospect in light of the fact that it will take you about 200 feet to stop (unless you hit a tree). At no time should you stop pedaling unless you are jamming on the brakes. As you approach some of the more wicked curves you are conscious of a few fifty-foot, side-to-side skid marks. Amateur tracks. A definite "groove" is visible on most of the corners, worn into the surface by the passage of many knobby tires.

A roller-coaster section gives you a new thrill as the bike becomes weightless just when you want the tires on the ground. Into a dip and the bike slides sideways, then corrects itself pointed in exactly the right direction. Cutting all corners as closely as possible, you receive a whack or two from overhanging branches.

As your adrenalin pump goes into overdrive, your reflexes and vision improve immeasurably. You are aware of every pebble on the road, even though they are whipping past. You are totally alone; the only spectators are at the bottom. You dare not lose your concentration for an instant, but the danger of that is slight. You are definitely getting off.

Sliding into an off-camber, eroded turn you make a micro miscalculation. Out of control, you must make a rapid decision, off the edge, or lay it down. Lay it down . . . damn. Torn shirt, bloody elbow. No time to mess with that now (the shirt was old, so was the elbow), how's the bike? Okay . . . jump on it and feed the chain back on with your hand as you coast the first few yards. Back in gear you really stand on it to make up time.

Near the bottom of the course is a series of switchbacks and you are vaguely aware that

you are being photographed as you try for maximum cornering speed. Out of the switchbacks in a cloud of dust and into the final straightaway. Jam on the brakes to keep a lump in the road from launching you off the edge. Now there are several dozen people along the sides of the course, earlier riders, girlfriends, and a few locals. Last corner . . . and roaring past the big rock that marks the finish, you skid 50 feet to the flashiest possible stop, then throw down your bike and run over to the timer, who instantly gives you your time. It is the best so far, but your elation is reduced by the arrival of the next rider somewhat less than two minutes later. As the last half-dozen riders finish, the times continue to go down, and the last finisher records the best time, some twenty seconds better than yours. Any time under five minutes is respectable, but the record stands at 4:22.

chapter 12

THE WORD GETS OUT

Joe Breeze completed his sweep of 1978 with a third win at Repack on December 30. This was a low-key event with no poster, and only 11 riders showed up for the race. The next one three weeks later would be big.

A TV station employee who lived in Fairfax told someone at KPIX in San Francisco about our activities, suggesting we might be worth a few minutes on a local program called *Evening Magazine*. They tracked me down, and I agreed to put on a race for their cameras on January 20, 1979.

Pete Barrett did a poster, and the word was out that there was a TV shoot. Turnout was huge. A framebuilder named Tom Ritchey, who had seen Joe's first Breezer earlier that month, came up from his home in Palo Alto, 50 miles south of Marin, to take part. Since Tom didn't have a bike of his own, he used Wende Cragg's green Excelsior for the race, and he rode a very creditable 5:17.51 on his first trip down the course.

Wende Cragg holding her Breezer and Larry Cragg's Breezer on a rare snowy day on Mount Tamalpais, early 1979, on Railroad Grade at Ridgecrest Boulevard. Note the "No Bikes" sign. That was something new.

The camera crews had things we didn't, including a Jeep and a radio system. The production was big-time, and host Steve Fox interviewed me at the top, with a young Tom looking over my shoulder.

There was exciting crash footage when a rider flew over the edge with his Breezer bike, some say deliberately, directly over the cameraman, who kept his cool and tracked the bike as it slid down the hill.

As the course record holder, Gary started last and had a great day, nipping Joe by less than a second for a huge win in front of the cameras. This was the swan song for Gary's trusty Excelsior, which had already been welded back together a couple of times.

Interviewed afterwards, Gary gave a superlative answer to a silly question.

"Gary, why do they call you 'The Fish?'"

"I don't know, maybe because I wiggle in and out of things real well."

After the race a few of us spent the rest of the afternoon shooting background footage. Then we went home and waited to be on TV. The hours of raw footage were edited down to about 10 minutes, with the Steve Miller Band providing the sound track. It was breathless and over the top, just the way I like it. Although a San Francisco crew had shot the piece, local versions of *Evening Magazine* were syndicated all over the country, and the format provided a path to national exposure for interesting local stories. A few weeks after the initial airing in the Bay Area market, the piece was shown nationally on all the CBS affiliates, which meant it was seen again in the Bay Area. With my article titled "Clunkers Among the Hills" running simultaneously in *Bicycling*, the secret was starting to leak out.

The January race saw the first serious injury on Repack. The victim was a first-time rider who broke his wrist. Complicating his injury was the

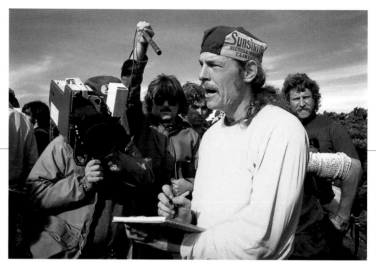

Above: Steve Fox from San Francisco's KPIX *Evening Magazine* interviewing me about Repack and the new sport, January 1979. Left to right: Steve Fox, me, Katie Ritchey, Tom Ritchey.

Right: Announcing the start times for the *Evening Magazine* camera. After the race, we rode home and waited to see ourselves on TV.

fact that he was a professional drummer who had just landed a juicy gig that he would not be able to play. None of this was caught on camera, and the rider tried to tough it out before his diagnosis and plaster cast, so it was days later before I even found out about the injury.

I had my own injury problems that year. My only previous fracture had been three years earlier on the trail we now called Broken Hand, and after getting a cast put on it, I had gone to work that night without missing a beat. My new injury, though, happened not on a bike but a skateboard. I had picked up a board in 1975 when Ray Flores had shown me a urethane skateboard wheel, and by 1979 I was hitting the skate parks regularly. At the age of 33 I was always the oldest person anyone ever saw skating vertical at the parks, and I was always the biggest. From my travels with the band, I had memberships in skate parks all over California. When I raced on Repack I wore the gloves, kneepads, and elbow pads I used for skateboarding, although I didn't wear the helmet.

I had done all my skateboarding without serious injury, but in the spring of 1979 my luck ran out, and I broke my leg in a skate park. After the doctor put the cast on, he told me not to put weight on the leg until the cast came off six weeks

Swapping post-race tales at the bottom of Repack in January 1979.

later. A week of crutches was all I could stand. With the help of a friend who shaped a wooden sole for my cast and helped me attach it, I started walking on it anyway. When I got down to a week to go before the doctor was going to remove it, I cut off the cast with my Swiss Army knife and went for a bike ride.

While I was laid up that spring, though, I wrote another article about the new bikes. I sent it to several publications, and it was accepted by an outdoor magazine called *Mariah.* By the time it was published in the September 1979 issue, *Mariah* had merged with *Outside,* and my piece ran in the first joint issue under the title "Built to Take It." It featured photos by Larry and Wende Cragg and Gary, including a photo of three of Joe's bikes.

The editors had done so many revisions that I didn't recognize my own words, and I found myself saying stuff I knew was untrue. I was unhappy with the article when it ran, but when it's out, it's out. I didn't mind the $400 payment, though, and I was two for two in magazine sales.

Gary was busy also. In need of a bike, he had hedged his bet. He knew a few other people in our crowd who had been inspired by the Breeze bikes and who didn't want to wait six months until Joe built more. Three people besides Gary wanted

bikes, so Gary ordered two each from two builders, Jeffrey Richman and Tom. Whatever got there first was his and then he could get rid of the others.

Tom was 22 years old and had retired from racing after being a dominant junior rider, winning senior races while still a junior. The reason for the switch from rider to builder was simple: money. There was no way to make money riding a bike in the mid-1970s, at least not the kind of money he could make turning out bikes by the truckload from a shop in his garage. Tom had built his first frame at the age of 14, and while that particular one had not been a ringing success, in the years since he had become one of America's premier frame builders and had probably built more frames in that span than any other American. Tom was

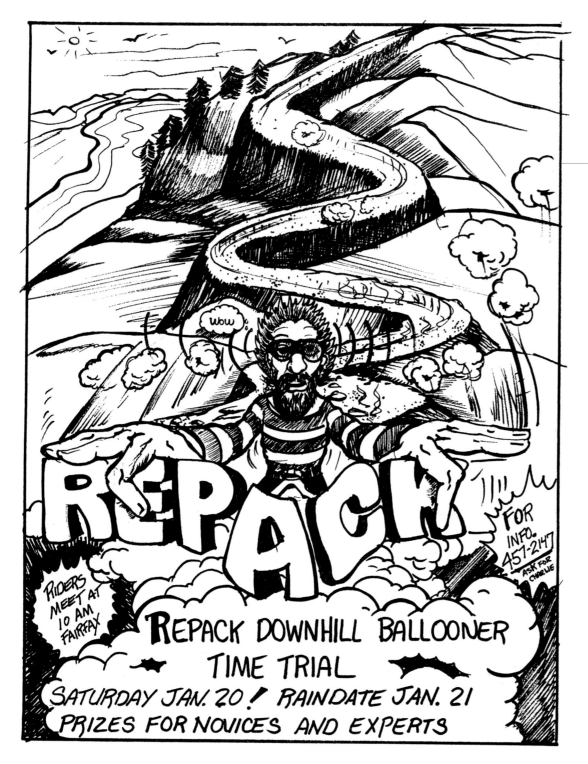

Pete Barrett's Repack poster for January 20, 1979. This is the race that KPIX filmed for *Evening Magazine*.

exceptionally talented and remarkably prolific, and he sold his custom road frames through the Palo Alto Bike Shop.

At that time most road bike frames were built with lugs, short metal sleeves at the corners of a bicycle frame that hold the tubing, which is then brazed into place with silver or brass. Tom built lugged frames, and he also built frames without lugs by mitering the tubes and brazing them together directly, a method that is more demanding of the builder and requires more fixtures but allows tubing of any size to be joined at any angle without being restricted to the sizes and angles of the lugs on the market.

Joe had brazed his 10 off-road frames because he used what the bicycle industry soon took to calling "oversize" tubing, meaning it had a larger diameter than the standard tubing used on road bicycles. So before he built the frames, Joe had to design and build the required tooling. Another reason it had taken so long to build those 10 frames was the number of welds it took to add the twin laterals. Joe had already calculated that the process could be sped up and weight could be saved by eliminating the twin laterals and beefing up the rest of the frame, but he hadn't yet built any frames along those lines.

Joe and Otis Guy were planning a tandem cross-country bicycle record attempt in 1979, and they were having Tom build the frame. In early January, Joe had taken his first Breezer to Tom's shop to show him a detail that he wanted Tom to use in the tandem. Tom expressed interest in making a fat-tire bike, so Joe mentioned his calculations showing that a standard diamond frame was a better design than one that included the twin laterals. Later that month, Tom took part in the filmed Repack race, where he saw six Breezers in action.

In addition to what he learned from Joe, Tom had input from Gary, who had a good idea of what he wanted. The result was three Ritchey frames completed in the spring of 1979. Tom kept a frame for himself, Gary got one, and the third went to a friend of Gary's named James MacWay. Jeffrey Richman came through a few weeks later, but by then Gary had his Ritchey assembled and would sell the two Richman frames to Mike Castelli, who had accompanied us to Crested Butte, and Mike's wife, Sheila.

When Tom had ridden Wende's bike at Repack in January, the clamp on the stem had loosened, and the handlebars had rotated. Later on, thinking about the problem like a framebuilder, he made a set of one-piece triangulated bars that bicycle raconteur and our future associate John Finley Scott would dub "Bullmoose," now the generic name for the obsolete design. During its brief

reign, this handlebar style was iconic for anything called a "mountain bike."

A frame isn't a bike, and the parts to complete the machine were a somewhat eclectic collection. There was no way the two Richman frames and the other Ritchey could be ridden without Gary's help, so he directed the owners as they purchased their parts at the bike shop and then helped build wheels and assemble the bikes.

That summer, a major prayer of ours was answered when aluminum, 26 × 2.125 wheel rims came on the market. Not only were they literally pounds lighter than the old steel Schwinn S-2 rims but they had much better friction for rim brakes as well, especially when wet. The aluminum rims, from Ukai, were anodized in colors such as blue or black, and our rim brakes quickly polished them to silver on the sides.

The Koski brothers were busy that summer too, and the first of their frames, made by Mert Lawwill, had been assembled. Joe had orders for more bikes as well, and he was gearing up for another production run.

In August I put on another Repack event. Gary made it two in a row and swept 1979 with another close win over his biggest rival, Joe. It was Gary's first race on the Ritchey and his first win on it.

Unleashing the booty to a cheering throng after Repack 18, October 1978.

Right: Four bikes in front of the Two Beans and a Pod coffee house near our MountainBikes office on San Anselmo Avenue, mid-1979. Left to right: 1940 Schwinn rehabbed by Alan Bonds, my 1978 Breezer number 2, late-1978 Jeffrey Richman number 1 owned by Michael Castelli, 1979 Ritchey number 2 owned by Gary Fisher.

Below: My 1979 Klunker Award, from the second Klunker Banquet Awards, 1979, for being "Captain Repack." Ceramics by Bob Klock, glazing by Pete Barrett, embroidery by Wende Cragg.

As it turned out, that August ride would be the last Repack race for more than four years. The rider who had broken his wrist in January during a Repack race had sued the TV crew who had filmed the event. He might have sued me also, but there would have been no point in it since I didn't have enough money to change his life one iota. He went where the money was, and that was the TV station. His claim for damages was that the camera crew had distracted him and caused his injury. The TV station had better attorneys, however, and it prevailed in court. The station had offered the victim $5,000 and his medical costs to settle, and he had turned it down, so in the end he got nothing.

That was the end for me. What had started as a lark had turned serious. Since I never charged anything for the event, all I ever got out of it was the prestige of being the promoter, and now that was tarnished. I did not want to worry about total strangers getting injured at my events, and I shut down the Repack race and turned my attention to other efforts.

In late 1979 Denise and I moved from the house at 1320 San Anselmo Avenue to a house a few blocks from downtown Fairfax, where I would live for the duration of my bicycle adventure, another 12 years or so. My new house at 288 Bolinas Road in Fairfax would serve as the first regular meeting place for the National Off-Road Bicycle Association (NORBA) a few years later.

Below: This clip from the Marin County Court Reporter tells the tale: KPIX was off the hook, but I was spooked and swore off race promotion for the foreseeable future.

Right: Pete's Repack poster for August 11, 1979.

Marin County COURT REPORTER
Page 2   Friday, July 11, 1980

LEGAL BRIEFS

Bicycle accident responsibility denied

Video tapes were admitted into evidence and shown to the Court in the personal injury case of ▓▓▓▓ v. KPIX Television, Inc. (Westinghouse Broadcasting Co.).

This matter involved an accident which occurred on the Mt. Tamalpais fire trail known as "Repack Hill" during a "Clunker" bicycle race (Clunkers are balloon-tire bicycles which have a specially reinforced frame for cross-country racing).

Marin resident ▓▓▓▓ asserted that a vehicle belonging to KPIX blocked his way as he was negotiating a turn on the race course, causing him to fall and injure his wrist.

The defendant, KPIX, maintained that, "plaintiff was a part-time maintenance man and sometime short-order cook and drummer. Claims he fell from his bicycle while trying to avoid 'defendant's' equipment 'truck' which he says was 'upon' the trail in his way. Plaintiff maintained that the jeep carrying the KPIX film crew was not in plaintiff's way, was not on the trail when plaintiff passed it and fell. Rather, plaintiff fell after he passed the Jeep which was parked off the trail when, because of his own recklessness, he lost control of his bicycle in a hairpin turn and crashed into a tree branch hanging over the trail."

The KPIX videotape crew was on Mt. Tamalpais filming portions of the race for the "Evening Magazine" show.

The complaint by plaintiff ▓▓▓▓ was dismissed with prejudice.

chapter 13

THE RITCHEY MOUNTAINBIKE

In September 1979 I went back to Crested Butte with Joe Breeze, Wende Cragg, Gary Fisher, new Ritchey owner James MacWay, and Chris McManus, a friend of Joe's who was mounted on a one-speed, coaster brake dinosaur. We traveled in two vehicles, a rented station wagon with four people inside and the bikes on top and James's classic old Porsche with one passenger. Unfortunately, within shouting distance of Crested Butte the Porsche blew an oil plug, quickly followed by the engine. James had to leave it in a service station that had never seen a Porsche, and we all crowded into the wagon to finish the drive.

In addition to our six riders, another two loads of Marin clunker riders made the trek, including a couple of the Koski brothers with their new bikes made in Mert Lawwill's shop, for a total of 18 from Marin. When we got to Crested Butte, the change that had taken place in a single year was more than amazing.

Right: The Marin County crew stretches after the long drive to Crested Butte, Colorado, for the Fourth Annual Crested Butte to Aspen Pearl Pass Tour, September 1979. Left to right: Gary Fisher, James MacWay, me, Joe Breeze, Wende Cragg.

Bottom: Heading up Paradise Divide out of Crested Butte, September 1979. Left to right: Joe, me, Gary, and James. Wende's Breezer is over to the right.

While the crew that had originated the ride into Aspen had been blue-collar, hard-drinking firefighters, the town had another faction, the telemark skiers. Telemark skiing is a Nordic technique for skiing downhill that uses only the toe binding from skinny cross-country skis. A cross-country lift ticket was cheaper than a downhill ticket at the Crested Butte ski area; the assumption was that a cross-country skier would not be making a dozen runs in a day. By telemarking, locals saved money with a skinny-ski ticket while getting in just as many runs as the downhillers. In the process, they pioneered that style of telemark skiing in the United States.

Mountain biking was a perfect summer sport for the same crowd. After we had introduced it to the town a year earlier, the locals had caught up with us very quickly. The Clunker Tour sponsors at the Grubstake Saloon were ready for us this time, and the crew had more than doubled, although once again half the total riders were from Marin.

Fat Tire Flyer • The Ritchey MountainBike

Richard Nilsen, who had inspired us to come out a year earlier, was back, and this time he was on real fat-tire equipment to replace his touring bike. Alan Bonds flew into Aspen with his bike and rode it over the Maroon Bells into Crested Butte. It was a much more demanding ride to make in one day than he had expected, and he rolled into Crested Butte late in the afternoon exhausted and shattered.

The Koskis had brought with them a crowd of Cove Bike Shop regulars equipped with the latest advance in clunker technology since the arrival of aluminum rims. They had gumwall, 26 × 2.125–inch, Mitsuboshi Cruiser Mitt tires that were half the weight of the old Uniroyal Nobby tires we were still using. These gumwall tires were made for street riding and had minimal knobs, so they didn't look suitable for rugged, off-road use. The Cove riders used the new tires to ride the relatively good road to the overnight campsite and then, before the climb to the summit, swapped them for Uniroyal tires like ours, which they had stashed in the gear trucked up to the camp.

Rick Verplank, whose spontaneous adventure three years earlier had led to this point, fired a shotgun to send us off. At the top of Pearl Pass, we posed once again for the obligatory group photo.

A few months later the photo appeared on the cover of the April 1980 issue of *Bicycling* magazine.

Since the Porsche was not ready to return to California, the six of us jammed ourselves and our bikes into and around the station wagon for the trip home. Camping in Austin, Nevada, we were caught in a rainstorm that forced four big men to sleep in a two-man tent along with 3 or 4 inches of water. The situation was so ridiculously uncomfortable that we couldn't help laughing hysterically about it all night.

A few weeks after we returned from Crested Butte, Gary called me up and asked me to come over to his cottage in Fairfax. He told me that Tom Ritchey had made some more frames like the one he was riding, and he wanted to show them to me. When I got there, Gary opened the trunk of his battered BMW and showed me the frames. There were nine of them nestled in there, and they were as beautifully made as my Colnago. Gary explained that Tom had become very interested in this new kind of bike and had made a few more.

Although there was an avid crew of off-road riders down in Tom's area near Palo Alto, led by legendary local Jobst Brandt, they hit their trails either on road bikes or similarly set up rugged bikes equipped with 650B tires and drop handlebars. Tom hadn't

The start line and banner of the Fourth Annual (but third actual) Pearl Pass Tour, outside the Grubstake Saloon on Elk Avenue in Crested Butte, September 1979.

My first business card,
designed by Pete Barrett.

been able to sell any of the new style of flat-handlebar, big-tire bikes to anyone in his area. Since he knew Gary had access to riders who wanted bikes like Gary's, he had offered them to Gary on spec to see whether Gary could help get rid of them.

Nine bikes were a lot of bikes, and Tom wanted about $400 apiece for the frames if Gary was able to sell them. These frames were not at all cheap, and they only represented a starting point to a bike. As we looked at the booty, Gary asked a simple question with lifelong consequences. "Do you want to help me sell these frames?"

It was too easy to say yes, and I did. We did the minimum amount of company organization that was possible and then we were in business. We counted the cash that the two of us had on our persons at that moment, about $200. We took that money to the nearest bank, and we opened a joint business account.

We had a company name that we wanted to use. The term *mountain bike* had recently entered our personal lexicon. The bikes had been *clunkers* until Joe had taken them out of that category with his beautiful nickel-plated frames. Now there were several versions of custom off-road bikes: Joe's, Tom's, the Lawwill-Knight ProCruiser (from a Koski design), and Jeffrey Richman's, all similar

in quality to our road bikes. They could hardly be called "clunkers," but they didn't yet have a general name. When I took up cycling, the road bike had been just "the bike" because there was only one kind. Then I had owned a "clunker" as well. Now, when we had to differentiate in conversations as to which we were riding of the two beautiful bikes we owned, we spoke of our "road bikes" or our "mountain bikes." "Mountain Bikes" seemed like a great name for our company. Just to make it clear that it was a brand name and not just a general term, we soon made it one word and used a cute spelling, MountainBikes.

Gary and I went to Palo Alto so I could meet Tom. He had been at my January race and appears in photos standing behind me while I was interviewed by the TV crew, but if we had had a conversation back then, I didn't remember it. He was working in the machine shop in his garage when Gary introduced me, and the three of us talked in the most general terms about what would need to happen to get rid of those nine frames and more. Tom made frames and forks. He would deliver them to us already painted, with the new "Bullmoose" one-piece bar and stem. Gary and I would get the parts, assemble the bikes, find the customers, and pay Tom for the framesets. What could be simpler?

Ritchey number 1, from
Tom Ritchey's collection.
Tom's beautiful fillet brazing and
no-frills design are on full display.

Me hefting Ritchey number 2 up a steep trail
for a MountainBikes promotion shot.

While the discussion was going on, Tom turned out a couple of small bike parts on his lathe without appearing to measure anything, then fitted them right into place.

Pete Barrett designed a business card for us, depicting the rear wheel of a fat-tire bike on top of a snow-capped peak. We needed to be able to get mail, so we rented a post office box. A business card, a checking account, and a post office box address do not add up to a company, and $200 wasn't enough to equip even one of the bikes. Yet we were indisputably in the mountain bike business.

Gary and I stashed the frames at his house and went about the business of getting rid of them. On the plus side, we had nine frames and $200. On the minus side, we had nothing except those things, including a business location. We didn't have any place for a phone to ring except our houses, and any of three people answered at mine, so we used Gary's phone number.

We needed customers who would pay us in advance for the bike, which we determined would cost about $1,200. We would take that money to the bike shop and buy the parts we needed over the counter. We assembled the first few bikes at the house I shared with Kent Bostick and Pete on San Anselmo Avenue, and Gary took photos of one of our first completed bikes in the room where most families ate dinner but where we assembled bikes.

At the time, you could buy a Tour de France racing bike for less money than we wanted for a bike with $3 tires. We really needed to charge even more, but we had already pushed the ceiling as hard as possible. It took a lot of faith to hand over that kind of money to two guys with a zero track record. Besides, look at them. Because his hippie appearance was a hindrance for working in Europe with the bike team coached by Mike Neel, Gary had recently chopped off the 2 feet of hair he sported when I met him. I had no need for that kind of grooming, and I left mine long. I adopted the Fu Manchu mustache look, along with Gary, Joe, and Tom (who to this day has sported the same hirsute look). Few who looked at Gary and me would have mistaken us for solid citizens.

Nevertheless, we managed to find a few customers. My uncle, an engineer who worked on oil-drilling sites all over the world, ponied up for a bike and waited a few weeks for it, as did a local firefighter who worked with Otis Guy. We weren't making any money, but we were putting bikes under people and starting to find ways of drawing attention to the bikes and ourselves. I didn't even have a Ritchey myself when I started selling them,

Head-on toward the camera
aboard Ritchey number 2.

and it would be well into the next year before I had one of my own.

We took photos of Gary's bike with Gary's camera, a medium-format Hasselblad left over from the days in the '60s when he shot images of rock stars. We had one bike to use for the photos, Gary's, and one camera, also Gary's. I could ride a bike, but I had never used that kind of camera, so I served as the model on Gary's bike while he took the photos. One action shot had me toting the bike up a hill on my shoulder; another had me holding it at arm's length to show how light I could make it look. For my star turn, I wore ordinary Levis and a yellow T-shirt that Bob Burrowes had printed up. On the front was a photograph of Bob in action on Repack and the logo "Marin County Klunkers." On the back it read, "I'd rather be klunking."

When Thanksgiving rolled around, I had Pete draw up another poster for the Appetite Seminar, and the turnout was a couple dozen riders, including a San Francisco bicyclist named Darryl Skrabak riding a Jack Taylor cyclocross bike.

Darryl now and then contributed to a local free tabloid called *City Sports*. If Darryl hadn't been there and written about it, I might have forgotten that ride by now. It started raining during the

Mert Lawwill's ProCruiser, based on a design by the Koski brothers, came out in 1979.

ing for months. The miseries visited upon the participants will be dwelt upon at length, and recounted repeatedly, and expanded into tales, and thence into legend. It will be recalled as one of the great ones.

Because it was the worst.

Darryl took a photograph of Gary on his Ritchey bike and captioned it "Gary Fisher on his super-low-geared klunker." This was the first photograph of the Ritchey bike to hit print. Farther down in the piece, Darryl used our company name in print for the first time. "Ritchey is now party to a fledgling Kelly and Fisher concern known as MountainBikes, which markets Ritchey's frames and other klunker equipment."

That fall we received a visit from Bob Hadley, editor of *Bicycle Motocross Action*. We had nothing remotely to do with BMX and did not count it among our influences. It was most likely Mert's involvement in framebuilding for the Koskis that got Hadley's attention, since even in retirement Mert was a national hero and icon for motorcyclists. Mert had been a national champion motorcycle racer and had a starring role in a documentary film with Steve McQueen, *On Any Sunday*. By this time, Mert and the Koskis had separated,

ride, the mud peeling up off the road in sheets on our tires. The inclement conditions and the mud-clogged machinery turned the ride into a desperate forced march by hypothermic riders. As the leader, I was responsible, so I herded the miserable crew around the loop and then went home, warmed up, and tried to forget the day.

Darryl found the adventure charming in retrospect and wrote a paean to the ride that he titled "Working Up an Appetite." The *City Sports* editor at first derided Darryl's story and planned to spike it until members of the advertising department mentioned that they had already sold ads to bike

shops based on the expectation that it would run. It appeared in the December 1979/January 1980 issue of *City Sports*. It starts with this:

There are events that become adventures, and adventures that become ordeals, and ordeals in which things go from bad to worse, and the worse things become, the better they are.

It was that way at the Appetite Seminar held Thanksgiving Day in the Marin hills. This unheralded event was plain awful. It was the worst Seminar ever, and it was the Fifth Annual. It will fuel Marin bench rac-

Gary putting his second Ritchey MountainBike through its paces.

and each was working on bikes independently of the other. The Koskis would call their next design Trailmaster, and Mert continued producing the original Koski design as the ProCruiser.

The BMX magazine sent a photographer to take action shots, and Joe gave them the action they needed for a motor-drive photo sequence of a sideways pitch. The price of the bikes stunned Hadley; his eventual article was titled "Loaded for Bear and Ungodly Expensive: Full Bore Cruisers."

Despite his thin credentials in mountain biking, Mert got most of Hadley's attention for his Koski-designed ProCruiser. Mert claimed sales of his first 75 bikes for about $500 apiece, with the next 100 on their way. After that Hadley mentioned us: "The only other people who are producing pure klunkers are Joe Breeze and Tom Ritchey. Each has built around ten bikes. The Breezer and the Ritchey sell for an incredible $1,200 . . . which gives you an idea of the quality of the workmanship and components that are put into these bikes."

What to call them?

We asked Mert, Joe Breeze, Gary Fisher, Charles Kelly, and the owners of the Cove Bike Shop in Tiburon—the people at the heart of this brand-new pastime—what they thought these bikes should be called.

Of all the names that have been applied at various times for these bikes—Klunkers, Ballooners, Bombers, Downhillers, Mountain Bikes, Trail Bikes, Tankers, Cruisers, Cow Trailers, the consensus of opinion is that they should be called Mountain Bikes. And when you think about it, that name fits like a glove.

BMX was being marketed to parents as a "safe" sport for kids, and those kids were the target audience for the magazine. Our lack of helmets called

Our MountainBikes ad from 1980.

for a scolding in the article. A photograph of Mert sliding a ProCruiser sideways is captioned "Mert Lawwill, still hookin' it on, even without his Harley. But no helmet. Tsk, tsk, tsk, Mert."

A writer named Dean Bradley, who worked for the other major BMX publication, *BMX Plus!*, was the next to notice us, and in the February 1980 issue he reviewed what he called the "Richey [*sic*] Mountain Bike." Bradley led off the article with a remarkable prediction. "This month's 26-inch test bike is called a Mountain Bike. Chances are that you've never heard of it before, but believe me, you will be hearing a lot about this revolutionary bike in the future." The rest of the article went on in the same vein. Dean loved the bikes and gushed over them in the article.

In keeping with magazine tradition, the *BMX Plus!* advertising department leaned on us to take out an ad since Dean was giving us a lot of positive publicity in the article. This was our first print advertising, and we didn't have anything prepared. We didn't have Pete's graphics as a separate piece of art, so we sent the magazine's art department a business card and told them what we wanted the ad to say:

MOUNTAIN BIKES
The Trail Blazers
26 × 2.125 18 Speeds 28 lb.
Advanced Off-Road
Bicycle Technology
Custom Framesets—Bikes
Conversion Kits for Beach
Bike to Mountain Cruiser

Write or Call
For FREE Catalog:
Mountain Bikes
P.O. Box 405
Fairfax, CA 94930
(415) 456-1898

Really? A free catalog?

APPETITE SEMINAR

The Appetite Seminar started on Thanksgiving Day, 1975, when a half-dozen of us rode our one-speed, coaster brake bikes around the Pine Mountain Loop. In those days much of the climbing was bypassed with a truck ride to the trailhead of the Pine Mountain Fire Road, but the primitive gear still guaranteed a lot of walking and pushing. The idea was to work up an appetite for a big Thanksgiving dinner. Like so many first events, it started as a lark, with no thought we might do it again in a year.

The ride became a tradition immediately. By the following year, multiple-gear clunkers were starting to hit the trails, and the ride grew.

In 1978 I promoted the ride with a poster giving a date, time, and meeting place. I publicized the Appetite Seminar with posters for several more years. Even with promotion, the group was a manageable size, usually consisting of a couple dozen riders. I would lead the ride, leaving from the appointed meeting place at the Fairfax Theater parking lot at around the time the poster suggested. The group would travel together, and several regular stopping points became established.

The second year that I promoted the ride, it changed from funky fun to a legendary event. As we hit the trail, it started to rain. The rain turned driving and steady, and the ceremonial stops on hilltops were forgotten. I had to keep the slowest riders moving because I felt responsible for them, so I herded the back end while the stronger riders lit out for home. The Appetite Seminar in 1979 was two hours of freezing rain and caked mud and no way out but forward.

On the 1980 Appetite Seminar one of the riders suffered a clunker tragedy. He had flexed his wheel,

Pete Barrett's poster for the fifth Appetite Seminar, 1979.

Announcement for the sixth annual Appetite Seminar.

and all the spokes had popped out of one side of his Sturmey-Archer drum brake hub. I cemented some sort of reputation by sitting down and rebuilding his wheel on the spot. At that time, I was building most of the wheels at MountainBikes, so it took me only 20 minutes to fix this one, and doing so made me very popular with one rider. Dave Epperson documented the episode with photos for his article in *Action Now*.

In 1981 a woman living in San Francisco heard about the Appetite Seminar from Darryl Skrabak, who had written about the ride two years earlier. She accompanied him, riding from San Francisco on a Raleigh three-speed woman's bike with a wicker basket on the handlebars. For most women, tackling the 20 miles to the start of the ride would have been more than enough, but this was Jacquie Phelan, who would become the first women's mountain bike champion. Jacquie went the distance of the Appetite Seminar and then rode back to San Francisco afterward, a massive feat on her limited equipment. She confesses that it wore her out to a degree she had not yet encountered.

Darryl had told Jacquie to introduce herself to me during the ride, and she did so while the group stopped on a hilltop now known as Smoker's Knoll. Dave Epperson, standing on a nearby hilltop with a long lens, captured the moment of the introduction in a photo later published in *Bicycling* magazine.

During another Appetite Seminar I met a rider on a cyclocross bike. He was a stranger to me, and his bike was not really suited for the ride, but he was obviously a dedicated rider. While we rode together he hit a log lying across the trail and turned his front wheel into a taco. With the skinny, delicate rim, that meant he was going to have a long walk home. He removed the wheel and stared at it glumly. I was ready to try a crude technique of bending the wheel back into shape by pushing on the bent rim, but when he handed it to me, all I did was shake it by the bent spots, and it popped back into round. After handling it for only a few seconds, I gave the now straightened wheel back to its astonished owner, and he finished the ride on it. This was the most miraculous repair I have ever performed. That rider eventually saw the light and switched to a mountain bike. He has remained a cyclist and a friend ever since.

For a few more years I put out posters and promoted the ride. It became the mountain bike social event of the season. As the number of riders grew, it reached a point where even if I was the "leader," I was no longer in control. I didn't even know everyone in the group I purported to lead.

One Thanksgiving morning in the mid-1980s, the town of Fairfax was overrun by mountain bikers massing at the traditional meeting place, or attempting to. By then there were too many for everyone to hang out in the theater parking lot. Riders swirled through the center of town while they waited for my signal to ride out. The action attracted the attention of the local constabulary.

A police car stopped across the road from the parking lot. An officer climbed out and surveyed the busy scene. He asked loudly, "Who's in charge here?"

The answer to a question like that hinges on the meaning of "in charge." I was not exactly in control and definitely not "in charge" by any conventional definition.

I abdicated on the spot. I no longer wanted the responsibility for a lot of people I didn't know whose actions were beyond my control. Of course, my resignation was not yet public. Someone might have the impression that as the promoter I was also "in charge" and point me out. I did not care to explain semantic subtleties to anyone.

At the back of the theater parking lot is an alley, and from the alley a short footpath cuts over to a residential street. I gave a little high sign to a few friends, who picked up on my direction. I rode quietly toward the alley with them, sneaking onto the path so I could start the ride with a small group of people I knew and leave the officer to figure out who might still be in charge. After a block or so, I looked back and saw a line of riders a block long. Everyone had followed me, the ride was on, and I still seemed to be leading it. From the perspective of the police officer, dozens of riders had vanished in a matter of seconds.

Promotion or not, the Appetite Seminar had become a tradition. With the absence of leadership, riders showed up anytime they chose and followed the tracks of whoever had gone ahead of them. Numbers grew into the hundreds.

For a while there were political repercussions about the Appetite Seminar. It followed a legal road on public land, but the numbers suggested organization, and officialdom still wanted to know who was "in charge." With this many people, someone had to be, but for several years I rode elsewhere on that day, secure in the knowledge that every working ranger was on Pine Mountain and that my absence would not keep the ride from taking place.

In recent years the political tide has turned. The town of Fairfax has become a popular Bay Area mountain bike destination. So much of the town's economy stems from the popularity of mountain biking that the Appetite Seminar is now celebrated, sponsored, and supported by commercial interests and tolerated by land managers.

The original Appetite Seminar has remained a tradition, likely the longest-running annual event in the culture of mountain biking. Hun-

Seventh annual Appetite Seminar poster, 1981.

dreds of riders follow the route on the chosen day, not in a single group but as a parade of small groups over several hours.

Riders used to attend from far-flung areas, but now that the Thanksgiving holiday has become established as a day for such celebrations, similar "Turkey Day" rides take place all over Northern California. The fourth Thursday in November is as close to a national holiday for mountain bikers as we are likely to get.

chapter 14

THE FIRST MOUNTAINBIKE

It was time to compose that "free catalog" that we had so rashly offered in our first print ad. To get it started, we took a 75-mile drive northeast.

John Finley Scott was older than Gary Fisher and I and a lifelong bicyclist. In 1953, while still a college student, he had assembled what he called a "Woodsie Bike" at about the time Dick Kircher and Bobby Mushen were teaching me to solo on a two-wheeler. The bike he put together then was a slim-tire, diamond-frame Schwinn World widened to accept Uniroyal Nobby tires. He added flat handlebars and extra-low derailleur gearing. John's Woodsie Bike would have passed muster as a legitimate mountain bike when I met him 26 years later.

John was a professor of sociology at the University of California–Davis campus. We had met him in the fall of 1979 through Tom Ritchey. He had done well for himself and was an investor in several bicycle-related ventures (he later bought

The MountainBike, branded with our new company name. Wide-range gearing with thumbshifters, cantilever brakes, aluminum rims, and Tom Ritchey's impeccable construction, adding up to about 33 pounds. A beautiful machine in every way.

The first MountainBike brochure
carried this photo of the bike.

the Cupertino Bike Shop from its legendary owner, Spence Wolf). John was a friend of Tom's, and he employed a framebuilder named John Padgett who worked on bikes at John Scott's property in Davis. John Scott had the largest personal bike collection of anyone I ever met, all kept in a barn on the property. I didn't count them, but he told me that he owned about 60 bikes, all acquired for personal use.

John Scott had a lot of toys in addition to bikes, and he loved to find uses for them. One attraction in particular was a new office machine called a word processor made by Hewlett-Packard (HP). It wasn't portable, and it was at John's place in Davis, an hour's drive from Marin, so Gary and I went there to use it. The device was the size of a large dinner table, with a keyboard on top, and stored the processed words on a drive that used disks the size of dinner plates. My mom had made me take typing in summer school, so I was able to use the HP keyboard properly. The words that I typed appeared in glowing green letters on a screen instead of on paper, and if I wanted, I could change things later without typing everything over again from scratch. I could save my work to use again, and the word processor justified the print on a clacking daisy-wheel printer. It was an amazing device, and I

wanted one, but it cost $13,000, it filled an entire room, and John let me use his, so I put it off.

The first effort was a flyer announcing our existence, printed at an instant print place called Sir Speedy because John Scott owned stock in the company. On one side was a photo of the bike. On the other was a description that Gary and I composed by shouting lines at each other while I typed:

The MountainBike is a lightweight, extremely rugged bicycle built to go anywhere. The 26 × 2.125 balloon tires give superb traction and soak up the roughest terrain. The multiple gearing and light weight make for unbelievable climbing ability while the heavy-duty tandem brakes give you the confidence you need to take on any descent.

The MountainBike is hand-crafted by Tom Ritchey to the exacting standards of the finest road racing machines. Tom Ritchey is a former member of the United States Junior World's team and during that time he established himself as one of the premier riders in the country. Since then he has built hundreds of racing frames, both single and tandem, while perfecting the art of lugless construction and the use of oversize tubing.

Western America. This new cycling concept has been featured in Bicycling, MARIAH/Outside, CoEvolution Quarterly, BMX Action and BMX Plus as well as the nationally syndicated television program, Evening Magazine.

The MOUNTAIN BIKE is a lightweight, extremely rugged bicycle built to go anywhere. The 26 x 2.125 balloon tires give superb traction and soak up the roughest terrain. The multiple gearing and light weight make for unbelievable climbing ability while the heavy duty tandem brakes give you the confidence you need to take on any descent.

The MOUNTAIN BIKE frame is hand crafted by Tom Ritchey to the exacting standards of the finest road racing machines. Tom Ritchey rode with the United States Junior World's team in 1974, and established himself as one of the premier road riders in the country. Since then he has built hundreds of racing frames, both single and tandem, while perfecting the art of lugless construction and the use of oversize tubing.

The MOUNTAIN BIKE is the culmination of a six year program of research and development which began with the construction of the first multi-geared balloon tired bikes. These original historic hybrids proved to be the most efficient human powered form of transportation for off-road use and since then have been the subject of continuous improvement from the early "European/American crossbreeds" to today's highly refined machine.

MOUNTAIN BIKE frame geometry and components have been developed and tested under the most extreme conditions possible, from rugged rides in the Sierras and the Rockies to all-out downhill racing. MOUNTAIN BIKES are the originators and will always be the innovators in the field.

The MOUNTAIN BIKE combines the best features from European cyclo-cross, BMX, road racing bikes, and the trusty old ballooners that most adults grew up with. The MOUNTAIN BIKE rider is free to explore rough trails or dirt roads with approximately the same environmental impact as a hiker.

For the BMX rider who is outgrowing his 20" bicycle, the MOUNTAIN BIKE offers an alternative to motorcycles as an adult sport, and additionally fills the gap between BMX bikes and high quality road bikes.

The MOUNTAIN BIKE satisfies the adult rider's desire for quality equipment while providing the ruggedness and stability of the 26 x 2.125 tire. High performance and ease of handling make this the ideal off-road or on-road all around vehicle.

The Tom Ritchey Mountain Bike Frameset represents the state of the art in hand-brazed custom balloon tire bicycle frames. Made by hand one at a time, these frames are built to the standards of the finest racing bicycles and tandems, using the best components and materials. Frame geometry has been carefully selected to give the most stable ride under the most trying conditions, uphill, downhill, wet, on any road surface or on no road at all. Fabricated with lugless (brazed) joints from carefully selected oversize double-butted chrome-manganese and chrome-molybdenum tubing. All fittings are brazed on, including: water bottle mounts, cable guides, and cantilever brake bosses. Available in sizes from 19"-24" in a variety of Imron enamel finishes. Comes with custom Tom Ritchey sealed bearing bottom bracket, Campagnolo dropouts, quick-release seatbolt for 27.0 mm seatpost. Custom tapered-blade fork with Tange heavy duty blades and custom (extra wide) crown. Tapered fork blades absorb shock far better than BMX-style forks found on most balloon-tired bikes. Reynolds steering tube, Campagnolo or Shimano dropouts. Frame complete with fork and bottom bracket: $625

All custom options considered with $100 non-refundable deposit.

TOM RITCHEY CUSTOM HANDLERAR/STEM

The Tom Ritchey one-piece handlebar and stem is stronger and lighter than any other combination available. The traditional "gooseneck" stem is replaced by triangulated chrome-moly struts. Chrome-plated Chrome-moly custom bar/stem: $98

TOM RITCHEY CUSTOM SEATPOST/SADDLE

The Tom Ritchey custom seatpost/saddle (at 19 oz.) is incomparably light. The saddle is an Avocet Touring II (or your choice) rebuilt on a 1" aluminum tube and then clamped to the custom seatpost. The extra-long seatpost allows for maximum extension without danger of damaging the frame. (Specify seat angle.) Custom Seatpost and Saddle (Avocet T-II): $98

The MountainBike order form. Fill it out, send it in, and wait for the delivery truck to arrive.

The MountainBike is the culmination of a six-year program of research and development which began with the construction of the first multi-geared balloon-tired bikes. These original historic hybrids proved to be the most efficient human-powered form of transportation and since then have become the subject of continuous improvement from non-conforming crossbreeds to today's highly refined machine.

MountainBike frame geometry and components are developed and tested under the most extreme conditions possible, ranging from rugged rides in the Sierras and the Rockies to all-out downhill racing. MountainBikes are the originators and will always be the innovators in the field.

Our first address was a box number at the Fairfax Post Office. A month or so into the project we found a business location in San Anselmo. It was much closer to the Fairfax Post Office than the San Anselmo Post Office, so we kept the Fairfax mailing address. We had been eyeing the location because a garage in a commercial building next to our regular coffeehouse was empty. Terrible for just any business, 1501 San Anselmo Avenue was perfect for ours.

MOUNTAIN BIKE ORDER BLANK

Mountain Bike frame. Size: 19"__20"__21"__ 22"__23"__24"__

Color: specify_____

Custom frame fittings_____

_____

Chris King Headset. Black____Silver____

TA Cyclotourist Crankset. Length of Arms: 170___ 175__180__185__

Chainrings: Double, 32/48T__Triple, 26/36/48____

Other_____

Pedals: KKT Lightning, Red__Blue__Gold___
        Sun Tour MP 1000, Red__Blue__Gold___

Chain: Regina Oro___Sedis-sport___Uniglide___

Freewheel (6-speed): Sun Tour Winner, 13-26___ 13-30___14-34___

Rear Derailleur: Huret DUOPAR, Titanium/aluminum alloy___Steel/aluminum alloy___Sun Tour VX (long arm) ___

Front derailleurs: Sun Tour Compe V___ Sun Tour VX___

Rims: Aluminum alloy 26 x 1.75, Silver___Red___ Gold__Blue__

Saddle: Avocet Men's Touring I__Women's Touring I__Men's Touring II__Women's Touring II__

Complete MOUNTAIN BIKE including Ritchey custom seatpost/saddle, Ritchey handlebar/stem, KKT Lightning pedals, and Huret DUOPAR Steel/aluminum derailleur, transportation paid. Price: $1300.00
California residents add 6% sales tax.
$100 non-refundable deposit required on all custom orders.

Because MOUNTAIN BIKES are subject to use under unusually severe "limit-of-the-design" conditions, we are unable to provide any general warranty against failure of components in "normal use." However, we believe that we offer the best off-road bicycles available today, and to that end we offer an indefinite warranty of our framesets against manufacturing defects. Our policy in component selection is one of continuous improvement. We want to hear of any problems MOUNTAIN BIKE owners have with components, especially if the problem appears to be inherent in off-road operation. In cases where, in our judgment, the component is unserviceable for conservative off-road use we will provide adjustments at our expense.
We stand behind our products.

When the commuter train system had run through the Ross Valley, Lansdale Station had been a stop on the line. Our building had been a grocery store convenient to commuters getting off the train before the system was shut down and the tracks torn out during the 1940s. The part of the building we wanted was the former loading dock, an enclosed garage wide enough for a truck built before 1930 to back into. At 50 feet long and only 10 feet wide, it had a concrete floor near the street. Halfway back there was a step up to a wooden floor and then a separate room at the other end that we could use for an office. We pried open the door to an abandoned cellar that had once held huge blocks of ice and stored meat and was now simply an enormous room. The shop had a double garage door onto the street and a side door that led into a yard with 6-foot weeds.

We moved in. Gary brought all his tools and hung them on the wall. The bike workstand went in the middle of the floor. Our very own bike shop to mess around in whenever we wanted, where we could build the coolest bikes in the world. We couldn't get there early enough or stay too late.

John Scott had purchased a huge pile of TA cranksets for his own bike shop. They had the exact triple-chainring setup we needed, with a tiny 26-tooth inner ring. After Tom's contribution of frames on spec, John became our only other investor by turning over this valuable inventory for our use, in exchange for a handwritten IOU and a vague promise to pay for them eventually. For the next year we used them on bikes or sold them for needed cash.

Gary's experience working at Bob Hovey's Wheels Unlimited Bike Shop was invaluable as we started the business, since I had no experience in retail anything. We immediately took out the resale permit that would allow us to purchase our supplies from wholesalers, but having the license and making the purchases were two different things. To our suppliers we looked like a couple of hobbyists who were hoping to indulge our passion at less than retail prices.

Gary knew which suppliers handled the different components we needed, but some required a large minimum order before they would accept our business. Since there was no single source of supply for the variety of items on our shopping list, we did business with a dozen or so suppliers, each with different minimum requirements.

Our biggest score was Original Equipment Manufacturer (OEM) status with Magura, the German motorcycle company that made the brake levers we specified for our bikes. Buying these levers at less than wholesale, we became wholesalers ourselves for this one component. The levers came in two sizes, a short lever for the clutch and a longer one for the motorcycle front brake. By flipping over one lever from each of two sets, we could create two matched sets, one with long levers for the bigger bikes and a shorter set for riders with smaller hands.

Since the parts for our bikes came from so many different countries, we had to get them from a lot of different importers. The brakes, chains, and derailleurs were French; the brake levers were from Germany; the Campagnolo headsets were Italian; the Ukai or Araya rims, MKS or SunTour MP-1000 pedals, SunTour freewheel, and shift levers were from Japan; and the spokes were Swiss. We had a number of American suppliers as well. Hubs came from Phil Wood or Cook Brothers. Our bottom-bracket spindles were custom made for us by either Chris King or Cook Brothers. The bottom-bracket bearings were a common size of cartridge bearing, 10 × 17 × 35 mm. We ordered them from a bearing supply house, and they were probably the most inexpensive components on the bikes other than the brake and derailleur cables. Avocet was the saddle of choice, mounted either on a French Laprade seatpost or the SR Laprade, a licensed Japanese copy that was nowhere near as nicely finished but far less expensive.

At first we had to make do with the $3 Uniroyal Nobby tires. The first suitable 26-inch tire after the Cruiser Mitt was the CyclePro Snakebelly, which was more of a BMX tire than a real mountain bike tire. The Snakebelly was much lighter than the Nobby, but far more fragile.

One result of our tinkering was a modification of existing bicycle standards. At that time the standard rear spacing between the dropouts for a five-speed cluster on a road bike was 120 mm. Six-speed blocks had just come into use, upping the width to 125 mm. These were measurements built around a very skinny tire. The wider tires on our bikes forced the chainline farther outward from the frame. We used hubs manufactured to a tandem specification of 130 mm, which fixed the chainline problem and had the additional benefit of reducing the amount of "dish" in the wheel. This spacing became the standard for fat-tire bikes as soon as every other manufacturer ran into the same problems.

The modification of the chainline limited our choice in front derailleurs, at least until the manufacturers caught up. We used a Simplex or some-times a SunTour Spirt because they had enough travel to compensate for the greater distance.

The rear derailleur had to be Huret Duopar. Whatever we used back there had to have a long arm to handle the wide range of gearing, and it had to be able to shift down under load. The Duopar managed those chores admirably, although it also had two minor drawbacks. It was really expensive, and it was not very tough. In order to accomplish its complex task, it was hinged and pivoted in a lot of places. It was easy to catch it on an obstacle and tie it in a knot.

Joe Breeze had used Dia-Compe cantilever brakes on his bikes. Mafac tandem cantilever brakes were the best we could find initially, although by modern disc brake stopping standards they barely worked. Mafac had the longest lever arms of any on the market, coupled to big brake pads that made a lot of contact. We had to modify them before we could use them because once again the bigger tire created complications. On the front pads, we sawed off about a half-inch at one end; on the rear pads, we filed one corner so the pads would open far enough to admit an inflated tire.

Connecting motorcycle brake levers to bicycle brakes required an adaptor of some sort; we usually installed a little brass shim to give the lead

Joe aboard a Series II Breezer.

The 1980 Trailmaster, designed by Erik Koski. Its large-diameter frame tubes, stout fork, and sturdy construction made it a tough, bulletproof bike.

knob on the bicycle cable a purchase in the larger brake-lever slot. We ordered custom cables from a motorcycle supply house, but it wasn't long before we began making our own.

The bottom bracket was not a standard, threaded version; it was a couple of our big cartridge bearings on a custom-made spindle. The tools Gary used to tap the circular bearing into place were a ball-peen hammer and a big socket that fit neatly inside the BB shell.

At first we were still forced to use two right-hand SunTour thumb shifters because they were made for five-speed bikes. The left side or front shifter was just a right-hand shifter turned around, which gave the controls an asymmetrical look.

Frames, forks, and handlebars all came from Tom. Usually he would send them over to the

paint shop, Jevelot of Mountain View, and I would drive down in the big moving van and pick up the painted products.

As Gary and I got our business off the ground throughout 1980, we were not alone in the Marin community in making these revolutionary bikes. Joe had begun what became a production run of 25 "Series II" Breezer bikes, diamond frames without the twin laterals of the first production run. Most of these were sold through the Koski brothers at the Cove Bike Shop, although Gary and I sold one or two. We had considered adding Joe's bikes to our catalog, but Joe would not have been able to supply us as many bikes as Tom could. It was not that we were averse to getting our frames from several sources—it was the fact that there was no other source like Tom.

Mert Lawwill was still manufacturing his Pro-Cruiser, but his bikes were heavy and long, good for descending but not for climbing. In cross-country races of the sort then taking place, a fast climber gained more time pedaling uphill than he lost by being a poor descender. The race results alone showed that ProCruisers were not competitive.

The Koski brothers had their own design for a bike similar to ours, and in many respects their Trailmaster was superior. The fork was much stouter than the Ritchey version, and the tube set for the frame had a larger diameter, making the bikes more rigid without adding significant weight. The Trailmaster, which came out in 1980, was bulletproof and much tougher than the first generation of Ritchey MountainBike frames. The Koski design for the dropout on these bikes was a revolutionary approach to a simple part and is still in use.

By organizing our sources of supply for the eclectic collection of necessary parts, we made ourselves valuable to our putative competitors, Joe and the Koskis. In fact there was no such thing as competition among us, because every bike that any of us rolled out was sold before the air was in the tires. Marketing was not a problem.

The only problem with the Trailmaster turned out to be getting one. Trailmaster frames were manufactured by Dave Garoutte of DKG Industries, a local machinist who worked on a wide variety of fabrication projects. Tom had been building nothing but bike frames nonstop for about eight years, and he had honed his methods to the point where there was no one else in the United States at the time building as many bicycle frames of his quality. Because of our business arrangement, Tom had the luxury of concentrating on frame production, while Gary and I took care of every

other aspect—finding the components, assembling the bikes, and handling marketing and sales. Time Tom spent on the telephone took away from production, so we tried to keep it to a minimum. As a result of this level of industry, no one else in our tiny market niche could keep up with us. The demand for Trailmasters and Breezers was probably equal to the demand for our bikes, but the wait was endless by comparison, and only about 100 Trailmasters and 75 Series II and III Breezers ever hit the trails.

Breezer riders line up with a mix of Series I and II bikes during the Fifth Annual Crested Butte to Aspen Tour in September 1980. Left to right: Wende Cragg, Denise Caramagno, Tim Schuyler, Joe Breeze, Dave Sigman, Steve Potts, and Erik Koski.

chapter 15

WIDENING THE VIEW

Gary Fisher and I found a knack for self-promotion early on. It started with the printed matter. We went back to John Finley Scott's and used his word processor to make up a true catalog to fulfill our promise from the first publicity sheet. In it we listed Tom Ritchey's bikes and all the other components for clunkers and cruisers. On the back page was an order form for a bike with many options of colors or components. Our first flyer and the ad in *BMX Plus!* had produced responses, and we needed something to send out. We understood that a mailing list was a good thing to have.

It was obvious that we had to take immediate steps to protect our company name, because we knew that MountainBikes was a good one and that we were definitely the first people to use it. The cute spelling was intended to set it off as more than just a phrase. Gary and I considered our company to be "MountainBikes," and we had

Pete Barrett's poster for the Ballooner Blastoff race held on January 6, 1980.

come up with the name together. The relationship between the two of us and Tom was never clearly defined, but Gary and I considered our company to be MountainBikes and Tom's company to be independent of ours. As it turned out, it wasn't quite that simple.

I looked for an attorney to handle our trademark and found that there were two in Marin County specializing in such things. I chose the one who was the shortest bike ride away. We held a brief meeting, and he asked for $125 to file the two-page application, which looked to me like 10 minutes of legal services. It was a painful amount to give up that early in the undertaking but obviously necessary. I had to show him a sample of the "mark," the decal we had made with the name on it, and demonstrate that it had been used on something shipped across state lines, also easy to show since one of our first customers had been in New Mexico. We filed the application.

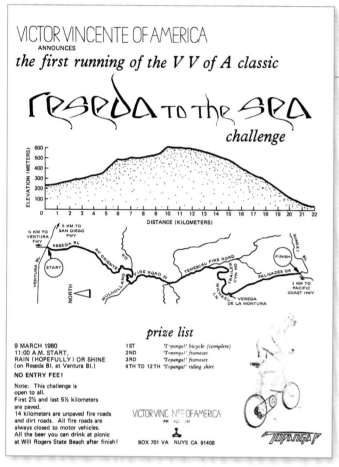

Poster for Victor Vincente of America's Reseda to the Sea Challenge race held on March 9, 1980.

We didn't have a storefront yet, so customers had to beat on the doors of our workshop to get in. We wanted the locals to know where those doors were located. To introduce and publicize our new business, Gary and I sponsored a ride in January 1980 that we called the "Ballooner Blastoff," a lap around our regular Thanksgiving Day course on Pine Mountain. Pete Barrett drew up the poster, of course. At first we did not realize how many frames Tom could turn out, and we wanted to make sure the riders on "classic" equipment were still being served and that we would get their business as well.

The two BMX magazines with stories about our bike had come out, and we were finally noticed outside the Bay Area. I picked up a few more writing gigs, which was a double bonus since I could use the stories I was paid for writing to advance our company's commercial goals. *Bicycling* magazine bought my story about the ride from Crested Butte to Aspen and used the photo from Pearl Pass on the cover of the April 1980 issue. Dean Bradley at *BMX Plus!* asked me to write a column, thinking that there would be a crossover audience, but I only lasted a couple of issues. BMX and mountain biking may have looked similar, but they do not attract the same people, and I couldn't write for an audi-

ence half my age whose idea of cycling was riding laps on a vacant lot. I traded for ad space instead of being paid and retired from the BMX magazine gig. Despite the fact that we were advertising mountain bikes in a BMX magazine, the ad space paid off by getting us noticed in Southern California.

There was no mountain bike racing scene outside of Marin County until that year. But as soon as it became possible to build bikes light enough to consider riding up hills, racing took off in places where downhill racing had yet to catch on. Racing was the ideal venue to publicize our bikes, because not only did MountainBikes have the best equipment but also we had by far the best rider in the person of Gary. The first race we attended outside Marin County took place in Southern California in March 1980.

Before the Araya and Ukai alloy, 26-inch rims became available in the middle of 1979, a few builders had experimented with off-road bikes that used alloy, 20-inch rims made for BMX. The rims were light, and there were aggressive tires made for them, while the 26-inch riders were stuck with steel rims and the outdated and heavy Uniroyal Nobby. You could easily take 6 pounds or more off a bike if you built it around the little wheels. Craig Mitchell had designed bikes around 20-inch

Victor posing with his 'Topanga!'
It was designed to use
lightweight 20-inch wheels.

wheels in Marin County, and Victor Vincente of America had done so in Southern California.

Victor Vincente of America was the nom de guerre of Michael Hiltner, a 1960 Olympic cycling team member who pushed the envelope in all aspects of his life, none more than in cycling. Several years earlier he claimed the first coast-to-coast bicycle record by riding the distance and calling it his. Then he turned around and rode home so he could claim the record for both directions.

For his off-road exploits, Victor had designed a bike he called the 'Topanga!' It had 20-inch wheels and lightweight, BMX tires. Victor had seen our ad in *BMX Plus!*, leading him to contact us with information about his bikes and to ask whether we might like to distribute them. At the time we were open to anything in the way of suppliers, and we were happy to have a look at the bikes. Victor also sent us a flyer for his first big race in March, "Reseda to the Sea." He was offering a 'Topanga!' bike for the winner and using his event to showcase the superiority of his lightweight design.

Road trip.

Being friends with John had many unusual benefits. Among them was the coolest bicycle toy anyone had ever conceived, a double-decker London bus reconfigured for bicycle transport. He had upgraded the drivetrain with a Cummins diesel truck engine that was loafing at 70 mph, pulling the light bus instead of 20 tons of wheat. The seats had been removed from the lower passenger section, and bike hooks had been installed on the ceiling. All passengers rode in the upper compartment, reached via spiral stairway. Most of the seats upstairs had been removed too and replaced by large, foam mattresses. There was easily room for 20 people to lounge comfortably. The driver sat in a tiny compartment on the right side of the front end wearing ear protection because the big truck engine sat only a few feet away.

John had purchased and remodeled the bus for the purpose of supporting "super tours," touring rides on road bikes with riders unencumbered by gear. With a bus that could move all the riders and their bikes, the tour could start and finish anywhere, and the bus could act as the sag wagon for each day's ride. John said he would take us to Los Angeles for the Reseda to the Sea race.

With transportation in place, we rounded up a crew consisting of Gary, Joe, Wende Cragg, Denise Caramagno, and myself, plus John and some of his friends from Davis. Since I did not yet have a Ritchey bike, I was still riding my Breezer, and Denise rode a borrowed Breezer.

We drove south on March 8. My brother, Jim, lived in Los Angeles, so we parked the behemoth in front of his cottage, which was half the size of our transportation, and the race crew slept all over the bus and on Jim's floor. After abusing Jim's plumbing the next morning, we headed over to Reseda.

I don't know what crossed local minds when a double-decker bus pulled up and unloaded three Breezers and a Ritchey from among the machinery hanging in our cargo section. As we had done in Crested Butte earlier, we made a grand entrance that suggested a team of quasiprofessionals.

Victor turned out to be a bearded hippie cyclist cut from a different bolt of the same cloth as Gary and I. He planned to use his race as a showcase for his 'Topanga!' bike just as Gary and I promoted local events to show off our own products. He had

On the way to the Reseda race, near Los Angeles. We all went on John Finley Scott's double-decker London bus. Left to right: me, Joe Breeze (near the bus), Denise Caramagno, Gary Fisher, Craig Mitchell, Peter Brooks, and Kent Bostick.

a young rider named Todd Deangelis who would ride the 'Topanga!', hopefully to victory. As it turned out, though, the actual north-south showdown was between Gary and a SoCal cyclocross rider, Ron Skarin, a member of the North Hollywood Wheelmen.

Ron was a prominent racer in multiple disciplines and had to be considered the favorite. He had won 10 national titles on the banked track and had won road races as well, including two victories at the Tour of Somerville in New Jersey. At the time of Reseda to the Sea, he was director of the United States Cycling Federation (USCF), the official sanctioning body for traditional bicycle racing at that time. On March 9, 1980, he brought a cyclocross bike to a gunfight.

There was no more casual race start in history than the one we saw that morning. Victor assembled the mob at an intersection and issued instructions in the middle of the street with no regard for auto traffic. He described the route, which started and ended on paved streets, and without a formal signal everyone shoved off and started racing amid the auto traffic.

As Gary described his part of the race, which took place far out of my sight, Ron had a decided advantage on the paved approach to the dirt road because of his lighter bike, and his advantage continued on the dirt climb. As soon as they crested and started down toward the ocean, however, the same clunky Uniroyal tires that had made the climb tough for Gary became his advantage because Gary could fly at maximum velocity while Ron picked his way across rocks. Gary won easily, and Southern California was on alert that MountainBikes were perfect for that sort of racing. It would be more than a year before Gary collected his prize of the 'Topanga!' bike.

I met a young man at the race who had brought a bike of his own ineffective, fat-tire design. He was interested in what was taking place in the Bay Area, which to him seemed years ahead of the state of the art in Southern California. He had come out to see if there was a story, and shortly afterward I saw his article titled "Cruiser Bikes: Off-Road to Happiness" in a trade magazine called *Bicycle Dealer Showcase*. It was one of the first he ever had published but far from the last. The young man's name was Mike Shermer; now he is better known as Dr. Michael Shermer (Ph.D.), author of multiple books, *Scientific American* columnist, and founder of the Skeptics Society. He is also a five-time finisher of the Race Across America.

While other riders either saddled up and rode back over the course to cars on the other side of the ridge or called friends for rides, John brought the bus around to pick us up. We partied on Victor's home-brewed beer for a couple of hours, then piled back into the bus thinking that this adventure was in the books. Somewhere along Interstate 5 as it winds up into the hills toward Tejon Pass, John ordered the bus pulled over, and we took a 10-minute relief break. After the passengers were back in the upper compartment, the bus pulled out and headed north.

We had gone about 20 miles up the road when a California Highway Patrol (CHP) helicopter swooped down and began flying parallel to the bus. It was obvious that we were the object of attention, and there was someone speaking over a public-address system from the chopper, but there was no way for us to understand the message over the noise of the aircraft and the deafening bus engine. Some who had been openly drinking beer

quietly put it away. Since John typically rode with the driver in the earsplitting pilot house, someone went down to alert him about our visitor. The messenger was back in 2 seconds.

"John's not down there."

Everyone was accounted for on the flagship except the admiral. When the crowd of riders had re-entered the bus after the break, the driver had assumed John had gotten on with everyone else and had retired to the upper compartment as he sometimes did. In the upper compartment we had assumed that John was riding with the driver as he usually did and had given the order to pull out. Now we had a pretty good idea what the CHP message was.

We found a truck stop and pulled in. I was delegated to make the call from a phone booth. I looked up the nearest CHP office and spent $1 to call it. The officer who took the call knew exactly which double-decker bus with the missing owner I was speaking of. He advised me that John had caught a ride with a trucker, and we just needed to stay put; he would catch us.

After an uncomfortable half hour, John arrived, climbing down from the cab of a big rig that he had somehow flagged down. He was enraged, but he didn't have a convenient target among our

crowd since none of us had been assigned to take a roll call after our stop. The driver was more culpable, but John still needed him, so the professor of sociology grumbled about human nature for a while but didn't scold anyone directly.

Arriving back in Marin County around 10 p.m., we unloaded our bikes and settled up with John. He did a little arithmetic and gave us the tab for fuel. For our two-day, 800-mile round trip, each of us owed him $12.

In June we mounted another expedition, to the Central Coast Clunker Classic in San Luis Obispo, promoted by Glenn Odell. Gary cleaned house again and would go on to take the inaugural Whiskeytown Downhill in Redding and the second annual Reseda to the Sea race in 1981. That made a clean sweep of the first "classic" mountain bike races, and of course Gary also held the course record on Repack. In the early 1980s, Gary was by far the best off-road rider in the world, although admittedly that world encompassed only a few dozen participants.

On the other hand, in the 1980 Northern California Cyclocross Championships, Gary rode his Ritchey MountainBike to second place overall, down only 16 seconds to future professional rider Gavin Chilcott, who was then a junior and took

Mark Edwards with Breezer number 2 and me holding my Ritchey modified for road riding at the Hekaton Century in Dublin, California, September 9, 1981.

that title home while Gary settled for the senior championship. Pitting a MountainBike against dedicated cyclocross bikes was generally a losing proposition, as Joe and I had found earlier, and it's to Gary's credit as an all-around cyclist that he prevailed.

And Gary wasn't alone. A few weeks later, on December 21, Velo-Club Tamalpais (VCT) member Kenny Fuetsch rode a Breezer to the handicapped win at the venerable Tilden Park Cyclocross, while another VCT member, Joe Ryan, had the best time from scratch on a traditional cyclocross bike. A year earlier, Gordon Burns of Santa Rosa had ridden a Jeffrey Richman off-road bike for the win at the same event.

Just as the Repack races had defined a new approach to high-quality bicycles, the burgeoning cross-country racing scene in California put the stamp of invincibility on the Ritchey Mountain-Bike. If there was one in the race, the winner rode it. In Southern California, Monte Ward, Tim Rysdale, and Jim Samuelson, a trio of MountainBike owners calling themselves the Ritchey Wrecking Crew, competed only among themselves for win, place, and show. You could get bikes of similar quality in Marin County if you wanted a Trailmaster or a Breezer, but Ritchey MountainBikes were

going out to locations all over the West, and outside of Marin there was nothing else like them.

The first few production runs of Ritchey MountainBikes were built to a standard that was hardly necessary. Simply put, the fabrication was world-class. The tubing for Ritchey MountainBikes was delivered from the foundry to Tom's property on Skyline Road above Palo Alto. It came in 20-foot lengths and in several diameters. Tom made jigs for cutting, bending, and mitering tubing that made it possible for an untrained worker to do it. He hired a helper to do all the tasks that didn't require his personal skill. Tom handled the torch, and he could do it all day as long as someone kept him provided with tubing to join.

Tom could make a lot of bikes, and yet he still made each one as beautifully as any handmade bike in the world. The construction quality was unsurpassed, the paint was immaculate, and the components were the best we could find for their purposes.

Forks, however, were a problem. There was no available cast crown like the ones Tom used on his road bikes. Tom came up with a design using two flat plates attached to the steering tube, but it was more complicated to make than the rest of the frame put together.

Until the Ritchey MountainBike changed the bicycle market, if you had an unlimited amount of money and went into a bike shop wanting the best bike you could get, you ended up with only one thing, a Tour de France racing bike. Only a fraction of the cycling population can even ride such a delicate machine, which is made for riders who have a follow car full of spare bikes and wheels.

The Ritchey MountainBike cost more than a road racing bike. A lot more. It was built to the same standards as that Tour de France bike, but anyone could ride it, and it would take you anywhere. Not that just anybody bought one, because it took a lot of money, and you had to wait a while to get it. Our customers were a very small slice of the market, but there were enough of them to keep us busy. Even though we sold one of the most expensive bikes then available, we couldn't keep up with the demand.

The word about our bikes reached a San Francisco financier and bicycle enthusiast named Thom Weisel. His secretary called and said that her boss had heard about our bikes and decided he wanted one. How much were they, and when could she pick it up? We explained that it didn't work that way. You gave us some money, you looked at a checklist and made a dozen selections and then you waited a month or so. That was unacceptable,

she replied. How much would it cost to make it happen faster? You can't make it happen faster, we said. Apparently this was not the kind of news she wanted to take to her boss. He was, of course, the same Thomas Weisel who later created the Montgomery Securities cycling team, which morphed into the U.S. Postal Team, which counted Lance Armstrong as one of its riders.

One custom order became what we called the "Alaska Bike." The customer was ordering from New York, and he was working on producing a Broadway show called *Alaska*. He had decided that he needed one of our bikes for the show, although it was not quite clear in what capacity it would be used. He sent us promotional T-shirts for the show, with a North Star that lit up. Obviously it would be a major publicity coup if we could get a bike on the Broadway stage. The bike had to be one of a kind, though. We went all out, with a special paint job, custom everything, and gold-anodized components. We even gold-anodized the aluminum spoke nipples.

But after a dozen phone calls and decisions about the order, the customer never sent money. After we realized he was trying to scam us out of a bike, we made the Alaska into our display model for an upcoming bicycle trade show.

Gary and others were dominating the racing circuit, but my racing skills were a long way from being competitive. I took it on myself to demonstrate our bikes on recreational rides. Specifically, century rides, or 100-mile, supported, recreational road rides that draw hundreds of cyclists. Anyone who can go 100 miles in a day is a reasonably dedicated rider and probably spent more on machinery than the average bike owner. These were exactly the kind of people who needed to see our bikes.

I prepared my bike specifically for this kind of riding. The Mitsuboshi Cruiser Mitt tire had come on the market in 1980, the first available lightweight balloon tire. It was strictly a street tire, with a hard rubber ridge running down the center line. I outfitted my bike with a pair pumped up to a rock-hard 80 psi. Overinflating the tires made them as big as my leg. I modified the gearing on my bike with a close-ratio cluster and put my road pedals on the bike so I could wear cleated cycling shoes. At an event where virtually everyone else was on a bike with drop handlebars and sew-up tires, the Ritchey MountainBike was a traffic stopper.

The biggest disadvantage of my balloon-tire bike compared with a road bike was that the heavier wheels limited acceleration. With the thin, rubber ridge down the center and high-pressure inflation,

though, the rolling resistance of the Cruiser Mitt was negligible.

A century ride is not a sprint. You get rolling and keep rolling, and I had plenty of experience riding in pacelines. I would join the fastest group I saw and do more than my share on the front to make sure I was welcome. If a faster group came by, I would join it. On a ride that went over what was billed as the steepest grade in Napa County, road cyclists were reduced to pushing bikes with 42-tooth road chainrings, their cleats scratching on the slick asphalt, while I shifted into my tiny 26-tooth third chainring and rode straight up the hill.

At the end of the ride, people with Colnagos and Cinellis and the like had to get a look at the fat-tire bike they hadn't been able to keep up with, and that gave me an opportunity to talk about it.

Eventually I built a MountainBike strictly for the purpose of century rides so that I didn't have to swap equipment around on my usual bike. We used every trick in our arsenal on that bike to make it exceptionally light and fast. We used packing tape instead of a rim strip, latex inner tubes, alloy spoke nipples, and the lightest rims we had found, made by Ambrosio in Italy. A road bike gear cluster and road pedals completed the package and perhaps created the prototype for a modern town bike.

THE LONG BEACH BIKE SHOW, 1981

In recent years, the bicycle industry's big trade show has been held in September, but in the early '80s the big West Coast bike show was held early in the year. By 1981 Gary and I were ready to go.

Gary had attended a few trade shows in connection with his work at *Bicycling*, but he had never been an exhibitor. We paid for the cheapest possible space, a 100-square-foot undecorated slab of concrete at the farthest fringe of the Long Beach Convention Center.

According to the house rules, if we brought in more than we could carry by ourselves, we had to hire union help to move it. Our "exhibit" consisted of a card table, two small boxes of cheaply printed literature, and two bikes. The bikes we displayed were a tandem MountainBike and the Alaska Bike we had created for a stage show in New York.

There were two other representatives of the new movement at the 1981 bike show. Jeff Lindsay, one of our regular customers for the special supplies he needed, was there with a bike he called the Mountain Goat. Jeff, from Chico, California, had been among the first after Tom Ritchey to enter our market. Chico is a three-hour drive north of the Bay Area, and it had its own local off-road tradition, including a race called the "Bidwell Bump" that began about the same time the first Repack races were taking place. Jeff was probably the most prolific craftsman after Tom, and his Mountain Goats employed his own unique design for the frames, using oval tubing.

The other off-road exhibitor was Victor Vincente of America, showing a 'Topanga!' bike similar to the one Gary had won at the first Reseda to the Sea race a year earlier. Victor had a unique exhibit. Our bikes were clean and polished, but his display bike was covered with mud and sat in a tray of dirt. Victor lounged nearby in a comfortable chair. Victor was still using the 20-inch wheel design, but the future was obvious. Bigger wheels were on their way.

I was overwhelmed by my first taste of the trade show. Big companies spent lots of money attracting eyeballs. We were theoretically competing against pumping disco sound tracks and models in skin-tight outfits.

But in truth, we weren't. Our only "competition" was our friends, Victor and Jeff. Nobody else had what we had. We didn't need models and flash-ing lights because anyone who responded to those wouldn't get what we were doing anyway. No one over the age of about 40 responded at all to our exhibit. Teenagers and 20-somethings, a minority at the show, stopped and stared. They got it immediately.

High-quality frame, check. Lots of gears, check. Big tires, check. Big brakes, check. I want one. HOW MUCH?

The trade show is where bike dealers meet the manufacturers and wholesalers to figure out what they will order for the upcoming season. Bike dealers generally buy wholesale and sell for more, but there wasn't a lot of room for profit on top of what our bikes cost us to build. The shop owners asked the obvious question: What was our "dealer program"? But we didn't really have a dealer program; we were a couple of guys in a rented garage who put together this new kind of bike. We were just there to meet people, show our bikes, and find suppliers for the stuff we now needed in great quantity.

One of the biggest displays belonged to a major component company, with a loud soundtrack accompanying an endless and repetitive video narration explaining that by making derailleurs and brakes more aerody-namic, the rider could shave a percent or two from his wind resistance. It seemed symbolic that the bike industry in 1981 was so desperate for a new direction that enormous sums had been spent, first on the research and development to develop the slick-profile components and then on the marketing, to convince bike dealers to sell these products to average riders who would never need the extra percent or two of performance they had just spent their money on.

As Gary and I stood in our bare-bones booth, holding court with bike fanatics in jeans and T-shirts and being ignored by the better-dressed element, a very important and well-dressed figure in the bike industry wandered over to take a look. He knew enough about bikes to understand what he was seeing, and in a moment of kind condescension he offered us advice.

"I love your passion, guys," he said, "but I've been in the bike business a long time. The future of the bike industry is aerodynamic components."

MOUNTAINBIKES

At first the company consisted solely of Gary Fisher and me. For a few months in 1980 it would have been hard to find a more idyllic life for a couple of bike junkies. We had our own shop, which meant no more assembling bikes in the buildings where we lived. We had all the tools we needed, we were best friends, and in our funky space we were creating some of the coolest bicycles on the planet. We knew it, and word was getting out. That summer, the Marin County weekly, the *Pacific Sun*, ran an article about us titled "Clunker Capital of the World."

The two of us were quickly overwhelmed, however, because demand was insatiable. Eventually we realized we needed an employee. Gary and I were adept at building the bikes, but keeping track of the money was a different set of skills. We needed a bookkeeper, but we didn't have much money to hire one. We posted an ad on a bulletin board at the College of Marin. We got one response.

New Ritchey MountainBikes ready to ship outside our shop at 1501 San Anselmo Avenue.

When there is only one applicant, the interview process doesn't take long. Dave Sahn was not actually a bookkeeper, as it turned out; instead, he was a guy who was taking a class in bookkeeping. But he was the only person who applied, and he took what we offered him. He got the job and lasted for 10 years at it, a lot longer than I did. Gary and I didn't make it easy for Dave. Sometimes we would grab some money out of petty cash to pick up some groceries on our way home, leaving an IOU of course, and the tax implications of this kind of behavior drove him crazy.

My dog, Amelia, was the unofficial shop dog. About the time Gary and I opened the shop, my girlfriend, Denise Caramagno, and I moved to a house in Fairfax, about 1 mile from the shop. In the morning I would ride my bike to the shop, and about 10 minutes later Amelia would arrive. She knew the route, and from following me on the bike she had been trained to run on the sidewalk and stay out of traffic. She never got busted by a dog-catcher on her daily trek.

One thing that I knew we needed was a computer. Our mailing list was growing, and we needed a way to keep track of it. Some amazing little desk-top units had arrived on the market, and they did "word processing" just like John Finley Scott's clanking, steam-driven, $13,000 machine did, and they could do mailing lists and the like. And they only cost, um, about $2,000.

Gulp.

We bit the bullet and bought one. When the computer arrived, we found we had another problem. Someone had to write a program for our mailing lists. We hired a programmer, and she sat and wrote us a script to do exactly that. But printing the labels from the list turned out to be a complication. I finally sent the floppy disks to a friend who worked in Silicon Valley, and he printed up our first mailing list.

The computer world was evolving just as fast then as our bike world was, and within months we had solved our mailing list problems with commercial software. I thought computers were supposed to be fast, but it took our little Apple II+ a half-hour to sort 500 names on a mailing list. When I first encountered database software, I realized that I could use it to identify every part in our inventory and attach all sorts of useful information to the files, like what it cost and where we got it. Then we could print the whole thing up and use it for reference.

As the business grew we added people, and we added space. One of the other tenants in our building moved out, and we took over the store-front and made an office space. Now we had a place where we could display our bikes and a neater area with desks for Gary, Dave, and me.

We gradually added a few more employees in the shop area. It started with the subassemblies.

Anybody could assemble a drivetrain—crank, chain, derailleurs—with a little instruction. You didn't need to be a master mechanic to mount tires or install brakes. Making brake cables was a pain, but somebody had to do it. We hired some of our friends to work on those routine tasks, but we also had several expert bike mechanics who enjoyed building what was at the time the bicycle equivalent of a Rolls-Royce. I still built most of the wheels. After building so many of the same kind, I could build a set in less than a half-hour. Reaching into a big box of loose spokes, I could grab 36 just by the feel of the handful.

The business never really ran efficiently because we always had supply problems of one kind or another. Sometimes bikes sat and waited for one part before they could be shipped out. Sometimes the lack of a certain part idled our employees.

Despite the problems, our product was undeniably the biggest thing to hit the market. At first we had handled every bike as a custom order, with the customer choosing from a list of components and selecting a color from the Imron paint chart (Imron was a tough, polyurethane enamel that provided a durable finish). But Gary and I had almost no input on what Tom Ritchey did in his shop. We could sell everything he made,

but he tinkered a lot with the design. For example, several different versions of his twin-plate fork crowns arrived with no advance notice. And then there were things we asked for but didn't see through to completion. One such idea was a rubber boot over the seatpost to keep it clean. Tom cut a groove around the top of the seat tube as an anchor point for the boot. But we never had the rubber parts made, and the groove never had a function.

In order to kick up production and reduce the price of our bikes, in 1982 Tom offered us a standardized design available in two colors, blue or gray, and two sizes. He cut back on the flawless cosmetics of the bronze welding, although it took a close comparison to discover the difference. If the top of the line was the "Everest" model, we needed a slightly lesser mountain to describe the less-exalted alternative, so this bike became the McKinley. Forks from Tange, a supplier in Japan, got Tom off the hook for the most complicated fabrication. Giving the customer a choice of a less expensive fork allowed us to lower the price even more.

Gary and I were hardly the only people marketing the new style of off-road bike. Jeffrey Richman had built a couple at the same time Tom was building his first off-road bikes. Joe Breeze had built his

second generation of Breezers in 1980, redesigned without the twin laterals. The Koski brothers had orders for their Trailmaster. Mert Lawwill had his ProCruiser, a bike destined to be collectible in the future because of its dead-end design. Victor Vincente of America had updated his design to use 26-inch wheels, and his new bikes looked a lot more like ours.

Jeff Lindsay, of Mountain Goat Cycles in Chico, was our closest competitor in terms of production, but there was no real competition in a market where every bike was sold long before it was available. In 1980 a rider named Scot Nicol joined us on our caravan to Crested Butte and came back so inspired by what he had seen that after apprenticing with Joe he began building frames himself and founded the Ibis bicycle company in 1981. Ross Shafer was an employee of Santana Cycles, which built custom tandems. Starting in 1981 with a bike using 650B tires, he quickly got on board, opening a fat-tire company called Salsa Cycles.

Also in 1981, Joe and his friend Steve Potts, who had been studying framebuilding with Joe, took their Breezers to New Zealand for a touring vacation. Steve was so inspired that within a year he was turning out his own fine mountain bike frames. He also became a founding partner of Wilderness Trail Bikes.

Charlie Cunningham had been an iconoclast in Marin County. No less a dedicated cyclist than the rest of us, he rode his hand-built, skinny-tire bike on all the same trails we did, but he didn't race downhill. There was no doubt that he could cover more ground on the lighter bike, but it would not have been competitive on Repack. Charlie was not part of the clunker crowd and didn't hide his disdain for the crude machinery. He made custom components and sold them through local bike shops. I had one of his seatposts on my Colnago racing bike. After light rims and tires became available for mountain bikes, however, Charlie found that there was a market for any bike that used them. Charlie transferred his use of large-diameter welded and heat-treated aluminum tubing to off-road bikes and was able to build some of the lightest bikes of that era. His production was minimal compared with Tom's, but his adherents were fanatical. Within a few years, Cannondale and Klein would provide the ultimate form of flattery by building off-road frames of oversized, aluminum tubing.

One of our original suppliers was Specialized Bicycle Imports, a small company started by Mike Sinyard that sold us Japanese components. In early 1981, his company brought out the first decent balloon tire for our purposes. Until the Specialized Stumpjumper tire appeared, the CyclePro Snake-belly had been the only dirt tire on the market. The Specialized tire was much better, with large lugs. It was made for real dirt, not a BMX track.

The Stumpjumper tire took off immediately. We were buying them in huge numbers. Specialized became one of our biggest suppliers.

A few months later we got a call from Mike. He asked about getting some bikes for himself and his employees. It was hard to refuse a big order from a major source, even though he asked for a wholesale discount from the street price. We were already selling every bike we could build at full retail price, and culling a few from the herd to sell at a discount was not appealing. But Specialized was a big supplier, and we needed to find a solution.

At the time we had a few bikes that might be regarded as "seconds." Tom had done a production run of frames for his friend and ours, John Scott. They were different from the frames Tom supplied to us, incorporating a slightly sloping top tube with the slope going downhill toward the front—that is, lower at the head tube than at the seat tube. Because Tom hated making forks, he sold the frames alone to John, and John hired his friend and framebuilder, John Padgett, to fabricate the forks.

John Padgett had no idea that the top tube was supposed to slope, so he built extra-long forks that made the bike level. This resulted in a couple of extra inches of clearance between the front tire and the fork crown and a slack steering angle. John Scott lost interest in the project before it was completed, and the "Padgett bikes" ended up at our shop. When one of our employees wanted a bike, we would sell him one of the Padgett bikes at a steep discount.

Specialized got four of the Padgett bikes.

In 1982 Specialized introduced the Stumpjumper, a virtually identical copy of the Ritchey MountainBike but set up for mass production. The initial model had a cast fork crown designed to resemble Tom's biplane fork, and the geometry reproduced that of the Padgett bike. The component group was nearly identical. Although there was a slight difference in the way the chainstay was bent, the only obvious change was that the Stumpjumper used Tomaselli motorcycle brake levers from Italy rather than the German ones on our bikes. A sticker on the chainstay assured us that it was "Designed by Tim Neenan," who was a custom builder in Santa Cruz, not far from Specialized headquarters.

If you say so.

September 1983 *California Bicyclist* cover with yours truly touted as "The World's Foremost Authority." They said it, not me.

At about the same time as the Stumpjumper came on the market, Univega introduced the Alpina Sport. Like the Stumpjumper, it was a factory copy of a Ritchey MountainBike. The Alpina Sport was the result of a suggestion by James McLean to Univega, including specifications. James was a bicycle sales rep and also owned a Ritchey MountainBike. He had been one of the first riders in Santa Barbara to venture off road and was a competent racer in his own right. He offered to represent our bike while traveling his sales route, but we didn't really need a sales rep because we couldn't keep up with our sales as it was. Even without a contract, James showed off his Ritchey MountainBike everywhere he went and sold the idea of making a factory version to Univega.

Both bikes opened the door for mass production, and within a year every major bicycle manufacturer had an entry into the market. Prior to that, Schwinn had come out with a sort of BMX-on-steroids model called the King Sting. Murray of Ohio, a company that produced department-store bikes, came out with the Murray Baja at just more than $100, which had a similar look to our bikes but was built so cheaply that performance was nonexistent. Nearly every one of the better bikes was a copy of the Ritchey MountainBike. With only a few

exceptions, the triangular Bullmoose handlebars became the signature style all over the industry, even though they had been an ad hoc design and far from the best way to mount a handlebar.

The MountainBikes design had taken over the bicycle industry. By 1987, the concept that Gary and I had introduced to the market would sell more bikes than traditional drop-bar 10-speeds.

In 1983, every American publication covering the world of bicycles discovered the mountain bike market. The trade magazine *Bicycle Dealer Showcase* featured an article in its May 1983 issue titled "The Mountain Bike Market: Where Do We Go from Here?" The article quoted a number of spokespeople from major bike companies, including Specialized, Trek, Bianchi, and Ross, all of whom were optimistic about the expanding market. Framebuilders Jeff Lindsay (identified in the article as Tom Lindsay) and Richard Cunningham of Mantis were quoted as representative examples of the custom builders with innovative designs who were shaping the market for the big bicycle companies.

The contrary point of view, and worst in hindsight, came from a Raleigh company spokesman. "Not everyone in the mountain bike market is enthusiastic, however," the article noted. "Lloyd

Docter of Raleigh Cycle of America reacted to the recent onslaught of mountain bikes this way: 'We don't believe there is a significant market for mountain bikes. We do have a mountain bike in our line, but the bulk of our quote unquote mountain bike entry is not at all geared to the traditional mountain bike market. That market is like all fads in the bicycle business. It doesn't take effort to display one sample at the New York Show.'"

While we were in a parking lot after a trade show packing our exhibit into a van, a Bianchi employee wheeled out that company's new entry in the market, to put in his own truck. Gary spotted it and asked whether he could have a look. The Bianchi employee knew who Gary was and was proud to hand it over.

In the space of 30 seconds or so, Gary bounced it off a few curbs, did a few jumps, and returned it to the ashen employee with a tire-scrubbing slide.

"Well, what do you think?" asked the Bianchi man.

Gary said, "It'll cost you a hundred bucks to find out."

CRESTED BUTTE, 1982

In 1982 the annual trek to Crested Butte loomed. We had chartered a bus the previous year in order to get as many of our friends and customers out there as efficiently as possible. That had turned out to be a little more of an adventure than we cared to repeat.

A year later, MountainBikes was at its peak in name recognition, and the only people Gary and I wanted to get to Crested Butte were the two of us. So we rented an airplane.

It was a Cessna 210 piloted by our friend Doug White, owner of a specialty component company called White Industries that made beautifully engineered parts such as wheel hubs. Doug had a pilot's license, and it turned out that you can rent planes just like you can rent cars. So we did.

The plane was rated as a six-seater, so the three of us and a couple of dismantled bikes were well inside the limit. Doug went down a checklist of what seemed to be a couple hundred items and then we were off, flying as far as Fallon, Nevada.

We could see a storm system ahead that was moving east just a little slower than we were. Rather than fly into the back end of it, we figured we would drop into one of the towns on our route and have a spot of lunch. Doug set us down at the Fallon Airport, which consisted of a runway and a shack roughly 20 miles from the town of Fallon. In the shack was a pay phone, and next to the phone was a list of casinos you could call to get a shuttle into the town. I called one at random, and I was told a driver would come and get us. The economy of Fallon is recreational, including but not limited to gambling. People who fly to central Nevada in private planes generally have recreation in mind, so local businesses make it easy to get there.

In about the time it takes to drive between the casino and the airstrip, a rent-a-cop arrived in a casino car. He gave us a ride to the place that had sent him out, where we retired to the coffee shop. We spent about $10 on a light lunch. We didn't gamble at all. We lingered over coffee while the weather moved ahead of us, then we found our chauffeur for the ride back. He drove 80 miles so we could have a salad and a cup of coffee.

We caught up with the weather again in Utah as night fell, so Doug set us down in Green River. Once again it was an unattended airstrip that anyone could land on, but this one was at the edge of the town, so we tied down the plane and walked to a nearby motel.

The next day Doug got us to the approximate location of Crested Butte and Gunnison, where there are airstrips, but the skies were socked in with clouds, and Doug was understandably reluctant to drop through them in an area studded with 14,000-foot peaks. The closest place we could find where a hole in the cloud cover allowed us to land was Montrose, so Gary and I rented a car there and drove to Crested Butte. Doug spent the next week or so flying around Colorado while Gary and I took part in the annual Crested Butte festivities.

Gary and I had arranged for Doug to pick us up in Aspen at the end of the annual ride over Pearl Pass, and from there we would return directly to the Bay Area. Because of this arrangement, Gary and I skipped the ride back to Crested Butte on a chartered bus, so we were not involved in the accident when that bus plunged off the road and rolled down a hillside, injuring a number of our friends.

chapter 17

FAT TIRE FLYER

Like so many other aspects of my bicycle adventure, the *Fat Tire Flyer* was not a serious undertaking at the start. When it first appeared, I was already a year into the MountainBikes business. I didn't need another time-consuming project. It was a conflict of interest. I charged others to advertise their products and put ads for MountainBikes in for nothing. Without any magazine experience other than a few freelance sales and without meaning to be one, I was suddenly an editor.

During the summer of 1980 MountainBikes was just getting rolling. For the first time there were public rumblings of conflicts between the new breed of bicyclists and the hikers and equestrians who were the primary users of the fire roads and trails where mountain bikes had suddenly appeared.

Some of us in the new cycling community had been members of Velo-Club Tamalpais (VCT).

Cover of the first *Fat Tire Flyer*.

We thought, for a week at least, that a club for our new form of sport would be a good idea. As it happened, the primary reason for founding VCT had been to meet the United States Cycling Federation (USCF) club requirement for road racers. Mountain bikers had no such incentive.

A dozen or so people met at Wende Cragg's house during the summer of 1980 to discuss the prospect of a club for off-road riders. Only two orders of business were completed at the meeting. We chose a grandiose name, the Marin County Wilderness Wheelers. And we decided that we would have a newsletter.

No evidence of any further club activity exists. I was the only person in the room who had been published, with a total of two magazine articles and a couple of paragraphs in *Velo-News* (as it was spelled then) to my credit. Putting together a little newsletter for my friends sounded like fun. What should we call it?

There were only two kinds of bikes in our world, skinny-tire bikes and fat-tire bikes. If this was a newsletter for the latter, the title should suggest it, and Denise Caramagno came up with the winner on her first try.

When she suggested *Fat Tire Flyer*, no vote was necessary. It passed by acclamation.

Its function fully satisfied by choosing the title of the newsletter, the club never met again.

Denise and I put together a cute little newsletter. It was eight pages, cheaply photocopied on letter-size paper, folded in the middle, and stapled. Text was typed on a manual typewriter, and titles were made with Letraset press-on letters. The average church or PTA newsletter was nicer looking and contained more useful information. The *Fat Tire Flyer* didn't have much news value, since any of the few dozen people who saw it probably already knew everything we had to report. Other than lists of race results and the schedule for upcoming events, there

Banner for the Clunker Connection race at Sorich Park, San Anselmo.

wasn't much to report about an activity in which everyone knew everyone else.

The *Fat Tire Flyer* might have disappeared along with the Marin County Wilderness Wheelers, except that when we put the first issue together, Denise and I had assumed the club would meet again. In the upper corner it was clearly identified as "Issue One." Issue One implies that there will be Issue Two.

In Crested Butte that fall Denise and I distributed copies of our first effort. Since it was cheap enough to print, when we returned we published number two.

And so on.

After Issue Two, there wasn't any obvious stopping point. People asked when the next issue would come out. Eventually, it would. We claimed to be bimonthly, but there was no calendar year in which six issues appeared.

It was natural to use the *Fat Tire Flyer* as the platform for mountain bike events. Denise and I promoted recreational rides as well as a couple of races. In 1981 we had a Valentine's Day ride and hosted a cross-country race in San Anselmo as part of a town celebration called Country Fair Days. With a little help from friends on the Grateful Dead sound crew, we set up a public-address system and radio contact with checkpoints around the course. Our amplified comments annoyed the other occupants of the baseball field, a small, traveling troupe of acrobats who called themselves Cirque du Soleil.

The winner of that cross-country race turned out to be multiple national cyclocross champion Laurence Malone, who borrowed a suitable bike and edged out local Charlie Cunningham. To the crowd's dismay, the 3rd place rider, Clark Roberts, was on a cyclocross bike. Clark saw the light and became a professional mountain bike racer a few years later.

Later that year we made the annual Thanksgiving Day ride one of our promotions, with a two-page ad in the *Fat Tire Flyer*. In 1982 we repeated our cross-country race.

Our cheap printing made it difficult to use photographs. Fortunately the world is full of cartoonists, and cartoons reproduce very well in photocopies. Much of the *Flyer*'s popularity—if not most of it—came from our cartoons. The first of these was an instant legend, *Ricky Cha*, drawn by Anthony Martin. This strip concerned the activities of a Rastafarian mountain biker whose riding ritual included lighting a large spliff. His catchphrases went viral in the subculture: the greeting "Cha mon," the admonition "Always be cruisen'!" and the expletive "Holy Bembwato!"

The first *Ricky Cha* cartoon, drawn by Anthony Martin for the *Fat Tire Flyer*.

Other cartoons followed. Kevin Coffey created an anthropomorphic mountain bike named Mud-Pup whose adventures with his rider, Edie, allowed the artist to comment on the movement from the bike's point of view.

In early 1981, Specialized Bicycle Imports introduced its revolutionary new tire, the Stumpjumper. The *Fat Tire Flyer* was an obvious place to announce it, and our ad rates were cheap enough. At that time, Specialized was a wholesale distributor, and the company hadn't needed much in the way of print advertising. There was no publicity photograph or prepared copy for this new tire, so our artist, Dave Bohn, sketched the tire for the ad and laid out the copy with Letraset.

Like MountainBikes, the *Fat Tire Flyer* was a business before it had a business plan, and by then it was too late to put one together. For all the same reasons that MountainBikes eventually failed, the *Fat Tire Flyer* would eventually fall apart. Unlike MountainBikes, though, for a half-decade the *Fat Tire Flyer* had absolutely no competition, which did a lot to compensate for its other failings, such as irregular publication schedules. For better or worse and almost in spite of itself, the *Fat Tire Flyer* created the only cohesive record of mountain biking until 1986.

Kevin Coffey's *MudPup* made the March/April 1984 cover of the *Fat Tire Flyer*.

After six issues in the original cheap, photo-copied format we got help from a commercial artist. Dave Bohn created what would become our logo, the *Fat Tire Flyer* banner title.

Our eighth issue went to a full-size format. Abandoning the typewriter, we had the type set and used a commercial printer rather than a copy shop. Now that we could reproduce photographs, we put Marc Horwitz on the cover. In the photo he is pulling his custom-built "tofu trailer" behind his Trailmaster, delivering tofu to local health-food stores. Unfortunately we chose cheap newsprint paper to keep our printing cost down, and the result was a fragile, easily torn magazine whose paper started turning yellow almost before the ink was on it. From the next issue on, we spent the money it took to print the *Flyer* on good paper that would last.

Moving up to the larger format signaled that the *Fat Tire Flyer* was ready to be a real magazine. Learning as we went along, we started having the magazine laid out by commercial designers.

We were the only vehicle for advertisers to reach a tiny market, and we were fortunate to have advertisers trying to reach that market. Readers were sending money and asking for subscriptions. The *Fat Tire Flyer* created its own momentum and took Denise and me along for the ride.

The *Fat Tire Flyer* became more of a business when Denise and I ended our personal relationship in 1982, because then it became the only thing we did together. Suddenly the *Fat Tire Flyer* was more than just a goofy newsletter with cute writing but thin content and some cartoons. We had accepted money for subscriptions and advertising. People expected something for their money, and we were now obliged to deliver it. Like it or not, we had created another business, parallel to MountainBikes and run out of the same facility. I was using the MountainBikes computer to handle the mailing list and to write the magazine.

We kept at it and learned the craft of putting out a magazine. The *Fat Tire Flyer* got a big boost when I left MountainBikes in 1983. Now the magazine was my main project and my voice in the mountain bike world. By that time the sport had exploded because of the introduction of mass-produced bikes. It was an exciting time to be the publication of record.

When the *Fat Tire Flyer* came on the market, there were hundreds of small magazines catering to their own relatively small readerships. We found a publisher who specialized in exactly the type of magazine we put out and who could handle printing and mailing for us. I wrote under several names

in the *Flyer* to keep it from looking like one person wrote most of it, but the voice was always the same, so the noms des plumes probably didn't fool anyone.

Now that anyone can have a blog and publish anything, the value of access to a printing press has been severely diluted. In paper-and-ink days, though, almost no one got to publish anything he or she pleased. Articles that I wrote for the big magazines had to fit a certain format. I had no trouble delivering that format, but I also had my own magazine, a platform rarely granted to writers. I was the voice of the sport by default. That voice was irreverent and unfiltered, and I spoke with the authority of someone who had been involved in the sport from the earliest days. The *Fat Tire Flyer* inspired an avid following.

In the summer of 1984, SunTour, a Japanese company that made components such as derailleurs and cranksets that worked well on mountain bikes, promoted the first Japanese mountain bike championships. Representing the *Fat Tire Flyer*, Denise and I went to Japan along with Tom Ritchey, professional racer Dale Stetina, and Dale's wife, Anne. It was news to me that I was expected to compete in a championship for Japanese riders. "Participate" would be a better word. As visitors and presumably experienced riders, Tom, Dale,

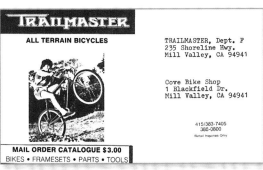

Top: Specialized Stumpjumper tire ad pieced together by Dave Bohn for the *Fat Tire Flyer*, 1981.

Bottom: The artwork we used for a Trailmaster ad in the *Fat Tire Flyer*.

Top: David Ross was the house artist who designed the *Fat Tire Flyer* logo.

Bottom: The first edition of the full-size *Fat Tire Flyer* was laid out in a landscape format with the staples at the top.

and I were not eligible for prizes. Fortunately, the "cross-country" event was largely downhill and about 2 miles long. I was riding on a borrowed bike and wearing a T-shirt, shorts, and no helmet. I managed to lose half a minute to Tom, who takes all competition seriously.

Like MountainBikes, the *Fat Tire Flyer* never had a defined business arrangement between the two principals. Denise and I worked together and got the magazine out. It didn't make enough money to argue over. Denise was an equal partner and had the right to dispose of her interest. In 1985 Denise sold her share of the *Fat Tire Flyer*, and I had a new partner, Don Mertle, who assumed the role of publisher.

A second-floor office space became available in Fairfax at this time, directly across the hall from the offices of the local newspaper, the *Fax*.

We moved the operation into the commercial space, and I finally had room to assemble what became the files leading to this book. Our new office location proved to be a major asset, since the staff of the *Fax* could help us with layout while we learned the art, saving us the cost of having the magazine assembled by a paid professional. I learned the venerable techniques of laying out copy for offset printing. A professional typesetter a

block away set our type, a job that went the way of buggy-whip manufacturing within just a few years. A copy center on the first floor of our building gave us access to a photocopier much better than anything we cared to buy, and we made liberal use of it in composing the magazine.

It was fun to learn the analog craft of publishing before it was obliterated by the digital version. The creative process of putting out the magazine involved much more than writing or editing the stories. We gathered the copy and artwork and arranged it into pages by physically sticking it to preprinted layout sheets with melted beeswax. The layouts would then go to the printer, which would photograph them to create the printing plates. Our unschooled, ad hoc approach gave the *Fat Tire Flyer* a unique look all its own.

For the next two years Don and I barnstormed around the West to various mountain bike events, returning to Marin to get the magazine out. I handled layout and kept track of subscriptions in addition to handling the editorial aspects. Our layout boards went to a printer in Missouri along with the mailing labels. The printer also mailed the subscription copies for us. The next issue could not go out until we found the money to pay the printer for the last one. The occasional delay in getting the money

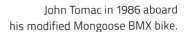

John Tomac in 1986 aboard his modified Mongoose BMX bike.

together to go to press made it impossible to keep up with bimonthly publication. Without explicitly claiming to be a quarterly, in practice we were.

At the same time that I was editing the *Fat Tire Flyer*, I was also contributing to consumer publications, including *Cyclist*, *Velo-News*, and *Bicycling*, and the trade publications *American Bicyclist* and *Motorcyclist*. I could sell a story to a regular publication to finance the travel and then write it up completely differently for the *Fat Tire Flyer*.

By 1985 the *Fat Tire Flyer* was well-known in racing circles. It was still possible to know just about every rider on the circuit, which was then mostly in the West, and my own name still carried a little weight. The press is welcome everywhere, and the host buys the beer.

Don Mertle and I had our first adventure as the *Fat Tire Flyer* at the initial Kamikaze Downhill at Mammoth Mountain (described later in this book in Chapter 22), where Don Douglass fanned the dying ember of downhill racing back to a white-hot flame.

After the Kamikaze, Don and I headed off to Crested Butte in what had become an annual migration for many of us in Marin County. In 1985 I couldn't imagine a year when I wouldn't be riding over Pearl Pass. Being the only publication

Fat Tire Flyer

Volume 6, Number 4

Jacquie Phelan leads Cindy Whitehead at the 1986 Sierra Plumbline race on the cover of the *Fat Tire Flyer*.

for mountain bikers allowed us to "scoop" the traditional press on several stories. In a 1985 issue we published an unsolicited story by a contributor named Todd Campbell who had discovered a unique mountain bike challenge in a remote part of Utah, the so-called Moab slickrock. In another issue we published a photo of a a kid named John Tomac riding a hastily converted BMX bike in his first mountain bike race.

The racing circuit had become well-established by the mid-1980s. The people who traveled around to all the venues became an intimate club who met for bike events all over the country. The pro category consisted of a couple dozen riders, and there was only one representative of the press. In an article about the sale of the National Off-Road Bicycle Association (NORBA) in 1987, I described the traveling party as the "small band of bike junkies who masquerade as the pro element, and the equally disreputable journalists who magnify their accomplishments."

The summer of 1985 saw the first attempt by anyone else to reach the market for the *Fat Tire Flyer*. Mainstream cycling magazines such as *Bicycling* and *Bicycle Guide* were now covering mountain biking regularly, but none had made the switch to that market alone. In that year, Crested Butte

resident Hank Barlow brought out the initial issue of *Mountain Bike for the Adventure*. A year later the publishing company Daisy-HiTorque, which published BMX and motocross titles, jumped in with *Mountain Bike Action*, and Challenge Publications brought out *Mountain Biking*.

Even coming in five years later, these publications entered the market with more going for them than the *Fat Tire Flyer*. From the beginning, the *Flyer* was patched together, underfinanced, and unstructured. It was put together by people who had no prior magazine experience. By the time other publishers entered the market the niche was established, and they had the opportunity to set up camp with a plan and financial resources as well as a professional production staff. The *Fat Tire Flyer* managed to stagger along for six years in the absence of competition, but now advertisers had somewhere else to go. The other publications looked slicker and came out on a far more regular schedule than ours.

A magazine is a harsh taskmaster. You never get done because as soon as one issue comes out, you have to think about the next. The two of us had to do everything it took to get out every issue.

The end of the *Fat Tire Flyer* came in the summer of 1987. Frustrated with the incompetence

A photo I took in 1986 . . .

. . . that was used to create this watercolor by Kristen Throop for the cover of the March 1986 issue of the *Fat Tire Flyer*. It was her first paid commission after graduating from art school.

that I was a big part of, I told Don that I was done with the project and that he could do as he wished with it. No more issues were ever printed. Because I felt terrible about having accepted payment for subscriptions that I could no longer fulfill, we eventually turned over our subscriber list to Hank Barlow's magazine, *Mountain Bike for the Adventure*.

Business problems notwithstanding, the *Fat Tire Flyer* was the most artistic statement I ever had the opportunity to make. As the final arbiter of what appeared in it, I could say anything I wanted. Even though we solicited stories from the readership, I wrote much of it myself under several different names. The *Flyer* spoke in the first person, a voice of its own that never appeared in any of the work I sold to the other bicycle magazines. None of the art that we used on our cover would have appeared on the cover of any other bike magazine of the day, and conversely, the stereotyped photographs that graced the covers of other magazines would not have appeared on ours.

Consumer magazines cater to advertisers by writing about new products. For bicycle magazines, that means "testing" the latest bikes on the market. I tried to concentrate on the experience rather than the marketplace. I wanted to create a piece of literature whose value did not end with the next issue.

Unlike most bicycle magazines, the *Fat Tire Flyer* didn't review bicycles. I made fun of such reviews in an article titled "The Universal Bike Review," a satiric piece that remains relevant long after any of the real bicycle reviews that inspired it have been forgotten.

The *Fat Tire Flyer* is not the only small magazine that came and went. At the time it was published there were hundreds of enthusiast magazines in print for audiences of a few thousand readers. It was right for its time, and it was as bully a pulpit as anyone could wish for.

Faulty business model notwithstanding, the *Fat Tire Flyer* is the only documentation of one of the most interesting times of bicycle history. I don't regret the experience for a moment, nor do I miss it. It was a time when it was possible to know everyone and when a voice as small as a couple of guys who were making it up as they went along could still be heard.

NORBA

n 1979 I had shut down my Repack promotions. Downhill racing had outgrown that particular venue. I had received unwanted attention for a race that was originally a secret. Cross-country races seemed a little easier to manage. The *Fat Tire Flyer* was a handy platform, and Denise and I promoted several X-C races sponsored by our magazine. In other parts of California, race promotions sprang up as soon as enough of the local riders had the necessary equipment.

In addition to Victor Vincente of America in Los Angeles and our efforts in the Bay Area, there was the Central Coast Clunker Classic in San Luis Obispo promoted by Glenn Odell, the Whiskeytown Downhill in Redding promoted by Gary and Bonnie Larson, and the Coyote Derby in Redlands promoted by Jim Harlow. As the number of race promotions grew, some sort of organization linking these local efforts was inevitable. Race insurance was a pressing issue. I had seen a lawsuit arise

NORBA logo ideas
designed by Joe Breeze.

out of a rider's injury at Repack, and even though he lost his case, the writing was on the wall.

Rules were a secondary issue, but they were inseparable from the issue of insurance. Each promoter made his or her own rules. In the case of Victor Vincente of America, no rules were the best kind. After someone says "Go!," first one to the finish wins. That summed up the general attitude among the rest of the West Coast off-road racing crowd of a few dozen riders and a handful of promoters. Despite this casual attitude, the prospect of obtaining insurance required some attention to safety, if only a helmet requirement. The rule book could be short, but there had to be one if racing were to grow beyond the point it had already reached.

Although racing was a primary goal among the founders, not everyone who rode a mountain bike raced it. A third issue unrelated to competition was access to trails and open space. It was clear that

some degree of organization would be necessary if our views on the subject of where we could ride were to be heard.

The organizing catalyst was unlikely, a man named Jack Ingram who worked for a company called Panda Bikes. Panda Bikes was a BMX company and did not sell mountain bikes. Ingram was not himself a mountain biker or a cyclist of any stripe. Based on contacts made at previous trade shows, though, Jack called a meeting in January 1983 of a dozen or so high-profile mountain bikers in Northern California in order to discuss a sanctioning body.

The meeting took place at Jack's house in Lafayette, which was nowhere near the Bay Area hotbeds of mountain biking. I can only speculate as to Jack's motivation because he is deceased. Since he was not passionate about the sport himself, I have to conclude that his interest lay in heading off the infighting that was at the time taking place among several

BMX sanctioning bodies and assuming a leadership role in the promotion of mountain bike racing.

The BMX-sanctioning model was flawed for our purposes. There was a major difference between the kids who competed under BMX-sanctioned rules and the mountain bike racers. BMX was a complete commercial package marketed to kids by adults, with an infrastructure that included private race tracks, several magazines, and some big sponsors. Access to public lands was not an issue.

The kids who raced BMX didn't have much to say about the activities of the BMX organizations that sanctioned their races. In contrast, the members of the mountain bike community who attended the meeting at Jack's house were adults, racers as well as promoters, and had been invited on the basis of previous mountain biking activities. Everyone at the meeting had strong opinions about the direction of any proposed organization—with one glaring exception. Jack didn't know what took

Front and back of my first NORBA member card,
1983, now in the Smithsonian collection.

place at a mountain bike race because he had never been to one.

All the participants were enthusiastic about forming an organization, and we even came up with a name that had yet to be formalized, the National Off-Road Bicycle Association (NORBA). What most were not enthusiastic about was traveling so far out of the area where we lived to meet at the house of a man who didn't participate in the sport. Even though there was not enough of a structure to suggest that a vote took place, the next meeting and several that followed took place at my house in Fairfax. After that we held meetings at Joe Breeze's house in Mill Valley. Jack hosted one more meeting at his house, but he never gained any degree of influence over NORBA. He continued to attend meetings, but his only lasting contribution to NORBA turned out to be calling everyone for the first get-together.

I was chosen to create the race rules, along with Tom Hillard, promoter of the Punk Bike Enduro in nearby Santa Rosa. We were selected for the task because we were the only people at the meeting who had actually put on races. The reason

for our selection was partly geographical. Tom and I were not the only people in California who had promoted mountain bike races, but it was not possible for race promoters from other areas to attend regular meetings in Marin County. After the name of the organization was settled, Joe accepted the challenge of creating a logo.

NORBA needed a few formal documents in order to exist, such as bylaws and a statement of purpose. Since I had composed the same sort of documents for Velo-Club Tamalpais (VCT), it was no trouble for me to put them together. The statement of purpose read:

> The purpose of the National Off-Road Bicycle Association is to promote all aspects of responsible off-road bicycling. The Association will act as the unified national voice of off-road cyclists and as the sanctioning body for off-road racing.
>
> As the sanctioning body for racing, the Association will provide insurance against personal injury and property damage, will draft standard rules for off-road racing, and will insure access to public lands for off-road bicycles. By supporting competition, the Association will help improve the technical aspects of off-road bicycles.

The initial rule book that Tom and I came up with was brief, a little less than three typewritten pages. Most of the rules were procedural, such as course-marking standards, rules for who could race, race categories, and so on. There were only a few that applied to the riders, and these rules were heavily influenced by a recent national cyclo-cross event I had attended. The winning rider came with a half-dozen bikes and a similar number of mechanics and assistants who moved bikes around the course and allowed the racer to change bikes several times per lap to one suited to each type of terrain. Any racer who arrived with nothing more than a bike and a dream was not even in the same league, no matter how fast he was.

As mountain bikers, we had all experienced mechanical failures at inconvenient times, and we didn't have a pit crew to help us. Most of us felt that racing should duplicate the real experience and that the rider had to be responsible for his or her machinery. Limiting the rider to one bike and no external support reduced the advantage of a factory team with disposable bikes and a pit crew to maintain them, so that became part of the NORBA rule book.

The bike itself could be anything that met minimum standards. A "safety inspection" required that the bike have brakes on both wheels and have no parts deemed unsafe by the inspector. We debated a minimum tire size to make sure that the bikes were real mountain bikes, but we scrapped the idea in favor of letting the course dictate what worked best.

Riders were required to wear a hard-shell helmet and "footgear that covers the entire foot." There was no mention of other clothing being required.

There were three race rules:

1. You must finish with the same bike you started, including all parts on the bike.
2. All repairs must be done by the racer only.
3. All spare parts and tools must be carried on the bike.

NORBA meetings continued into the summer of 1983, but problems began to crop up right away. The structure was unwieldy since every decision required a vote. At the same time in my own life, MountainBikes was not doing well, and the *Fat Tire Flyer* was expanding into a real magazine. My attention was divided, as was that of several other NORBA founding members who had related businesses.

By the middle of 1983 two of the three initial goals of NORBA had been accomplished, although no lobbyist had been hired yet to address the land-access issue. There was a set of rules that reflected a new philosophy of bicycle competition and insurance to protect race promoters. Joe had created the logo, which remained in use for more than 20 years despite several changes in NORBA ownership. Now NORBA moved into a new phase. Who would run it, and for what reward?

Glenn Odell, who promoted the Central Coast Clunker Classic, followed our activities, but since he lived 200 miles south of the Bay Area, he had no way of participating in the meetings. In the spring of 1983, Glenn wrote to NORBA and made an interesting offer. He would like to run the association as a sole proprietorship, but if we didn't care to let him do that, he planned to start a rival organization.

To the eternal disgust of many who did not have to try to run NORBA, we agreed to the offer, after a negotiation that preserved participation in policy decisions by several of the founding members. On June 27, 1983, NORBA came under Glenn's control. Glenn's proprietorship only lasted a few years before NORBA was swallowed up by bigger interests, but he did at least as well as the founders had. He did excellent work on advocacy, and he also put on credible national championships.

Having a national organization for mountain bikers solved one problem and created another.

The final NORBA logo, designed by Joe, was used for over 20 years.

From the earliest days of mountain bike racing there had been a crossover of athletes. Road racers Joe, Gary Fisher, and Otis Guy held the top three times on Repack. In 1980 Gary won Victor Vincente of America's initial Reseda to the Sea race ahead of Ron Skarin, a prominent road racer with a number of national titles during the '70s. Ron is now honored by inclusion in the United States Bicycling Hall of Fame. He was also director of the United States Cycling Federation (USCF) in 1979 and 1980, the American affiliate of the Union Cycliste Internationale (UCI) that sanctions all road racing in the United States, which might explain why he raced off-road under the barely disguised name of Renaldo Skaroni.

In the early '80s the USCF had no reason to support mountain bike racing. It was not just another bicycling discipline—it was more of an UNdiscipline. There were no championships to be won, there were no real rules, there were no big sponsors, there were no big prizes. Riders wore outlandish costumes, and they rode machinery that was not restricted to a standardized design. The only connection to the rest of the world of bicycle racing was that USCF riders sometims crossed over to the Dark Side, and to the USCF way of thinking, that had to be controlled.

The numbers indicated that sooner or later the USCF would have to deal with the upstart organization. The first Rockhopper event in Santa Rosa's Annadel State Park took place in October 1982, a few months before the first NORBA meeting. Gary took the win from the 162 riders who showed up.

It took several years for the USCF to accept mountain bike racing as a separate sport with its own rules and participants. It was probably not stirring rhetoric that turned the tide but rather the sheer number of riders turning out to race off-road. Now that we have world road champions and Tour de France winners who came up through the ranks of mountain biking, it seems hard to imagine that there was ever such a conflict.

The presence of NORBA may have been a catalyst, or it may have been a reaction to pressure, but suddenly there were mountain bike races all over California. A few months later, in May 1983, the second Rockhopper event was held, and the ridership more than doubled to 374. Gary didn't get the win this time, but winner Gavin Chilcott rode Gary's bike to the new course record. In a harbinger of times to come, Ross Bicycles fielded a professional team in matching uniforms, the somewhat politically incorrectly named Ross Indians.

Pete Barrett's Repack poster for the race held October 8, 1983. Repack was back, and we were ready to show the new guys what we used to do.

The name of the race was a takeoff on "Stumpjumper," a trademark of Specialized. Race organizers later signed over the name Rockhopper to Specialized, and it became the name for a line of bikes.

Now that there was a national mountain biking body, national champions could be chosen. The titles were won in 1983 by USCF racers Steve Tilford and Jacquie Phelan. The inaugural championship was held very late in the year at Rancho Los Osos on the California Central Coast, an area not known for torrential rains. The event on December 10 was scheduled to be five laps of the course but was marred by a daylong deluge. Brake shoes were scoured away to nothing by the gritty mud, riders were complaining, and the race was declared over after three laps. The truncated race did not satisfy everyone that a champion had been chosen. Some complaints surfaced later, but on the day of the race no one accepted Gary's challenge to ride two more laps and claim the title.

In late 1983 Gary decided to promote another Repack race, this time with a NORBA sanction. It would be the first sanctioned mountain bike downhill race. I was initially skeptical that he could pull it off, but he got the land-use permit and scheduled the race for October 8. I assisted with the timing and assumed my usual role as announcer. The largest field to date, 61 riders, took part. Jimmy Deaton started what would become a Hall of Fame mountain bike racing career with his first win at the classic course.

A work party takes a break on NORBA Trail Day, Yolanda Trail, Mount Tamalpais, in 1984. Left to right: Matt Hebbard, Charlie Cunningham, John Aranson (Marin Conservation Corps), Conrad Oho, Mark Slate, Joe Riboli, and Joe Breeze (back to camera).

Joe, always a competitive downhiller, was just two seconds off Deaton's pace.

A few months later, in early 1984, I obtained a permit for my own NORBA-sanctioned promotion on Repack. The downhill race was scheduled to take place on May 19, the day before the fourth iteration of the popular Rockhopper race in Santa Rosa. The newly formed professional teams from Specialized and Fisher would be there along with the Ross team. Even Mike Sinyard, owner of Specialized, signed up to ride Repack.

With a decent budget to work with, I hired a professional race-timing crew and set up a public address system and radio communication. The biggest field ever of 94 riders showed up, creating a severe strain on logistics, but we pulled it off. Jimmy repeated as the last-ever Repack downhill champion.

The resulting publicity killed Repack forever. The hyperbolic descriptions of riders bouncing off rocks and trees outraged the land managers. The logistics of racing in a location originally chosen for secrecy were daunting. It became clear that insurance or no insurance, no permits would be issued in the future. The downhill sport had outgrown its birthplace, and its survival was in doubt. Where else could you ever pull off a race like Repack? The only possibility seemed to be a ski resort, but we had already heard that those areas did not welcome mountain bikers.

NORBA itself went through several more iterations before the USCF purchased it in 1989. Glenn Odell had run into financial problems instead of profits almost immediately and was forced to sell NORBA within a year of taking over. The new owners were also owners of a BMX-sanctioning body and did not have the USCF's ingrained opposition to bicycles with fat tires, and mountain bike racing took off under their management. The USCF could only watch between 1984 and 1989 as the number of mountain bike racers exploded past the number of riders participating in road and track racing.

The USCF would have saved itself millions by accepting mountain bike racing as a legitimate form of bicycle competition five years earlier. Instead, the federation had treated mountain bike racing like a moral failing, penalizing its own members for participation in NORBA events.

The USCF was the last bastion of road and track racing purity, but events forced the federation to act. By 1989 mountain bike racing had taken hold all over the world, and there were already two different versions of "world championships," the American version at Mammoth Moun-

tain in California and the other, where everyone else competed, in the Alps. In order to unify the sport, present a legitimate national team for international competition, and not at all coincidentally claim tens of thousands of new members, the USCF joined the modern world of international mountain bike racing by purchasing NORBA.

The sport that had originated at Repack 20 years before and had been outlined in the first NORBA meetings just 13 years earlier would become an official cycling competition in the 1996 Olympic Games.

chapter 19

THE 1982 COORS CLASSIC

first met Mike Neel after a bike race, probably in 1973. Mike, along with John Howard, the national champion at the time, had lapped the field twice in a local criterium, riding away from everyone else so easily that they did it while sitting up and chatting until one of them—I think it was John—had to win it in a sprint.

Gary Fisher knew Mike from the racing scene, so after the riders started drifting away toward vehicles in the parking lot, he introduced us, and Mike said, "You guys want to smoke a joint?" Mike liked smoking weed.

Mike identified with Gary and me because we were, after all, defining the limits of the term *hippie bike riders*, and that defined Mike also. I went to a few local races with him over the years, not as a rider but just because why not? Mike always did well and partied afterward. There is only one velodrome in the entire Bay Area, and it's a long way from Marin. The only time I went there was with

Mike, and I watched him have a pretty good day riding pursuit and sprints. When he was around on our side of the Bay he might ride with Gary, also a very good road rider. I don't recall that I ever actually rode with Mike, but I may have. He would definitely hang around to party after a training ride.

Time passed. Gary and I moved in the direction of mountain bikes, and Mike went pro and moved to Europe. We didn't see much of him for a few years.

By 1979, when Gary and I got into the mountain bike business for real, Mike had retired after a brief career with a few great rides. The most impressive to us was 10th place in the 1976 world championship road race in Ostuni, Italy, a placing he didn't think much of himself. He had used his time in Europe to make a number of commercial connections and had gone into the business of importing Italian cycling goods, including Sidi shoes. Gary and I were consumers of such goods,

and by then we had our own shop where we could order stuff wholesale. Over the space of a couple of years, Mike gave me a set of professional wheels for my Colnago and various items of expensive cycling clothing.

Forward to 1982 and the period after I broke up with my longtime girlfriend. My depression became annoying to Gary, who was by far my most full-time companion by dint of sharing an office. Gary had participated in the original Red Zinger race in Colorado, which had mutated into the Coors Classic, the biggest American stage race at the time. Mike was headed out there to coach a team, and it was a long drive that he wouldn't mind splitting two ways. The trip had commercial implications as well, because if I could take my Ritchey MountainBike, the product that Gary and I sold, I knew that I could show it to all sorts of cycling elites who were not then convinced that mountain biking had a future. Gary told me to grab my

Mike Neel knew more about bike racing than anyone else I had ever met. He was also a great storyteller and an analytic thinker.

sleeping bag and here's a couple of hundred dollars and get the fuck out of here. He said, "When you get there, look for a guy named Bill Woodul and introduce yourself. He'll take care of you."

So I threw my MountainBike into Mike's garishly painted Sidi van along with a few road bikes that he had brought, and the two of us headed for Colorado. It's a long drive, which we polished off in two days, and for those two days we talked bikes. It's not that we both didn't have other interests, but we didn't have any other interests at that time. The subject was bikes and bike racing. By the time we got to Boulder, Colorado, I knew a lot more about bike racing than I had when we left, and my education was just starting.

I also had gotten to know Mike even better than I could have imagined. He's very candid about things he's done, and some of the things he's done I wouldn't do myself. Mike is incredibly intelligent, one of the quickest and most analytical thinkers you could ever meet, and he's a great talker and storyteller. He knew all the pros in Europe, and he speaks four languages.

He was also a quick learner, a fact I learned from listening to some of his cycling stories. For example, Mike told me about the time he was riding in Mexico in a stage race. He's a big man for a bike racer—and an especially big man in a Mexican bike race where the riders are generally about 5 feet 3 or 4 inches. Mike said he was kind of pushing around people in the peloton just because he's big and he's aggressive, and he could.

At one point Mike was riding with his hands down in the drops, and a little guy rode up next to him and looked him in the eye to get his attention. Mike described him as an "old pro." The Mexican rider reached over and grabbed the brake cables where they looped over the handlebars on old-style brakes. Mike said, "I was frozen. He totally had me under control. I couldn't let go of the bars, and all he had to do was give them a shake and I was down in the ditch, and it didn't matter how big the guy was. Then he just let go and moved away, and I got the message."

Mike knew how to cheat on a climb. "Push on the other guy's knee. You steal all his momentum."

Because he was a coach, I challenged him to tell me something about bike riding I didn't know. Mike said, "Here's something I learned by watching Joop Zoetemelk," a Dutch rider who won the world championship in 1985. "All riders corner with the outside pedal down. Except Joop. He does it with the inside pedal down, but back of center so it doesn't hit the ground. That shifts your center of gravity to the inside of the turn and lets you take your first pedal stroke slightly earlier."

Mike was very conscious of doping and talked about it at length. He mentioned stars of the day he knew were using steroids and told me how to detect them from changes in appearance.

Mike explained why the coach and the athlete are not on an equal footing and how that leads to doping. "The athlete is looking for a career. He wants to ride for as many years as he can. The coach is looking for a performance, and he does not care about the rider after that. The coach can get more riders, but he needs that performance now, and he'll do whatever it takes to get it out of the rider."

Mike talked about the teams we would be meeting, who was on them, which riders were used for which jobs tactically, the deals he might have to make to advance his own interests. He talked about massage, feeding, strategy, mechanical stuff, head-case stuff, which riders were coachable (Bob Roll), and which riders were not (my former roommate Kent Bostick). He talked about the politics of the team, how the team riders were chosen, and the weird relationship he had to maintain with the sponsor in order to get paid. He talked about the structure of the race and how it was officiated.

Bill Woodul was in charge of Campagnolo's neutral support program. In addition to spinning wrenches and making repairs, he dispensed advice to riders in need, including Ramazan Galyaletdinov on this climb.

It was a total general rundown on what to expect when we got to Colorado. After a two-day briefing, the experience was far less overwhelming and easier to understand for someone who had never seen this kind of spectacle, and since I understood what was supposed to happen, it was not that difficult to find ways to make myself useful.

We got to Colorado a day or so before the action was to take place. I wasn't an official anything, and there were no accommodations with my name on them, but I had my sleeping bag, and I wasn't fussy about where I unrolled it. In a pinch that place could be inside the Sidi support van, which by now I had a key to so that Mike could send me on errands.

First order of business was to find Bill Woodul. I didn't know who he was, but he turned out to be the Campagnolo rep and the guy who drove the lead motorcycle on every stage. Bill was very well-connected, and when I introduced myself as Gary's partner, so was I.

Bill had some minor errand to take care of, and with nowhere else to go immediately, I hung around his temporary quarters while he went out. There was a knock on the door, so I answered it. It was a woman who was looking for Bill, and after two days of lectures on steroid abuse from Mike, I saw the living embodiment of every physical symptom he had described. This woman looked like an East German swimmer, and her voice was deeper than mine. As soon as I looked at her I pegged her for a steroid user, and I was right. Her name was Cindy Olivarri, and many years later she wrote a book describing the physical damage she had suffered as a steroid abuser.

Jonathan Boyer was on the Sidi/Mengoni team, and in the previous year he had ridden in his first Tour de France, the first American to do so. Jonathan was pretty sure he was all that, and to say that we did not get along when we first met would be an understatement. I made the mistake of complaining to Mike.

It was not something Mike wanted to hear. "I need him a lot more than I need you," Mike told me. "It's only for a few days. You can either get along with him or go somewhere else and stay out of everyone's way." Point taken. I apologized to Jonathan, and we managed to coexist for the rest of the race.

As the prologue time trial approached, I wandered into the room where Mike was preparing for the event. I found him sitting on the floor with a big box of cycling shoes, some rubber cement, and a pile of Sidi logo patches. He looked beyond distressed and almost didn't have time for the explanation, which was that all of the riders on his ad hoc team had shown up with their regular shoes, which of course were not necessarily Sidis. A cardinal rule for athletes is that you never change equipment right before an event, so giving all the riders new shoes was out of the question. But since Sidi was the sponsor, Mike was terrified that a rider would get photographed wearing another logo on his shoes. It really didn't matter whose shoes the riders were wearing; it just mattered that the label for this race said "Sidi." Mike was desperately trying

to cover up the existing logos with the Sidi patches, but it wasn't working. The patches just slid right off the shoes, and Mike was freaking out.

I told Mike to go do something important, like coaching, and give me the shoes and the use of the van; I would take care of the problem. I'm not sure how much faith he had in me, but he gave me the job. Grabbing a phone book, I found a shoe-repair place nearby and drove there with the box of shoes. I explained that I had an emergency and that I needed instant service, invoking the name of the Coors Classic, which was an overwhelmingly big deal in the town.

The manager called over a young woman who had been working at one of the industrial sewing machines and put her at my disposal. With her equipment and experience it was a ridiculously easy job, and for 10 minutes of her work I gave her $20. A little more than a half hour after accepting the task, I returned the box of shoes to Mike, every one of them sporting a handsome Sidi logo over the real brand name.

Making quick work of a problem that had seemed intractable a few minutes earlier cemented my role. Mike made me his unofficial assistant. He didn't make an announcement, but there were never enough people to deal with the many tasks

Jonathan Boyer was talented, and he knew it. He won the second stage of the 1982 Coors and eventually finished eighth overall.

Every stage of the Coors was tough; there was never a moment during the race to relax.

at hand, and I was capable and wasn't costing the team anything, so he put me to work. Somehow he obtained a meal pass for me, which entitled me to eat in the dormitory dining hall with the teams and the support crews. I had slept the first couple of nights in the team van, but now he let me roll out my sleeping bag on the floor of his room, and he started assigning errands for me to run.

As soon as the prologue was over, Mike said, "Come on. We have to go shopping." I had never thought about this aspect of bike racing. The mission was to pick up supplies for the next day's musettes (the bags of food that we'd pass out to the riders), and as we pushed a cart through the market, Mike ticked off the items we would need: bananas, oranges, peanuts, raisins, soft-bread rolls, marmalade, cream cheese, Coca-Cola, cheap spoons and table knives, foil. After this one day of on-the-job training, I took over shopping for the team.

Back in the room we were now sharing, Mike showed me how to prepare the food. He explained that it had to be easy to handle and should be no more than a couple of bites at a time. Oranges and bananas were peeled and sectioned, then wrapped in foil. Small, soft rolls were punctured and filled with cream cheese and marmalade. Cokes were put into water bottles, and the riders would drink them flat and warm. Riders had different food preferences, so each musette was labeled. Then Mike told me I was going to help feed the riders, a task I had never done. He warned me that I shouldn't hold out the musette until my rider was close, because a musette is a musette and riders from other teams would be just as happy to snatch one out of my hand.

The first day of actual road racing, Mike told me that I should go help the mechanics pump up tires, a daily chore that a monkey could perform. By taking that over, I gave the real mechanics more time to do skilled work, and not at all coincidentally, established my welcome with the team support crew.

After the tires were pumped and the riders were off, I joined the soigneurs in the team van, and we went out on the road course to the feed zone. My first hand-up was a terrifying experience.

All I saw approaching was a mass of shifting colors, then somehow a rider in the correct jersey found me and took the proffered bag. It got easier quickly. After a couple of tries things slowed down, and I got the knack. I found that I could make eye contact with my rider at a hundred yards or so, then watch as he moved to the side of the peloton. At the last second I would hold up the bag for him.

As soon as the first stage was over, Mike helped with the massage, another aspect of racing I had never thought about. The team had a masseuse, but if Mike helped her, the job got done faster. I watched, and Mike explained the technique to me as he rubbed the riders down, but this was one task I would not be trusted with. A few years later in the first Iditabike challenge, though, I was able to put this knowledge to good use helping out exhausted riders.

Every means I could find to be useful helped the team, and as the guy who always seemed to be with Mike, I had joined the exclusive little club that was the Sidi/Mengoni team. As a matter of course I started wearing team logo clothing, and one morning the Sidi company representative found me by the conspicuously labeled Sidi van, wearing Sidi shoes along with a Sidi logo shirt and cycling cap, and had me pose for a photo.

Every stage race has a "lanterne rouge," or red light, the last rider to finish, and in the 1982 Coors Classic it was Rick Baldwin, a friend who was on the Sidi team. I had met Rick through my roommate Kent Bostick, who would later make the Olympic team and hold a national road racing championship. Rick was primarily a sprinter, and his talents were not particularly well-suited to the mountainous stage race. He lost time every day in the mountains, but his worst stage was in Aspen on a lap course that featured a major climb on every 5-mile lap.

Standing with Mike, I watched Rick suffer far off the back, struggling up the climbs he was not built for. Mike explained that Rick was trying to stay inside the time limit. If Rick had to quit the race, he would not be available in the criterium and the team time trial, so the team needed him to stay on the bike. Rick was barely inside the cutoff time, riding just ahead of the invisible demon that threatened to make him retire.

At the end of the race, when Rick was awarded that lanterne rouge, I realized that it is an honor in itself because I had seen what it took for him to get it. Rick had probably suffered more than the race winner. With little to ride for except to support his team, Rick did not quit while other riders more tal-ented than he was and holding respectable General Classification (GC) times had taken off their numbers and retired. Simply put, the lanterne rouge is the guy with the least talent and the biggest heart, and that deserved recognition. With that award, Rick earned a lifetime of respect from me.

A subject that did not get into the story I later wrote for publication was my astonishment at the amount of drug use I saw at the race. It was not so much among the riders, although I did open a door and surprise a big-name cyclist with a long needle in his leg. Cocaine use was rampant among the support and sponsorship staff, who did not have to face doping controls and who were overworked and underpaid.

In 10 years working for a rock band I had seen plenty of cocaine, but being a cyclist I was not attracted to the result other people got, and I managed to avoid joining them. Before attending the Coors Classic I assumed that other people close to the sport felt the same way. Color me enlightened. After dinner one evening I accepted a ride back to the dorm from the owner of a company that was a major race sponsor. I embarrassed him mightily when I turned down his offer of cocaine. He had assumed that no one ever turned down free coke. The company he owned failed a little later.

chapter 20

THE IMAGE

While MountainBikes was going downhill slowly as a business, Gary Fisher and I, and Tom Ritchey by extension, were in a class by ourselves when it came to crafting an image. The Breezer and the Trailmaster were as mechanically impressive as our MountainBike, but when it came to promoting the products there was no contest.

We owned the media, not in the least because both Gary and I had contributed to *Bicycling* magazine and had the ear of the editorial staff. Outside of Marin County, few cyclists were even aware that there were bikes similar to the Ritchey Mountain-Bike, while ours were being gushed over in print by national publications.

An additional advantage was that while Breezers and Trailmasters were in limited supply, you could actually get a Ritchey MountainBike, and we were shipping them to all points in the West. The first time anyone who loved bikes saw one of

ours, the deal was done. The first production runs of frames were as beautiful an example of bicycle construction as you could find, although the need for greater volume led later to a slight sacrifice of the cosmetics. The graceful lines of the frame and perfect curves of the bronze-welded construction were like nothing else on the market.

We coined our first advertising slogan for our print ads. Capitalizing on the title of Tom Wolfe's recent best-seller, we asked, "Do you have the Right Stuff for cross-country? We do."

There was enough editorial interest in the new aspect of cycling to create a market for stories about it. Our activities were colorful and lived up to the California image of skateboarders and surfers. Gary and I were easy to find for interviews, and we had the look that fit the image. Or perhaps the image was derived from our look. Our names were often the only ones mentioned in articles about the new sport.

We were fortunate to get a bike into the hands of Dean Bradley, who published the first review of the Ritchey MountainBike in *BMX Plus!* (misspelled as the "Richey"). The bike he tested belonged to one of our first Southern California customers, Monte Ward. Monte's bike was one of the first nine that had launched the company.

Dean became a friend, and when he moved to the editorial position at a magazine called *Action Now*, he gave us another boost. A two-page photo spread featured our friend Monte on his Ritchey MountainBike along with his friend Jim Samuelson, ditto.

In a later article, Dean collected photos of all the bikes on the market in this new niche, excluding the Breezer and Trailmaster. He may have been aware of these two bikes, but he couldn't get any

Left: The original paste-up for an early MountainBikes ad was just a piece of letterhead stationery and some stick-on letters.

Above: A slightly more polished MountainBikes ad from May 1981.

Laguna's 3-speed cruiser.

Bassett's "Star Cruiser."

S & S "Bigfoot" 5-speed.

Powerlite.

Cook Bros. cruiser.

Champion racing frames.

Lawill's "Pro Cruiser" 5-speed.

Schwinn's 5-speed cruiser.

S.E. Racing's "OM-Flyer."

S & S "Newport" cruiser.

Richey Mountain Bike, 10-speed.

Laguna's 5-speed prototype.

BMX Products' "Kos Kruiser."

Littlejohn's "Fireroader."

A roundup of mountain bikes pictured in *Action Now* magazine. The publisher, Dean Bradley, couldn't get his hands on a Breezer or a Trailmaster in time for his photography.

examples to photograph. When compared with the modified beach cruisers and beefed-up BMXers that had been hastily entered into this new market niche, the Ritchey MountainBike was clearly the adult in a roomful of children.

I was able to generate frequent publicity with my magazine submissions because there were no other participants in the burgeoning movement who wrote about it regularly. My first articles had been published before we started the company and gave me the writing credentials I needed to become a regular contributor on the subject. I started writing for the bicycle trade magazines as well as the general magazines, such as *Bicycling*. By the end of 1980 I was also the editor of the *Fat Tire Flyer*. This was a major conflict of interest because I had a lot of good things to say about the products we were selling. The *Fat Tire Flyer* was the only thing in print on the subject, so I got away with it.

Through his connections with *Bicycling*, Gary got us a gig writing reviews of bicycle books for the *Next Whole Earth Catalog*. With our names right there in print, we were bona fide experts. Our local weekly, the *Pacific Sun*, profiled us in an article called "The Clunker Capital of the World." I had an article in *Velo-News* that included a photo of

Joe Breeze and Monte, both on Ritchey Mountain-Bikes. Bob Woodward profiled our company for his trade magazine, *National Outdoor Outfitters News*. In the July 1981 issue of the trade magazine *American Bicyclist and Motorcyclist*, I explained the new bikes. The article included a sidebar about the company. That was better for generating publicity than a paid ad.

The April 1980 issue of *Bicycling* had put the movement on the cover, with a shot of the riders at the top of Pearl Pass during the 1979 Crested Butte–Aspen ride. Both Gary and I appear in the photo, along with another dozen or so riders from Marin County. My story on the ride shown in the photo, "High Rollers in the Rockies," was one of the features inside.

In the fall of 1980 we once again mounted an expedition to Crested Butte. There were three vehicles in our little caravan, room enough for the regular crew of myself, Gary, Joe, and Wende Cragg, as well as Denise Caramagno, Monte, Berkeley bike shop owner Adlai Karim, iconoclastic Marin bike builder Charlie Cunningham, and new friend Scot Nicol along with his girlfriend, Ginny Allen.

On the way out to Colorado we camped at Capital Reef in Utah, where Wende caught this group shot.

San Rafael Reef, Utah, September 1980. We were on our way from Marin to Crested Butte. Left to right: Monte Ward, me, Joe Breeze, Gary Fisher, Scot Nicol, Charlie Cunningham, Denise Caramagno, Ginny Allen, and Adlai Karim.

Charlie got up early the next morning and cooked his customary breakfast slab, which involved stone-ground, whole-wheat flour and some liquids and required only a skillet and a heat source to cook. The skillet also served as the plate. Then Charlie got on his bike and headed east, saying we could pick him up whenever we caught him.

By our third visit to Crested Butte, we had become accepted members of the community. The tour had grown to 90 or so riders, and the Marin crew, which had made up half the crowd in 1979, still represented a third of the participants. The local participation had shifted from the bar crowd to the more athletic cross-country ski crowd. My story on the annual ride over Pearl Pass had been featured in *Bicycling* magazine with a cover photo of the crew at the top of Pearl Pass that included myself, Gary, Joe, Wende, and Alan Bonds.

In one of the more dramatic places to practice the sport, mountain biking had taken hold and established Crested Butte as the prime mountain bike destination. The local economy was tied to the ski resort, but the town revenue suffered in summer. With the arrival of mountain biking, a ski area that offered hiking and wildflower study in the summer suddenly had a new way to bring money into town.

We received international exposure through articles in Canada and the United Kingdom. I was able to insert a few subtle plugs for both my enterprises, MountainBikes and the *Fat Tire Flyer*, when I contributed the first article on mountain biking to the 1981 annual cycling almanac, *International Cycling Guide*. The quarterly *Bicycling News Canada* published several of my articles. The Rough-Stuff Fellowship house organ, *Rough-Stuff Journal*, was pleased to include my article on the 1981 Crested Butte–Aspen tour and noted the growing American interest in riding off-road on what they called tracks and byways: "The author is one of four RSF members we have in Northern Califor-

nia. This account is reproduced in full, exactly as received, American spelling included, and should give our British and European members a good insight into American-style rough-stuff.—Ed."

Our connections with *Bicycling* magazine were a huge boost. In addition to the editorial coverage, our bikes got on several covers. The June 1982 cover photo by Dave Epperson was shot in Crested Butte the previous fall. The four riders shown include me on one of three Ritcheys in the photo and Denise Caramagno on my original Breezer. A previous cover had shown Tom on one of his bikes, and yet another showed the *Bicycling* editorial staff on mountain bikes, with ours prominently featured.

In 1982 SunTour was fighting what eventually became a losing battle to be the dominant player in the growing mountain bike component market. As part of its market strategy, the company created a major presence at Fat Tire Bike Week in Crested Butte. No one from SunTour had been to Crested Butte before. When the SunTour executives arrived, I was hanging out with a few friends at one of the open-air eating establishments. Several dignified older Japanese men approached my bike, which was parked nearby. They admired the bike with a spirited discussion in Japanese. Then one of them hopped aboard and took it for a ride. It was too big for him,

and he hadn't asked permission or even ascertained whose it was. I was sure he wouldn't steal it, and in a few minutes he was back, very excited about the bike and curious to meet the owner. I was then introduced to Junzo Kawai, president of Maeda Industries, SunTour's parent company.

As part of the marketing program, SunTour put a lot of us on the payroll that week. Erik Koski, Neil Murdoch, Chris Allen, and I were all tapped to speak on various aspects of our sport to a reverent throng. The site was a local restaurant that was rented for the evening and closed to the general public. After a sumptuous meal for the invitees, Erik gave a historical overview of mountain biking. SunTour employee Chris explained why the company was so interested in coming to Crested Butte. Neil spoke about the new sport and its potential. I was the featured speaker, and my topic was the business of mountain bikes.

I had prepared carefully. My speech was written out word for word in longhand, unfortunately. I stepped up to the podium, looked at my notes, and realized that the light was so bad that I couldn't read a word of my prepared remarks.

So I winged it, trying to keep my original thoughts in order but eventually giving a disjointed version of them. My rambling speech was unfortunately taken seriously, possibly because English was a second language to many in attendance. My remarks were recorded and published word for word in the company newsletter, no doubt to be quoted around the water cooler. This might have been embarrassing for me if anyone outside Sun-Tour had ever seen it.

Most of the activities during Fat Tire Bike Week were not as formal. The evening after my disappointing appearance at the SunTour Symposium, I was invited to speak after a different sort of dinner. This was the pre-race, carbo-loading spaghetti dinner for everyone who had paid to go on the tour. No neckties in the room. Guys playing hacky-sack and riding "trials" inside the building. There was lots of pasta and beer and then Charlie Kelly would deliver the after-dinner remarks. We ate. We drank. Somebody introduced me, and I got up from a table and headed toward the podium.

In contrast to my presentation the previous evening, on this occasion I had no prepared remarks. In fact, I had not spent a single second preparing. As I approached the podium, no one in the room was more curious than I about what I might say. I got to the stage, where I had to turn around and speak into a microphone. I looked out over four or five dozen expectant, slightly flushed faces.

No one recorded or transcribed what I said, and I don't remember any of it, but it must have been good, because I laid 'em in the aisles.

A few months into 1980 we got some bad news from the attorney we had paid to trademark our name. It had cost us $125 to have him file a two-page application in his legal specialty. Most of the application consisted of our address. He had received a response from the U.S. Department of Commerce asking whether these bikes were made specifically to be used in the mountains. There were two possible answers, yes or no, and this was the question we had paid him $125 to know the answer to.

He choked. He responded that these were indeed bikes for use in the mountains.

The response from the Commerce Department was immediate. A feature of trademark law that I didn't know is that you can't trademark a description. They probably teach that on day one of Trademarks and Copyrights 101, but apparently our guy was hung over and missed that day. The proper answer was no, you can ride them in parking lots or on a race track. "MountainBikes" is the company name.

With our lawyer's affirmative answer, however, the trademark was denied.

Anyone could call a bike a mountain bike or a MountainBike or any similar combination. Fortunately for us, there were only three people who knew it: Gary, me, and our former lawyer. That gave us a chance to bluff the rest of the industry—for a while, anyway. Never mind that in public, riders were referring to any similar bikes as lowercase "mountain bikes." In print it was assumed that any use of the term was a reference to our company trademark. *Clunkers*, or the variant *klunkers*, no longer seemed appropriate for bikes that met the standards of fine European racing bikes, but that was the term used initially by publications. In the June 1982 issue of *Bicycling* there was an article titled "The Klunkers of Marin." Author John Schubert also referred to the new type of bikes interchangeably as "ballooners," a reference to the tire size. The article includes this sentence: "Klunkers, sometimes called mountain bikes (not to be confused with the company name Ritchey MountainBikes), are rugged off-road bikes."

Bicycling magazine was initially leery of using the term *mountain bike*, since Gary had worked for that publication. We were advertisers as well, even if our ad was tiny. Editor Chuck McCullough used his monthly column to suggest a poll among the readers to name this new creature that could not be called a mountain bike. The winner was announced in the next issue. They would be called All-Terrain Bicycles, or ATBs for short.

Sure they would.

Our secret didn't last long. The name ATB didn't catch on anywhere except in France, where to this day they call the bikes VTT, for "Velo-Tout-Terrain." In English that would be "All-Terrain Bicycle." Italians swing the other way. For them it's "mountain bike," even though their alphabet doesn't even use the letter k.

We lost control of our own name. The term *mountain bike* entered the lexicon as describing any bike with big wheels and big tires and flat handlebars. The rest of the bicycle industry caught on, probably because we never bothered to defend the mark for any use of the name.

The writing was on the wall and in print too. The May 1981 issue of *Bicycling* featured Tom and his dog, Bo, on the cover. Tom was riding his MountainBike across a field and wearing jeans like a proper lowercase mountain biker. This exposure was better than a full-page ad for our company, because neither Tom's longer history of building road bikes nor his brief but stellar racing career was the reason he made the cover. Tom was the MountainBike builder.

In the same issue, Schwinn advertised its Side-winder mountain bike, using the term generically. An article elsewhere in the issue was titled "Packing the Mountain Bike for Touring," although the author did not use the term *mountain bike* in the text.

Even I conceded the point eventually. In articles written for the trade magazines I used the term the way it is used now. Gary and I had contributed a term to the Oxford English Dictionary.

John Schubert's 1982 article in *Bicycling* showcased the Marin image, including the Trailmaster, Breezer, Ritchey MountainBike, and Jeff Lindsay's Mountain Goat, which was made 150 miles away in Chico. John also noted the transition of mountain biking to the rest of the world with the arrival of the Specialized Stumpjumper and the Uni-vega Alpina Sport. His article included what only seemed like a bold prediction if you didn't live in Marin County: "All this leads me to a startling conclusion: I predict klunkers will overtake dropped handlebar 10-speeds as America's favorite bicycles just as soon as enough manufacturers make them available in appropriate quantities and price levels. It's so much easier to enjoy yourself on a klunker than on a dropped-bar bike, and the klunker is so much more practical on our recession-era pot-holed roads, that klunkers will prevail."

Even *Car and Driver* noticed us in the January 1983 issue. An article identifying 10 best modes of transportation other than, well, cars, included this:

The most intriguing new self-propelled two-wheeler is something called an "off-road bicycle."

The off-road bike is actually a synthesis of three familiar designs: conventional, old-time, horn-on-the-tank bikes, ultra-light, hyper-expensive, low-bar touring bikes, and the popular little knobby-tired BMX-type units that thousands of kids are motocrossing.

A sterling example of this new genre is the Ritchey MountainBike. It doesn't look like much to the uninitiated, but it's packed with good stuff: a custom-built, lightweight frame, huge brakes from a tandem, an eighteen-speed gearset, sturdy balloon knobbies, and so much lightweight pro-racer componentry that it weighs but 30 pounds. (Mass-produced bikes of this size tip the scales at about 50 pounds.)

The MountainBike is to normal touring bikes as an NFL linebacker is to a ballerina—able to shrug off brutal abuse, yet quick and agile beyond your wildest dreams. You sit upright for maximum comfort and maneuverability, and the MountainBike is as adept at pounding over inner city potholes as it is silently carving up forest trails. That's why there's no shortage of orders—even at these prices. Suggested retail price: $820–1,529 depending upon options.

The culmination of the image-crafting might have been an article we found in a Japanese publication. Although we couldn't read the story, some of the words were in English, including the captions for a drawing that purported to represent how the typical California mountain biker dressed. It was clearly a drawing of Gary made from a photograph. He was dressed in boots, jeans, checked shirt, and knit hat, all helpfully identified with titles and little arrows. Even his personal style had gone generic and fed the image.

One of our customers sent us a photo of a helpful passerby holding a MountainBike far too big for him to ride on the Great Wall, circa 1981.

chapter 21

THE RIDE
OF A LIFETIME

The dissolution of MountainBikes was inevitable on the day it was formed. Before we started the company I had only been in Tom Ritchey's proximity once, at the January 1979 Repack race videotaped by the KPIX crew. If Gary Fisher introduced us then, I didn't remember it, but Tom appears in photos of the event standing close to me.

Tom had not expected to go into business with us when he built the nine frames he consigned to Gary, but he found that he had no connection to the market for them. He sold his road bikes through Palo Alto Bike Shop, but even though it sat a mere 50 miles from Marin County, there was zero demand for these strange bikes down there. He had nothing to lose by putting those frames in Gary's hands.

The initial project for Gary and me was to sell the nine frames, and at first we didn't look beyond that. Some of our friends had not been in on the

In order to carve out an identity separate from Tom Ritchey, Gary and I operated briefly in early 1983 as "Kelly-Fisher MountainBikes." After I left the company, it was shortened to "Fisher MountainBikes."

first wave of Breezers and were willing to spend whatever it took to catch up with the new technology. Here were some bikes we could put under them. We bought the parts for their assembly over the counter at the bike shop at retail prices, which made our profit margin just about zero, and we assembled them at my house. Adding the cost of the frame and the cost of the components, we established a retail price of $1,300. For half that amount you could have a very nice road bike.

To say we had a business plan would be an insult to real business plans. Our plan broke down to one sentence spoken by Gary: "Hey, Charlie, you want to help me sell these [nine] bikes?" From that moment on we were winging it every day. Only the fact that we owned our tiny market niche completely kept us going for as long as we did, from the fall of 1979 until I left the business in the summer of 1983. It is clear in retrospect that while we had marvelous talent for publicity, we had very little for

business. Nothing could have prepared us for our immediate future. We didn't have any idea what our business would become, because no one, not even we, would have ever guessed in 1979 that the noise made in our tiny workspace by a couple of hippie bike enthusiasts would be heard all over the world and would bring the world to us in numbers beyond any level of wild optimism.

When Gary and I started the business, we did not envision that Tom and the two of us would be joined in a largely undefined business arrangement. From our headquarters in San Anselmo we saw a market niche for our special knowledge of clunker conversion as well as a market for high-end bikes.

By 1980 we could get chrome-moly versions of the curved-tube clunker frames from BMX shops in Southern California such as Laguna and Cook Brothers. Made to be raced in the BMX Cruiser category, they were much tougher and lighter than the originals, and we thought we

could add those to our catalog and then sell the drum brakes and conversion kits for the 10-speed upgrade. As it turned out, however, we only sold a few of them and soon dropped the idea. The market was moving fast, and everyone wanted the new generation of diamond-frame bikes with cantilever brakes. Cantilever brakes didn't work on the old-style cruiser frame because the stays were so short that the rider's heel would hit the brake arms.

Still, Tom wasn't the only person building the new style of bikes, and we thought we might sell Breezers or Trailmasters too. We could have sold any high-quality frames that came our way, but in the end there was no source of supply for us like Tom, and for him there was no more voracious customer. "Ritchey MountainBike" had become the equivalent of "Rolls-Royce" in our market. If you knew the name of a single product in it, you knew ours.

Another ad for our bikes and catalog. Here we seem to be either "Kelly-Fisher" or "K & F." Either was fine as long as you sent a dollar with your request.

The nature of the name was a little murky. Gary and I were collectively "MountainBikes," and Tom was "Ritchey." It took all of us to get the bike out the door, and we all wanted to see our names on the product. So the product was the "Ritchey MountainBike."

At first the downtube decal was Tom's original design used on his road bikes, which consisted of the stylized word "Ritchey" and, in small letters, "Palo Alto." We had a small white sticker that said "MountainBikes" that was applied to the chainstays as well as to a lot of flat surfaces having nothing to do with bikes. Later we had a downtube decal made that combined both names. By doing so, we acknowledged that Tom's bikes were the only ones we sold.

Our company's growth was dictated by only one factor, which was how many frames we could get from Tom. The capitalization came in small part from the supply of TA cranksets that John Finley Scott had left with us, but primarily from the fact that Tom could take $20 worth of steel tubing and increase its value by a factor of 20 by turning it into a bike frame. As the business grew, and we had more and more bikes to sell, we had to hire employees and expand our rented space. The money for all that came from the value of the bike frames Tom provided to us, but as time went on, our payments to Tom never caught up with our debt to him.

Because of the ad hoc nature of our initial agreement, Gary and I had no proper lines of authority for making decisions, nor did we separate the aspects of our business responsibilities. There was no agreement on how we planned to share profits, if there were any, or what we expected to be paid. For our personal expenses, we would often take some money out of the till, leaving an IOU so that Dave Sahn, our harried bookkeeper, could keep track of it. Dave had a thankless and impossible job trying to maintain a ledger of how much the two principals were costing the company.

Despite the fact that we were not keeping up with our obligation to Tom, we sent him what we could when we had it. Over the period of three years, the amount we were in arrears grew and grew, until by 1983 our debt to Tom was in the neighborhood of $60,000. Everyone involved started to get nervous. Tom's only leverage to collect on the debt was to hold out his products until we paid. But if he did that, we would have been out of business immediately, and he would certainly not get paid with our doors shuttered. To be sure, by that time the market for Tom's bikes was established, and he would have had no trouble selling them himself, but if he cut us off he would be out a significant sum. None of us was sleeping well.

Gary and I started to have different visions of the company's future, and that led to further complications. The mass market had been kicked open by Specialized and joined in 1983 by every major bike company. Off-road bike sales were growing exponentially, but we were limited to the number of frames coming out of Tom's shop. Gary wanted to get into the mass market, with bikes made in a factory. I liked the idea of keeping the business relatively small and selling a few hundred really expensive bikes a year. Even though both Gary and I no longer personally assembled each bike, I could still walk back to the assembly area and be part of the process when I chose. If MountainBikes was just a place where a container full of bike boxes was unloaded and shipped out somewhere else, the hands-on aspect was gone. To my mind you might as well be selling plumbing supplies. Neither view is wrong, but they are totally different.

When we started the company, it was just the two of us in our tiny shop making the coolest bikes in the world. The only "future" we thought about was getting the next bike out the door. Three years later, it stopped being fun because I knew that Gary and I would argue over something. The situation was untenable, but there didn't seem to be any good way out of it.

Gary's father, A. Robert (Bob) Fisher, resolved the situation. In the space of three years, Gary's image as a ne'er-do-well hippie, light-show artist, and Grateful Dead Party Krew member had been transformed. Now Gary was a worldwide celebrity in a bike market whose potential was enormous. Bob was an architect who had done well for himself, and he and Gary made me an offer. They would buy me out of the company, and Bob would help Gary finance a production run of bikes from a factory in Taiwan. For Gary that would serve two purposes: First he would get into that mass market, and second, he would not be utterly dependent on Tom's goodwill.

It was an easy decision for me. I could stay in the business, owning my half of a $60,000 debt and fighting every day with a guy who had been my best friend for more than a decade, or I could take the offer and do something else. By then I had a fledgling magazine, and running the *Fat Tire Flyer* looked like more fun than arguing and owing money.

I took the offer, which was $2,500 in cash and the company's Apple II+ computer. I then happily moved into the next phase of my journey through the world of bicycling, being a magazine editor and the voice of the movement.

Gary and Tom maintained an uneasy relationship for about six more months, but that also drew to a close. Not being a party to the dissolution of their relationship, I have no opinion on it, except to note that it was probably doomed from the beginning. Having shared such a profound experience, Gary and I have come to appreciate the adventure we had together. We have long since gotten past our differences, and I have no issues with the way our partnership ended. It was a wonderful ride.

Whenever I see Tom, he tells me that I always say the same thing: "If I'm not the luckiest guy in the world, I don't care who is, because I'm close enough."

Gary in front of Fisher MountainBikes in 1985.

chapter 22

MAMMOTH KAMIKAZE

After the last Repack race in 1984, the discipline of descending was endangered. Despite the fact that the roots of the sport lay in downhill racing, the emphasis had shifted to cross-country events. Downhill racing required more elaborate officiating than cross-country, and no one anywhere else had put together a two-timer system like mine. It was possible for a promoter to put on a cross-country race nearly anywhere that had trails, but you needed a respectable mountain to create a challenging downhill course. That left out a huge part of the available off-road terrain.

Years earlier we had speculated about the use of a ski resort for downhill events. After all, resorts had lifts, and these lifts were serviced by access roads that usually served as the "bunny hill" for beginning skiers. When the snow melted, it seemed to us that the resorts would welcome some summer action.

Riders queue for the
Mammoth Mountain Kamikaze, 1985.

From a modern perspective, that seems like a no-brainer, but in the early '80s it wasn't quite so obvious. Our initial inquiries to ski-area representatives were received with words to the effect of "we are not in the business of allowing people to take life-threatening risks on our property." Apparently none of these people had ever seen a Warren Miller ski film.

In 1985 I had a call from Don Douglass. I had never met him, but I had heard of his business, Plumline, a bicycle clothing manufacturer. Don and his wife, Reanne, also published a series of bicycle guides to routes in the mountains of California.

Don had secured permission to move mountain bike downhill racing into the modern era. Mammoth Mountain, a ski resort in the southern Sierra Nevada, had agreed to let Don promote a downhill event as part of a three-day bicycle festival. The downhill race would start at the top of 11,000-foot Mammoth Mountain and would include 2,500 feet of descent over 3.5 miles. That's twice the elevation change and nearly twice the distance of Repack. Riders would be delivered to the starting line by a ski lift. Don was going to call his race the Kamikaze, the Japanese term for a suicide pilot. The name was probably distasteful, but it is now carved in stone.

Since I was the only person who had any experience in coordinating and timing downhill bicycle

Top: Riders at the top, waiting to descend the Kamikaze course.

Bottom: Note the Repack timer hanging on the official's neck. I'm flying the VCT colors while doing my best to help out or stay out of the way, depending on your point of view.

Cindy Whitehead at the Sierra 7500 in 1986. Her saddle has fallen off, but she continues, standing on the pedals to a first-place finish.

races, and since I already knew many people who would be interested in riding, and possibly because I had a magazine that would publicize the event, Don asked me to help him put on the Kamikaze. This was not an opportunity I was going to pass up. How long had riders dreamed of putting their bikes on a ski lift for a ride to the top of a mountain? Now it was going to happen.

I brought out the original Repack timers, and I worked at the starting line to organize the 300 riders who turned out. The Mammoth Kamikaze was by far the most popular mountain bike event in California to that date, and the riders lined up for hours to get their one chance. Unlike Repack, which has blind, off-camber turns and twists that keep speeds down, Mammoth Mountain is a place where the ultimate speed could be attained. The air is thin, and much of the road is dead straight and steep. As fast as a mountain bike can go, it can go that fast there. Jimmy Deaton made it a hat trick with a win following his domination at the last two Repack events and added another four titles after that, holding the record of five wins.

After the complications of timing an event at Repack without even the most rudimentary communication between start and finish, I had the luxury at Mammoth of being able to talk to someone

Downhilling at Mammoth.

at the finish line anytime I wanted to. This seminal event was Repack on steroids. I was looking forward to a continued presence at the Kamikaze, but that was my only appearance. A ski resort has plenty of experience in timing downhill events, so my "expertise" in timing racers on Repack while flying blind was not really necessary.

The day after the inaugural Kamikaze race saw the Sierra 7500, a 50-mile cross-country event with 7,500 feet of climbing, topping out at 11,000 feet. The longest course yet used for a mountain bike event had the closest finish, with Roy Rivers nipping reigning national champion Joe Murray by half a wheel in a sprint.

Having shown the resort how popular downhill mountain biking could be at a ski resort with

a lift to the top of the hill, Don was no longer necessary for the Kamikaze or for any other aspect of the Mammoth operation. Mammoth Mountain, like virtually every other ski area in the country, now includes a full-time summer program of lift-serviced downhill riding. The next year, 1986, Mammoth Mountain's own publicity and production staff took over the promotion of the downhill event, and although I was treated as an honored guest, it was clear that my input and participation were not invited, nor were Don's. Don was not done promoting races, but he was done at Mammoth Mountain.

Despite its instant popularity among the participants, the initial Kamikaze did not rate much ink in the mainstream cycling press other than my stories in the *Fat Tire Flyer* and *Cyclist*. Downhill racing was a radioactive subject for those whose only background was road racing. The riders wore everything except traditional bike clothing, including armor adapted from other sports. Why, they might as well have worn golf clothes in a tennis match or white shoes in November. It wasn't done.

The traditional world of cycling journalism, which had barely accepted cross-country mountain bike racing as a legitimate sport, was appalled. As my article in *Cyclist* noted, "Downhill racing is not as safe as, say, tennis. In tennis you might get hit by a ball. In downhill racing you might get hit by a mountain."

If Don had invited me to his race in order to ensure coverage, it was a sound decision, because that was all the coverage the race received. Apparently, though, that coverage was enough. The race's popularity exploded.

The Mammoth Kamikaze is now the oldest downhill mountain bike event, but Don has been largely ignored in the course of mountain bike history. I am not convinced that we would still have a downhill sport had Don not shown the initiative that he did. The 1985 Kamikaze marked my last active participation in a race promotion, a few months short of nine years after the first Repack race.

Despite being cut out of the action at Mammoth Mountain, Don was back the next year with an event called the Ultimate Kamikaze/Sierra 7500, which started with a bus ride to the crest of a 6,000-foot descent over 16 miles, the Silver Canyon Kamikaze. This was followed the next day by a repeat of the 50-mile race through the highest mountains in California, setting the stage for one of the most dramatic performances in bicycle competition history.

In addition to the extreme distance, there was a lot at stake in 1986 for two of the participants. Riding for the Ross team, Cindy Whitehead was having her career year, while Jacquie Phelan was defending her third National Off-Road Bicycle Association (NORBA) championship. Earlier in the season Cindy had become the first woman rider to crack the previously unbeatable Jacquie, winning by 4 minutes on the 35-mile Whiskeytown course. But a mile or so into the Sierra 7500, Cindy's saddle worked loose and fell off. She was close enough to the start that it would not have been a problem to quit the race while still close to the car. Instead, Cindy stayed on the bike and in the race, standing on her pedals for the rest of the 50-mile event.

Jacquie had her own problems at the race, injuring her ankle. At the end of the day, Cindy went the distance without her saddle and took home the trophy, a mountain biking legend for the ages. Later on that year, Cindy would dethrone three-time champion Jacquie and claim the national title.

Match that, Tour de France.

GIRO D'ITALIA

In the spring of 1985, John Francis, editor of *Cyclist* magazine, invited me to lunch with Tom Ritchey. Talk turned to Mike Neel, who had recently signed on to coach the 7-Eleven team in the Giro d'Italia, Italy's big three-week stage race. A little more than a year earlier, Mike had been completely out of cycling and had called me to see if I could put him in touch with Tom. Mike needed a job more than Tom needed a sales rep, but Mike got the job. Mike didn't stay long. He had used the opportunity to regain his position as the premier American cycling coach. Now he was poised to lead the first American team into a grand tour.

John said, "Charlie, would you like to go to the Giro d'Italia?"

What was this, a trick question? You might as well have asked a Japanese baseball fan, "Hey, you've heard of the World Series. Would you like to cover it?" Of course I would like to. I just didn't have any idea how it was done.

My Giro d'Italia
press badge, 1985.

I have no idea whether John had planned to ask his question before he invited us to lunch or whether it was spontaneous, but I took the offer without hesitation. Then I asked about the details. John left them all up to me. He named a price a couple of times higher than the usual article payment, which apparently included my expenses.

That was refreshing.

My next task was to figure out how to do it. The Giro schedule was not easily available in the United States in 1985. I corresponded with the local Italian consulate, and after some back and forth I got the dates and the schedule. I also got my visa. That seemed to settle everything, and I made no other advance preparations whatsoever.

Just before I left, Tom asked me to personally deliver a bike to Antonio Colombo, the owner of Columbus, Italy's largest and most prestigious supplier of tubing for bicycle frames, including most of the bikes in the Giro. It was just one more thing to

tote through airports, but I got the bike to Milan. Antonio was grateful, and he was a very good person to have on my side.

From Milan I took a train to Verona, where the Giro would start. Race headquarters were easy to find, and I made my first visit to *la sala stampa*, the press room.

Somehow I stumbled through the process of getting my press credentials. I was jet-lagged and had no idea how it was done. It did not help that all race business at that time was conducted in Italian. There were no subtitles. Everyone else at the press headquarters was a veteran of the European professional bike race circuit. They all knew the ropes. Every question I asked was dumb.

In its three-week route, the Giro d'Italia travels all around Italy. The organizers are helpful in telling you where it goes. There is a thick press packet with all that information, but they don't give you a ride. You're on your own to get from each start

to finish, one of those details I had not considered. The professional European journalists knew that, of course, and it was part of their game plan. They had hired cars or arranged carpools. Hotels? Another one of those pesky details. Fortunately the organizers realize that the press has to sleep in the towns inundated by the bike race. The organizers booked rooms for me, but I paid for them.

From the press HQ I found out where the 7-Eleven team was staying. I got myself over there and found a bunch of riders and mechanics sorting through bikes and boxes of cycling clothing. Mike was more than busy, but I prevailed on him to help me get through this complicated event I had gotten myself into. Mike didn't need the distraction, but I cashed in my favor from a year earlier when I had asked Tom Ritchey to give Mike a job, and Tom had done so.

The prologue time trial took place in the streets of Verona, ending in the ancient Roman

Francesco Moser crosses the line at
the Verona coliseum with the winning
time in the '85 Giro prologue time trial.

amphitheater. The 1984 winner, Francesco Moser,
was the crowd favorite. He was the last rider to
leave the start house, wearing the *maglia rosa*—
the pink jersey—as the previous year's winner. It
was the last time he ever wore that color. From
just outside the stadium you could track his progress through the city: A helicopter overhead and
the tidal wave of crowd noise showed precisely
where he was. I had a long time to set up my camera for the split second when he crossed the finish
line. It was the money shot, with the crumbling
ancient columns in the background.

Getting from the start of each stage to the finish turned out to be a challenge. I hitched rides in
the team support van, and on a couple of stages I
rode with Mike and the team trainer and mechanic
in the team follow car.

The soigneurs traveled ahead of the race in the
van and set up in the feed zones, then waited for
the race to show up. At least they got to see the
racers. When I rode in the team follow car, Mike
had one caveat. After the race starts, there will be
no respite for calls of nature. The car will stay in the
caravan in its specific position unless told on race
radio to move up. You've been warned.

A stage rolls out slowly, and along the way the
riders answer the calls of nature in groups, shoul-

dering aside a couple of roadside spectators to do so. A 7-Eleven rider dropped back to ask Mike, "Hey, do you have any toilet paper in the car?"

We didn't. The rider needed something to do the same job, and all we could give him was a canvas musette bag. He took off down a side road and shortly afterward worked his way past us to rejoin the peloton.

The best place to see the Giro, or any major bike race, is in your living room, watching on your TV. I traveled in the caravan, I had a press credential, and I didn't see much bike racing. At the finish of one stage I stood with a group of journalists in a wire cage directly at the finish line. Everyone there watched the sprint on a TV screen, even though it was taking place a few feet away. The cameraman, on a crane boom, had a better view than anyone else.

Team cars are kept in a strict order in the following caravan. That order is based on the team's overall General Classification, or GC. The 7-Eleven team was dead last in GC, which put us so far back in the caravan that we never saw any riders except those who had been dropped by the peloton. Mike kept us up on developments by translating the race radio chatter. Except for the screaming people lining the road, we might as well have been taking a slow drive across Italy.

At the finish of one stage I took a photo that no magazine would publish but that has since been spread all over the Internet. Just inside the barriers a distracted mechanic holds a bike with a shattered front wheel. On the pavement nearby is a pool of blood with a discarded bloody bit of gauze.

At the end of each stage I would visit the press room, where a couple dozen reporters were writing stories on typewriters provided to them. From there they could send copy by various electronic means to their publications. I don't know how they got their information, unless they were watching the race on TV.

I had no such chore. I was there for the catered food and the goodie bags handed out by the local chambers of commerce. My article would run months after the Giro was over, so daily results would not make compelling copy. The dramatic aspect for my story was the experiences of the first American team to test the European waters at the second-biggest stage race in the world after the Tour de France. All I had to do to pay for my Italian vacation was to get some photographs and write 2,000 words about what it was like to be there.

I abandoned the Giro before it rolled into Rome. The cost of the experience was beginning to eclipse the pay I was going to get.

Aftermath of a bad crash at the Giro.

chapter 24

AFTER
THE *FLYER*

At the end of 1987, a few months after the last issue of the *Fat Tire Flyer* was published, Hank Barlow sold his own magazine, *Mountain Bike for the Adventure*, to Rodale Press, publisher of *Bicycling*. Mountain bikes had become a big part of the bicycle market, and adherents of one discipline didn't care to read about the other. Rodale's newly acquired title would continue to address the mountain bike audience, leaving the road bike coverage to the flagship.

Operating from the East Coast and staffed with road riders, Rodale was not in a position to start its own mountain bike title, so it bought the one with the most credibility, not at all coincidentally the only one that was for sale. It is barely possible that in the quest for a quick piece of the off-road market, Rodale Press might have considered adding the *Fat Tire Flyer* audience to its circulation, but the issue was moot because the *Fat Tire Flyer*

The final issue of the *Fat Tire Flyer* featured an image that wrapped around from the front cover to the back.

no longer existed. I'm glad I didn't have to make a decision about selling my magazine, because there is no way it could have kept its unique voice under the editorial helm of Rodale.

The timing was not bad for me. Rodale hired me immediately as the West Coast editor of its new acquisition. Rodale's company headquarters in Emmaus, Pennsylvania, were a long way from the heart of mountain biking in the West, and the magazine needed someone who lived near the subject. A salaried position was a freelancer's dream. Paychecks came regularly, I didn't have to solicit editors for the opportunity to see my work published, and I would see it in every issue. Hank remained the editor in chief, but location worked against him. Crested Butte was a mountain bike paradise, but it was a long way from the West Coast's mountain bike activity and also a long distance from the magazine offices. Eventually Hank moved on from his editorial position, and in his absence I took over

the opening editorial to go along with my regular column and a feature in every issue.

With Rodale picking up my travel bills, I went to Iditabike, and I got around to covering the national championships. Still, evidence emerged here and there that I wasn't a good fit for my East Coast employers.

I rarely traveled to Pennsylvania, so the annual bicycle trade show in Las Vegas served as the meeting ground for the editorial staff. At one such meeting in 1989, story ideas were being tossed around, and I brought out one of my own. It was a fictional humor piece, I explained, about a guy who gets a little computer for his bike, and from then on every ride turns into a line on a spreadsheet.

The Grateful Dead's Bob Weir during a break on a ride we took in 1991.

ences between me and the rest of the staff were on display. I was the only male representative of the company who was not wearing a necktie, because I didn't own any (and still don't). I wore jeans and a T-shirt. My "mountain biker image" isn't cultivated. It's the way I dress, and it inspired a bit of harrumphing among my erstwhile associates.

Suddenly everyone in the booth stood up. The men adjusted neckties; the women checked their grooming. Antonio Colombo was approaching. He was a very important Italian manufacturer who owned Columbus, which made fine tubing for bicycle frames. He was also a big advertiser and the very same Antonio Colombo to whom I had personally delivered a Ritchey bicycle a couple of years earlier. Antonio's suit probably cost more than all the suits worn by the staffers in the booth added together. Ignoring all the tie-straightening editors, he walked up to the booth and stopped in front of me. He extended his hand and said, "Hello, Charlie. Nice to see you again."

Having had the final authority on virtually every aspect of the *Fat Tire Flyer*, I didn't anticipate the limits imposed on *Mountain Bike* by corporate ownership. I still thought I had some of my own authority. If the covers of the *Fat Tire Flyer* and of the original *Mountain Bike for the*

The guy knows to the inch how far he has ridden this year and to the 10th of a kilometer per hour how fast he did it. He gets so far into riding solely to generate numbers that his friends don't want to ride with him anymore.

All heads swiveled to a certain senior editor, a dedicated "training journal" type of guy, who was not amused. Apparently no one else thought it was funny either.

At the same trade show, I was hanging out in the Rodale Press booth, where a few of the differ-

Adventure had shown imagination, the covers for the new version were a study in risk aversion. To plead my case that we needed some diversity, I photocopied a dozen bike magazine covers, each of which featured an identically posed photograph. On each cover the rider approaches the 300-mm lens filling the exact same percentage of the frame. Flying hair and water are de rigueur. "Sell lines" are always arranged in a column on the left side of the cover, where they will be seen when the magazine is displayed on a news rack. This must be what they teach in Magazine Publishing 101, but I missed that semester. I accompanied my examples with a rather caustic explanation of what I liked and didn't like in bicycle magazine covers. For my troubles I was told that covers were not my department and that the company had people for that.

My wife, Mary, and I welcomed our daughter, Dana, into the world in July 1990, and my bicycle adventure came to an end almost exactly two decades after it started. The date is easy to pinpoint: It was the day I received my pink slip from Rodale Press, one week after Dana arrived.

As far as I knew, I had done the job I was asked to do, and no one had asked me to do less of something or more of something else. No explanation was ever supplied. I was just fired.

I had settled into a comfortable niche of going to all kinds of cycling events, getting the photos, and writing about what I saw. It was hard to imagine a more idyllic job. In most issues I wrote more copy than any of the other editors. I had a press pass wherever I went, and I went everywhere.

It was not my magazine, though. This was a lesson about putting my livelihood into the corporate hands of people who did not know me and did not care about anyone they didn't know. I was a number that had to be deleted from some spreadsheet, or perhaps my outspoken views had offended someone, either an advertiser or an editor.

I could still write for bike magazines, but the pay for freelance writing work is paltry and does not compare to a salaried editorial position. My failure to bring a little of the irreverent editorial voice from the *Fat Tire Flyer* to a mainstream magazine suggested that I was not cut out for that world. I wasn't about to get a suit and tie and try to become someone else.

If I was not a cycling journalist, there was no longer a place for me in the bike business. I wasn't about to start a new bike company from scratch. I probably could have found a position with one of the bike companies run by my friends, but selling someone else's bikes, no matter how nice, could never compare with starting MountainBikes and being a principal. When you've been in on the gold rush, the prospect of being a mere miner is not appealing.

In the six years since *California Bicyclist* magazine had described me on the cover as the "World's Foremost Authority" on mountain biking, I was back to being a recreational rider.

The last ride I took that was worthy of writing about was in 1992. It made a nice bookend for an adventure that began a little more than 20 years earlier when I met Gary Fisher at the Grateful Dead office. In the years since, Grateful Dead guitarist Bob Weir had become a mountain biker himself. Late one night Gary, Bob, and I rode to the top of Mount Tamalpais under a full moon, where we sat at the highest elevation in Marin County and solved a few of the world's problems.

It was a pretty good ride. I don't know what more anyone could ask of life.

HALL OF FAME

In 1988 the sanctioned sport of mountain biking was officially only 5 years old. The National Off-Road Bicycle Association (NORBA) had been formed in 1983. A "hall of fame" might have been premature, but by then mountain bikes were the dominant force in the bicycle market in every way. Mountain bikes were outselling other types of bikes. Mountain bike parts were being developed more quickly and were selling faster than road bike parts. And mountain bike racing was exploding all over the globe. More and more, it was a fat-tire world out there.

I received a press release that spring announcing plans for a hall of fame for mountain bikers and a museum of mountain bike history to be located in Crested Butte. My membership in the advisory committee and my suggestions for nominees were being solicited.

A total of 10 honorees were to be inducted in the initial ceremony, to be held that summer during Fat Tire Bike Week. Although I suspected my name might get tossed into the hat, the 10 nominations I came up with were Gary Fisher, Joe Breeze, Tom Ritchey, Jacquie Phelan, Glenn Odell, Steve Cook, Joe Murray, Erik Koski, Gary Larson, and Al Farrell. After the votes were tallied, the final list had my name on it, along with Gary Fisher, Joe Breeze, Tom Ritchey, Jacquie Phelan, Steve Cook, Joe Murray, Charlie Cunningham, Neil Murdoch, and Mike Sinyard. All those

Mountain Bike Hall of Fame ride, Crested Butte, July 1989. Foreground, left to right: Victor Vicente of America, Matt Hebbard, Dave Lindsey, Hank Barlow. Standing, left to right: Paul Anderson, Charlie Kelly, Joe Breeze, Don Cook, Carole Bauer, unknown, Wende Cragg, Karen Jansen, Gary Fisher, unknown, Rick Baldwin, Mark Slate, Mike Sinyard.

on my list who were not honored at the initial event eventually assumed the mantle.

Apparently some of the other members of the advisory board voted for me. The letter from Ray Ford informing me that I had been selected as a charter inductee also contained a request that I act as the master of ceremonies for the first induction ceremony. You don't have to offer me a microphone twice. I accepted, which put me in the interesting position of inducting myself.

Ten years later we discovered that one of the people I inducted in 1988, the Fat Tire Bike Week organizer we all knew as Neil Murdoch, was an imposter whose real name was Richard Gordon Bannister. Bannister had jumped bail in 1973 on a federal drug charge and fled to the mountains of Colorado, settling in a tiny, backwater ski town that hardly anyone had heard of. He assumed a new identity, which he borrowed from a real person, and over a period of 25 years became a prominent member of

the community. Seeking anonymity, the last thing he must have expected was to become famous under his assumed name.

When federal authorities tracked Bannister to Crested Butte later in 1998, he was able to flee the town just an hour before they arrived to make the scheduled arrest. He stayed on the lam for three more years before being arrested in New Mexico to serve his nine-year sentence.

As my contribution to the Mountain Bike Museum, I loaned my original Breezer bike for display and donated a complete set of the *Fat Tire Flyer* for its archive.

Dear Hall of Fame Member,

On behalf of the *Mountain Bike Hall of Fame* I want to let you know that the following 10 people have been chosen to be inducted this year:

Joe Breeze
Steve Cook
Charlie Cunningham
Gary Fisher
Charlie Kelly

Neil Murdoch
Joe Murray
Jacquie Phelan
Tom Ritchey
Mike Sinyard

We hope that you will be in Crested Butte for the ceremonies on Thursday night, September 15, and I want to remind you your membership does include entry to the event. However, due to the limited seating of the Performing Arts Center you need to let us know as soon as possible whether you will be attending as seating will be given out on a first-come, first-serve basis. Send a note to Hall of Fame, Box 845, Crested Butte, CO 81224 for your ticket of admission. Thanks again for your help and support!

Carol Bauer

Above: Notification letter to the 1998 charter inductees from MBHOF founder Carol Bauer.

Middle: The Mountain Bike Hall of Fame logo on a sticker.

Right: Congratulatory letter from Ray Ford of Fat Tire Bike Week in Crested Butte.

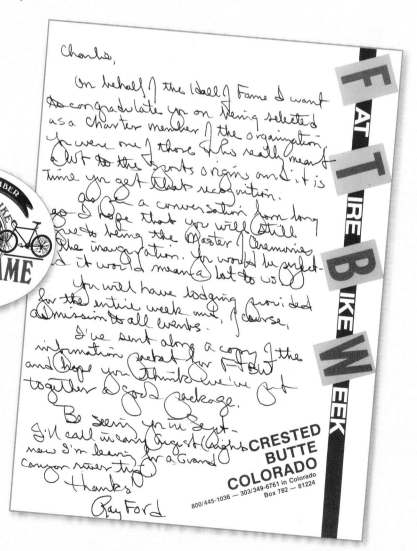

SOME CONCLUSIONS

A comment that I hear frequently that deserves to be addressed is "Why does Marin County claim the credit for this movement?" Followed by either "We rode trails on beat-up bikes when I was a kid" or a variation of "The Buffalo Soldiers rode bikes cross-country more than a hundred years ago!" Postwar Paris was the home of a club called Velo Cross Club Parisien, the members of which modified bikes and rode them in a fashion that would have been called mountain biking three decades later. Cyclocross was an established sport long before mountain biking.

All true, because dirt roads and basic off-road cycling machinery were available from the first days of the bicycle. A first-generation mountain bike looks suspiciously like a "safety" bicycle from the 1890s. Same diamond frame, same flat bars, similar big tires. When these bicycles appeared, most public roads didn't look much different from what many now consider mountain bike terrain. Suspension systems had already been devised, mostly to deal with the effects of solid tires on cobbled roads, before John Boyd Dunlop popularized the pneumatic tire he created for his son's tricycle in 1887.

The invention of the coaster brake in 1899 put all the elements in place for a basic Marin County bike of the 1970s. Apart from the different wheel standards and frame styles, a bicycle manufactured in 1900 was similar to the bikes that I started to ride on the trails in Marin 70 years later. They were nearly identical to the bikes—as I am reminded so often—that everyone else rode on trails when they were little. Bikes like this were available to several generations of kids, but mountain biking didn't emerge then. There must be more.

The features that identify a first-generation modern mountain bike—multiple gears and flat handlebars—were hardly a mystery. Our collaborator John Finley Scott had come up with a nearly identical basic design 20 years before we did. No doubt others had also, but the sport of mountain biking didn't crop up suddenly anywhere else. The "invention of the mountain bike" happened multiple times in multiple places, no matter what the machinery was called, but the sport that changed the direction of bicycle manufacturing only had to arise once.

The Cupertino riders who inspired us with derailleur gears on fat-tire bikes in 1974 had been racing their hybrid machines downhill before we thought to do so, although they hadn't come up with the time trial format. Had they pursued the idea, one of them might be writing this. But they did not. Instead, they managed to disappear so completely that it was decades before I talked to them again. They did not advance the sport beyond what they had already accomplished by the time of our first encounter.

A dozen people are not a movement. When the number of participants starts growing into triple digits, and especially when the growth rate is exponential, it's a movement. What took place in Marin County in the '70s was the creation of a culture of mountain biking, even before the machinery had arrived for it. The culture created the machinery.

More than the mechanical aspect, the Repack race gave the culture a focus and an immediate hierarchy. It united members of small regional groups who had previously had no reason to meet. It was so abusive of machinery that it helped define what was necessary for the sport. The competitive nature of the culture led participants to spend the money it took to update the design and create commercial potential.

The Cupertino riders were not road racers who were accustomed to finely tuned machinery, but many of the Marin riders were. The precision of the racing bikes of the time stood in stark contrast to a typical "klunker." The Marin riders craved a better off-road machine. Spurred on by the downhill competition, the development of custom off-road frames was inevitable in Marin County, and this is why Marin County gave birth to the modern version of the sport.

There had been a few other advances in bicycle technology since the invention of the coaster brake, including derailleur gears. Derailleur gears can't be used with a coaster brake, so rim brakes

had advanced accordingly. The first generation of diamond-frame mountain bikes incorporated elements already available but were assembled with a different philosophy than merely to look like a racing bike.

Some assistance was necessary from the bike industry. You can build a bike frame in a garage, but a rim or a tire is a different story. For rim brakes to be effective on mountain bikes, and to bring the wheel weight within reason, aluminum rims and modern tires were necessities, and the industry came through.

Finally, it took a few people with enough interest and experience to take the last step, to put the machinery on the market as a new product anyone could buy. That happened first in Marin County.

The explosion of the sport in Crested Butte demonstrates that the times were right for mountain biking. All that was required was the arrival of a mature technology brought by passionate proponents to a place with untapped potential, and the seed would grow.

As the '80s progressed, and mass-produced mountain bikes became the norm, there was still a demand for the handmade variety. Mountain biking created a cadre of small manufacturers who entered the market niche MountainBikes had established with our first bicycles. In California that list included Scot Nicol (Ibis), Keith Bontrager, Ross Shafer (Salsa), Steve Potts (Wilderness Trail Bikes), John Parker (Yeti), and Charlie Cunningham (Wilderness Trail Bikes). In the Eastern United States, Chris Chance had a dedicated following for Fat Chance bikes.

It seems safe to say that mountain bikes provided a market for handmade bicycle frames that dwarfed the demand for road bikes.

As more engineering talent turned toward the subject of off-road bicycling and built on the previous efforts, innovations in the form of improved brakes, drivetrains, and suspensions exploded onto the market. It had been 100 years since that much ferment had taken place, when the "safety" bicycle replaced the "penny-farthing" toward the end of the 19th century. It's interesting that the first "mountain bikes" resembled the first "safety bicycles," which became popular before paved roads linked every destination.

Before mountain bikes changed the direction of the bicycle market, bicycle design was largely dictated by the standards used by the Union Cycliste Internationale (UCI) governing body to define road bikes for the purpose of sanctioned competition. An inexpensive bicycle didn't have to look like a Tour de France race bike because it wasn't built for the same purpose, but even a cheap "10-speed" from the '70s retained the racing bike's drop-bar look. By contrast, the ruggedness and comfort of the mountain bike, with its flat bars, multiple gears, and big tires, were attractive to people who could not imagine riding a 10-speed.

Even today I see people riding inexpensive mountain bikes from 30 years ago, a testament both to the ruggedness of the design and to the decades of use that design inspired, even if the tires never saw dirt in all that time. But I do not see anyone riding a 30-year-old cheap road bike.

Despite being one of the originators of the sport, I was already in my late 20s when I took it up. I was never a motorcyclist. My generation predated BMX by a few years, and we never had the experience of that sort of acrobatic riding. Our early equipment was dodgy and not very rugged and would not have stood up for a minute under modern off-road stresses. No matter how good a cyclist I might have been for my age group, skills acquired that late in life don't compare with skills learned earlier.

Now it is a generation later, and there are adults who have grown up in a world that always had mountain bikes. From the first time they rode, through adolescence and beyond, they have polished their skills on bikes imbued with technology that puts our original bikes to shame. Growing up in a world where bikes have always been popular, they never had to give them up for a few years in order to act like grown-ups. Given a lifetime of experience on modern equipment, mountain bikers are now capable of feats that none of us ever imagined.

The sport we invented, downhill racing, is now a respected discipline. Mountain bike racing is an Olympic sport. It is among the most popular high school sports in Northern California. The trail I rode for the first time on a one-speed clunker is now part of a dedicated trail system for mountain bikes. The bike I ride on this trail today is everything anyone could ask for in a bicycle—with full suspension; wide-ratio gears; big, tough tires; and, best of all, brakes that work every time. I know I had a part in making this possible, but mountain biking is now such an overwhelming part of the cycling landscape that it is difficult to believe that it all sprang from a day when a few bicyclists with a goofy hobby decided to see who could ride the fastest down a steep hill.

APPENDIX

Clunkers Among the Hills

This was my first published work, and also the first story of its kind I ever tried to write. It was published in Bicycling *magazine in 1979. The prose is hyperbolic and breathless. I like to think I got better later on.*

It is a cool, clear morning in Northern California, but the five young men are sweating profusely as they push strangely modified bicycles up the steep hill. They are discussing the dirt road surface, which resembles a moonscape more than it does a road, and as they push their machines one or another will kick a rock to one side or fill a small depression with dirt.

These young men belong to the same breed that skis down cliffs, jumps out of airplanes, or rides skateboards down Everest; they have developed their own unique athletic challenge, a race which is known only to a few dozen locals and is referred to as "Repack." The road they are on is the racecourse.

After 35 minutes of hard climbing, scrambling and pushing, the five reach the top of the hill, where the road they are on intersects another rarely used fire road. There they are met by another fifteen or so riders, including a couple of high-energy ladies, who have taken a route only slightly easier to the top. The road becomes a tangled jumble of modified machinery as riders pile their bikes around the intersection.

Most of the crowd are in their twenties, but there are a few teenagers and one bearded individual who claims to be fifty, although no one believes him. All are wearing heavy shirts and pants and most are wearing leather gloves and Vibram-soled boots.

There seems to be a little method to this madness, however, as one of the group drags a very well-thumbed notebook out of a backpack along with a pair of electronic stopwatches. This notebook is the heart of the race, since it contains all previous race results as well as the phone numbers of all the local riders. (Races are not scheduled; they are held only when the cosmic alignment is right.) Names are taken and numbers are assigned according to experience. First-time riders and those with slow previous times are numbered first and the fastest are numbered last; each rider is then assigned a starting time, which is duly noted. A copy of the list is made and the watches are started simultaneously. One copy of the list and one of the watches is given to a scruffy looking "official timer" who then jumps on his machine and vanishes downhill.

For the next ten minutes or so the adrenalin content of the air increases noticeably as riders eat oranges, make minor adjustments, and talk excitedly among themselves. Finally the first name on the list is called and a nervous young man wheels up to the starting line, which is scraped across the road in the dirt. This is his first time down the course and he spends his last few seconds at the top asking questions about the course and not listening to the answers.

"Ten seconds . . . five seconds." The novice is so anxious that he applies full power a little early; however the starter has a firm grip on the rear wheel and releases it as he says, "Go!" The novice is thrown off-balance by his early start and wobbles for the first few yards before finding the throttle and disappearing over the first rise.

The sport that is going on here may never catch on with the American public, and its originators couldn't care less. They are here to get off. The bicycles in use are as unique as the sport; they are usually old Schwinns, although a few other rugged species are included. Highly modified, most are five- or ten-speeds with front and rear drum brakes, motorcycle brake levers, motocross bars, and the biggest knobby tires available. A few reactionaries still cling to their one- or two-speed coaster brake machines, but drum brakes and ten speeds seem to be the wave of the future. The machines are referred to as Clunkers, Bombers or Cruisers, depending on the owner's local affiliation, and there are probably not more than a few hundred of the advanced models in California.

Clunking seems to have started with the invention of the bicycle; certainly people have been riding old bikes on dirt roads as long as there have been old bikes. Recently, however, the old bikes have been successfully crossed with the ten-speed to produce a hybrid which is perfectly adapted to the fire roads and trails of the Northern California hills. In the process of field testing modifications the researchers have shattered every part to be found on a bicycle: rims, hubs, handlebars, cranks, seatposts, saddles, gears, chains, derailleurs, stems, pedals and frames have all been ground to fragments along with the exterior portions of a number of clunking enthusiasts. Any sacrifice in the name of science.

Early in the experimental stage it was realized that the hill now known as Repack was the ultimate field test for bike and rider. Repack is a rarely used fire road that loses 1300 feet of elevation in the two miles from top to bottom. In addition to its incredible steepness it features off-camber blind corners, deep erosion ruts, and a liberal sprinkling of fist-sized rocks. The name "Repack" stems from the coaster brake era; after a trip down the hill all the grease in a coaster brake turns to smoke and it is time to repack the hub.

While Clunkers somewhat resemble lightweight dirt motorcycles, the similarity is largely visual, and cornering at high speed is a unique form of body art. A motorcycle has large tires and shock absorbers, but a Clunker does not and it consequently tends to become airborne when it hits even very slight projections in the road surface. In a tight corner a Clunker does not have the instant acceleration that a motorcyclist uses to bring the rear end around, and the lack of shock absorbers causes it to skitter. Nevertheless, they can be ridden around curves much faster than seems possible by an expert rider. Interestingly, photographs have shown that the fastest riders raise the least dust on corners.

Another interesting feature of the ride is the fact that the handlebars can become extremely difficult to hold onto at high speed when the surface gets rough. There isn't much to take up the shock, and it is transmitted directly to your hands, making delicate braking operations rather difficult. At the end of a Repack ride the most noticeable feeling is the cramp in the hands caused by this abuse. In this area the coaster-brake reactionaries claim superiority since their brakes are foot-operated.

The styles displayed by the expert riders vary with the personalities involved. One of the fastest riders, Joe, is known as the "Mad Scientist." Joe has drawn up detailed maps of the course, which he studies carefully. On race day he walks up the course to check for new hazards, then he rides with a controlled fury that makes cornering on gravel at 40 mph look easy.

Another rider, George, occupies the other end of the stylistic spectrum. Called the "Mad Bomber" because of his Kamikaze approach, George rides an old one-speed coaster brake machine with no front brake. His style is characterized by 75-foot sideways slides going into curves, accompanied by miraculous recoveries from certain doom. On other roads, George rides under single pipe fire-road gates at 35–40 mph and claims distance jumps of 40 feet or more.

Returning to the top of the course we find that riders have been sent off at two minute intervals. The spacing is to prevent one rider from catching another, since passing on this course is not easy. The ability grouping prevents a slow rider from being followed by an extremely fast one who might catch up. The fastest riders are started last so the others get a chance to see the experts finish.

What is it like to ride this course? As the rider before you leaves, you have two minutes to prepare yourself. For a surprising number of this means a fast trip to the bushes for emergency urination. Wheeling up to the line with a minute to go you find your breathing a little strained, fast, and loud in your ears. "Thirty seconds." Squeeze brake levers to make sure they are adjusted for maximum grab. "Fifteen." You check for the eighth time to make sure you are in the right gear. "Ten." Up onto the pedals as the starter holds the rear wheel. "Five." The world shrinks and becomes twelve feet wide, stretched out in front of you. Conscious effort is required to hold back from an early start. "GO!" The wheel is released and the bike shoots forward as if propelled by a tightly wound spring.

The first 150 yards are level with a soft surface and then a slight uphill. It is imperative to ride this section as fast as possible since there is a two or three second difference between a fast rider and a slow one here.

Over the rise and into the first downhill and you are already gasping from the initial effort. No time to let up though, for this section is straight and even though it is steep you are still standing on your highest gear.

Blind left turn onto the steepest section, covered with ruts and loose rocks. Watch that little lump across the road because at this speed it will put you in the air and out of position for the next turn.

Now the road becomes a series of blind corners which all seem to look the same as you approach. This section favors the experienced Repack rider who can remember which corners to brake for and which ones can be taken wide open. Since Repack is in more or less a straight line at the top, most of the corners can be taken at full speed, which is a thrilling prospect in light of the fact that it will take you about 200 feet to stop (unless you hit a tree). At no time should you stop pedaling unless you are jamming on the brakes. As you approach some of the more wicked curves you are conscious of a few fifty-foot, side-to-side skidmarks. Amateur tracks. A definite "groove" is visible on most of the corners, worn into the surface by the passage of many knobby tires.

A roller-coaster section gives you a new thrill as the bike becomes weightless just when you want the tires on the ground. Into a dip and the bike slides sideways, then corrects itself pointed in exactly the right direction. Cutting all corners as closely as possible, you receive a whack or two from overhanging branches.

As your adrenalin pump goes into overdrive, your reflexes and vision improve immeasurably. You are aware of every pebble on the road, even though they are whipping past. You are totally alone; the only spectators are at the bottom. You dare not lose your concentration for an instant, but the danger of that is slight. You are definitely getting off.

Sliding into an off-camber, eroded turn you make a micro miscalculation. Out of control, you must make a rapid decision, off the edge, or lay it down. Lay it down . . . damn, torn shirt, bloody elbow. No time to mess with that now (the shirt was old, so was the elbow), how's the bike? Okay . . . jump on it and feed the chain back on with your hand as you coast the first few yards. Back in gear you really stand on it to make up time.

Near the bottom of the course is a series of switchbacks and you are vaguely aware that you are being photographed as you try for maximum cornering speed. Out of the switchbacks in a cloud of dust and into the final straightaway. Jam on the brakes to keep a lump in the road from launching you off the edge. Now there are several dozen people along the sides of the course, earlier riders, girlfriends, and a few locals. Last corner . . . and roaring past the big rock that marks the finish, you skid 50 feet to the flashiest possible stop, then throw down your bike and run over to the timer, who instantly gives you your time. It is the best so far, but your elation is reduced by the arrival of the next rider somewhat less than two minutes later. As the last half-dozen riders finish the times continue to go down, and the last finisher records the best time, some twenty seconds better than yours. Any time under five minutes is respectable, but the record stands at 4:22.

Now that the event is over the winners are announced, but no prizes are handed out. There are no entry fees, very few rules, and usually no prizes other than a round of beers, but no one seems to care. The finish line is a hubbub as adrenalized riders bounce around, reliving and describing at length their rides and various crashes. "I would have done better, but I crashed. . ." "I crashed twice and still did better than you. . ." "You should have seen it. . ." But no one did.

While the Repack race seems to define the essence of clunking, it is completely unique and is only one facet of the sport. Most Clunker riders are interested primarily in riding, rather than racing. In Northern California there is ample hill country, laced with fire roads and trails which are as good as freeways to Clunker riders. This is where the Clunker comes into its own, for these are not just downhill machines. Super-low gears enable a strong rider to climb most hills, and the true enthusiast sees nothing wrong with spending an hour pushing his bike up a steep hill in order to come flying down. The Clunker allows the rider to penetrate deeply into the hills, away from cars and most hikers. The ability to travel at 10–15 mph in total silence in rough country makes the Clunker the most effective backwoods transportation yet invented. It can be ridden on the narrowest hiking trails or carried if necessary over any obstacle.

As a means of local transportation the Clunker has a few drawbacks; weight (about 45 pounds) and high rolling resistance due to the balloon tires keep the cruising speed down to a mellow but very comfortable velocity, but for short distances it is a perfect vehicle as its lack of speed is offset by incredible braking, cornering and maneuverability. To the experienced rider there are no obstacles, and ditches, curbs, fallen trees, etc. become part of the enjoyment of riding. One need not worry excessively about tire damage since there is probably no tougher tire than the 2.125 balloon tire knobbies in general Clunker use.

Clunker technology, a field limited to a small number of mad cyclo-scientists, is still in its infancy. Plans are being developed for frames to be made of the same lightweight tubing used in racing bicycles. If the weight can be brought down and the frame redesigned for better handling, the machines in use now will become as obsolete as the bikes they were made from. In underdeveloped countries, such as this one, the Clunker has promise as low-cost, non-polluting transportation over any type of terrain.

Working Up an Appetite

This article by Darryl Skrabak, and used here with his permission, appeared in the January 1980 edition of City Sports. *According to Darryl, the editors had decided not to run the piece, but the ad department had sold space on the basis that it would appear. Money won the day, and this became the first use of the term "Mountain Bike" to appear in print.*

There are events that become adventures, and adventures that become ordeals, and ordeals in which things go from bad to worse, and the worse things become, the better they are.

It was that way at the Appetite Seminar held Thanksgiving Day in the Marin hills. This unheralded event was plain awful. It was the worst seminar ever, and it was the Fifth Annual. It will fuel Marin bench racing for months. The miseries visited upon the participants will be dwelt upon at length, and recounted repeatedly, and expanded into tales, and thence into legend. It will be recalled as one of the great ones.

Because it was the worst.

You had to be acquainted among the Marin bicycle underground to know about the Appetite Seminar—so named because its survivors work up one hell of an appetite for the Thanksgiving repast. Each year somewhat in advance of Thanksgiving, Charles Kelly, 34, who lives in Fairfax, gets out an instant-print flyer announcing the event. These flyers are furtively distributed to the cognoscenti. They lie obscurely on counters in the nether corners of select Marin bike shops. They are not remarkable art, but they have a certain style. Someday they will be minor collector's items.

It was not Charlie's fault things went bad. The beginning was fine. It was a brisk fall morning, as the weatherman had promised. Charlie showed up at the appointed hour, 9 a.m., at the appointed place, the Fairfax movie house parking lot. He did not rush proceedings, for the annual Equipment Review was under way. The E.R. is where people look over what the other guys have brought. In the early days what they brought was whatever old-timey fat-tired bicycles the thrift shops had to offer. They were called klunkers, because that's what they were.

These days they're still called klunkers. But they ain't. The old bikes—those undestroyed—have been lovingly worked over, fitted with low-range derailleur gearing, and super-strong handlebar stems that won't break off, leaving you holding handlebars unconnected to a bicycle hurtling down some rocky descent. Their wheels have drum brakes rarely to be found in the U.S.A. outside Marin County. The 26-inch rims are aluminum, also virtually unobtainable beyond Marin. Dirt motorcycle-style handlebars have been added, along with Magura-style motorcycle brake levers. The thumbshifters are stock SunTour, but like the rims and the brakes and a lot of other trick parts, you won't see them outside Marin, either.

Getting most scrutiny were the new specials. From the frame up these are designed for their particular element. They represent the state of a still developing art. None are cheap. Some are really dear, even by custom bike standards.

Klunkers they ain't, but they are called that because nobody has yet coined an acclaimed replacement term. This is to the embarrassment of the purveyors and manufacturers of finer klunkers, who would really prefer a more dignified appellation for their wares.

On review at the parking lot were historic reworked Schwinns, new heavy-duty Schwinns, also reworked, beach cruisers from L.A., and the custom frame machines. Examples of the latter were produced by Mert Lawwill of Tiburon, former national champion motorcycle racer (you saw him in film maker Bruce Brown's *On Any Sunday*), whose design was developed with the Koski brothers of the Cove Bike Shop in Tiburon; and by Menlo Park framebuilder Tom Ritchey, who joined forces with Kelly and bicycle road racer Gary Fisher to design his frame. Ritchey is now party to a fledgling Kelly and Fisher concern known as MountainBikes, which markets Ritchey's frames and other klunker equipment.

The Lawwill and Ritchey-based bikes you can buy. Others were on hand that you can't buy. These were one- or two-off specials. Of this breed were a couple by Joe Breeze, who is a machinist and half of the famed tandem team of Otis Guy and Joe Breeze, perennial winners of the annual Davis 200 miler; and a bike made and ridden by Craig Mitchell, owner and proprietor of Mitchell Engineering in Fairfax. In a more formal showing, his beautifully crafted 20-inch wheel bike would have won Most Different.

There was even a lone foreign entry, this a Jack Taylor from England. For years the renown Taylor firm has built frames for English backlaners who tour historic unpaved roads, and who have formed an association known as the Rough Stuff Fellowship. For years Holland Jones, owner of Fulton Street Cyclery in San Francisco, had been badgering Taylor to ship a roughstuff bike. That which arrived a few months ago is probably the first in the country.

All the klunkers—the Taylor and Tom Ritchey's personal bike excepting—had one feature in common. They were shod with the largest and knobbiest tread tires to be had (the Taylor and Ritchey bikes had middling thick tires). This is in stark contrast to the trend for conventional road bikes, whose tires have become increasingly skinnier—and more fragile.

Klunker tires are big for two reasons. Their cushioning effect helps the rest of the bike—and rider—to withstand treatment no ordinary bike could withstand. Klunkerites are prone to ride over logs, bash against rocks and unabashedly ride down stairways. It takes big tires—and a tough and non-squirrelly bike—to suffer that without wrecking.

The other reason big tires are favored is flotation. "High flotation" is a reference for those oversize tires stuck on four-wheel-drive rigs. Even 4WDs sink on soft stuff with regular tires. Big, wide tires "float" on top and prevent bog-downs.

The effect is the same for bicycles. Klunker bikes are the ORVs (off-road vehicles) of the non-motorized set. Off pavement it's better if your tires stay on top of loose surfaces, rather than sink in, which is what happens to skinny ten-speed tires. The result can be like getting a tire stuck in a streetcar track—disaster. Or it can be like just getting stuck in the mud, which is even less fun when the other guys are rapidly disappearing down the road, buoyed up by their fat tires.

It was mud which prevailed at the 1979 Appetite Seminar—but not until the event was well under way, and riders had got to the interior of Marin's backcountry. The initial leg was pavement, and the first dirt mostly rocks, and the rain hadn't started yet. But it would come.

The start seemed to occur without signal. By some common agreement the group bolted the parking lot, within seconds chasing up the Bolinas-Fairfax Road. This section proved to be a not inconsequential hill. The climb was severe enough to discourage some riders. Klunker bikes are heavy, and their weight, combined with the rolling resistance of fat tires, does not allow hills to be surmounted with the elan of a ten-speed on pavement.

"How much farther up the hill, Charlie?" breathless riders shouted to the event organizer.

"Not much farther," Kelly would reply reassuringly. (What else should he say?)

Some riders were hip to the hill. They piled into Ed Christiansen's Sunshine Bike Shop (Fairfax) van with Ed and his wife. Mrs. Christiansen was driving the empty van down the hill while the pedal-it-yourself brigade was still ascending.

At the summit there was pause for a group photograph. Some 31 klunkers and two skinny-tired ten-speeds (both of which managed the entire seminar) lined up in the traditional handlebar-to-handlebar pose.

Then the seminar began in earnest, off pavement and onto Pine Mountain Road, a fire road, following a loop route of connecting fire roads that Charlie Kelly reckoned would cover 15 or 20 miles.

Only a handful of the most capable riders, led by Repack race fast-timer Gary Fisher, remained aboard on the first rock-strewn hill. The rest were off and pushing. Then the rocks thinned and the grade flattened, and the surface, recently rendered dustless by the season's first rains, became much quicker.

"This is okay now," said Howie Hammermann, veteran of all four previous Seminars. "But wait until the winter rains. This stuff turns to mud that sticks to anything within ten feet of it."

That pronouncement, only partially hyperbolic, was prophetic. Within minutes rain commenced. Riders dove beneath a sheltering tree. Charlie advised of a route option: the Repack course was less than a mile away. It offered a fast shortcut back to town. More than a dozen chose this shunt, leaving 20 others who pressed on over the original route, hoping the rain was no more than a shower. Having believed the weather predictions, none had brought rain-gear.

Charlie had chosen a course easy to follow. There were no turn-offs, hence no wrong choices. There was only one "Y." That was marked by the first riders through, who dug arrows into the dirt with their boot heels to indicate the right direction.

By the time later riders arrived, the arrows had filled with rain-water. The rain did not let up. By mid-course it gave evidence of being serious about preventing another Marin drought. And by mid-course it was too late to turn back—it was just as far to return as to continue.

It was a tough course that Charlie laid out. The Appetite Seminar is supposed to be tough. It led over rugged ridges and mostly up and down. Even the flat stretches became difficult as the rain made the rocks slick and began to transform dirt to mud. This was, as Howie Hammermann had said, awful stuff. In consistency it resembled bread dough. It developed the adhesive properties of Elmer's Glue-All. It sucked at wheels that went through it, and it stuck to the wheels, so that they looked like wet clay sculptures.

Fortunately, for the riders slogging and pushing through the goo, it was early in the season. The roads were only getting their first soakings. Later, when the mud has some depth to it, a bike can be parked in it. The bike will stand, its tires firmly anchored, until its owner returns, rested enough to drag it out.

Atop Pine Mountain it is alleged there is a spectacular view of Tomales Bay. But the view was blocked by the low cloud shrouding the mountain. There is a rare stunted cypress forest, which normally would provide cause to stop and admire, while the naturalist of the group (there is always one in Marin) pointed out the wherefores and the curiosities. But the trouble with a stunted cypress forest, when it's raining, is that it doesn't offer any trees big enough to keep the rain off. And anyway the naturalist isn't around, having already split up the road, desperately trying to get back to Fairfax, to back home, to somewhere that's warm before he freezes to death.

It was damn cold up on that mountain. And the cold got worse on the descent. The windchill factor combined with the evaporative cooling of soaked clothes made for super refrigeration. Riders arrived back in town in a state of near hypothermia.

There was no post-Seminar gathering in Fairfax this year. The Marinites fled to their homes or to those of the nearest friends who could be prevailed upon for hot showers. The outlanders scrambled muddily into cars and vans as quickly as frozen limbs and digits would allow and cranked the heaters up full. And those with only their bicycles for transport huddled miserably at Old Uncle Gaylord's giving thanks the place was open on Thanksgiving, hands clenched numbly around cups of hot coffee, wearing the doubtful expressions of those who wonder if it will ever be possible to be warm again.

It was a debacle, Charlie and partner Gary Fisher agreed afterwards. No camaraderie. No gathering of the group for smokes and repartee. None of the sharing of admiration for best assault on the last rocky ascent, or best get-off on a cliff-side corner.

However, this is not altogether true. These good things are merely put off, pending recovery of the participants. They will be shared in the months to come, when klunker riders cross paths on the Marin backroads, or gather for bench racing in bike-shop backrooms and Marin watering holes. Then the terrible Seminar of '79 will be worked into the legend of the Marin dirt bike underground, gradually transformed from a debacle into the one where You Should've Been There. One of the All-Time Great Ones.

BMX Plus! Review

Dean Bradley was working as an editor for BMX Plus! *magazine when his friend Monte Ward bought one of the first nine Ritchey bikes that Gary and I sold. Monte took our parts list and assembled his own bike, which saved him a lot of time in getting it, so he was one of the first owners to put his bike on public display. These first nine bikes were built like fine European race bikes, and were as cosmetically perfect as their design was revolutionary. Dean's review in the February 1980 issue, reprinted here with his permission, was the first time our bikes had been noticed in print, immortalizing a misspelled name in the title. Reading it today from our current perspective, Mr. Bradley was spot-on in his appraisal.*

The Richey [sic] MountainBike
By Dean Bradley

This month's 26-inch test bike is called a Mountain Bike. Chances are you've never heard of it before, but believe me, you'll be hearing a lot about this revolutionary bicycle in the future. Don't let the Mountain Bike's name mislead you, this bike defies all classifications. It's not really BMX, it's not really a "cruiser," and it's definitely not like anything you've seen before. The Mountain Bike (hereinafter referred to as the MB) even goes so far as to challenge the definition of "bicycle."

The MB is a hybrid machine that combines BMX, light weight 10-speed road racers, European cyclo-cross, and the versatility of motorized trail bikes. The end result is, very possibly, the world's most versatile bicycle.

In the past, bicycle manufacturers have designed their bikes to serve a specific market and purpose. Three, five and ten speeds fit the needs of commuters, tourists, and road racers. Single speeds were confined to short distance recreational rides and light utility uses. More recently, 20-inch BMX bikes offered durability and agile handling, but were uncomfortable for distance rides. For many cycling enthusiasts this meant a veritable stable of bikes. Impressive to some, but financially impossible for most.

The MB offers its proud owner a bicycle for all cycling situations. Riders may confidently go anywhere. If you can't get there, the blame lies in you, not the machinery. At 28 pounds, the MB may be easily carried through sections that are completely impassible by anything but a hiker. Our test riders, being motorcycle trail riders and offroad car enthusiasts, were completely amazed. These bikes went where 4-wheel drives, motorcycles, and even tanks could not have gone. In our test rider's quest for exploration of true wilderness, only hikers and helicopters followed.

If you enjoy getting away from it all, enjoy bicycle riding, and have a flair for style, you should definitely check into the MB. Being the extremely versatile on/off road, street/trail commuters they are, the MBs are the obvious bicycle of the future.

The heart of the MB is the beautifully handcrafted Tom Richey [*sic*] frame set. The hand brazed, lugless construction combines chrome-moly and Reynolds 531 manganese-moly tubing. The forks incorporate a Reynolds steering tube with a custom, extra wide

crown, heavy duty Tange chrome-moly tapered blades, brazed on cantilever brake mounts, and Campagnolo drop outs.

The Ritchie frame features brazed on fittings (water bottle mounts, brake and derailleur, guides and stops) plus Campagnolo dropouts.

Many years ago, Mountain Biking was a new sport with untested equipment. Since then, however, years and countless dollars of research and development have gone into establishing a recommended proven parts list. Each component serves an integral part in the MB's extraordinary performance and overall versatility.

Due to the unpredictable terrain, including hills, and varying dirt surfaces, a super wide gearing range is mandatory. The TA Cyclo-tourist (or equivalent 175-185mm) with triple chainwheels 26/38/48 combined with 6-speed rear cluster offer 18 wide-range gears which proved to be more than ample for any riding situation.

Recommended derailleurs are Huret Duo-Par rear, and a Sun-Tour Spirit [*sic*] front. SunTour ratcheting thumb shifters provide positive shifting with a minimum of protrusion from the handlebars. Chris King sealed bearing headset, Phil Wood bottom bracket and hubs along with Bullseye sealed pulleys allow for years of maintenance-free riding in dirt, water, sand, and mud.

It's no surprise that a bicycle with the above mentioned conglomeration of parts will perform like no other two wheeler. Without going into great detail, it's sufficient to say that the MB handled and performed very impressively. *Very.* If you couldn't ride the section, the MB's low weight allowed for easy carrying. It went anywhere and rode over just about anything. After miles of punishment through cycling situations that, up 'til now, just weren't ridden over, on, or through, the MB emerged unscathed.

With little preventive maintenance, the MB will provide its owner with years of trouble free cross country cycling. Ultimately, the Mountain Bike challenges you to challenge Mother Nature and traditional cycling concepts. If you like challenges, you'll love the new Richey [*sic*] Mountain Bike.

On that note, our test comes to an end. . .

Unless of course you plan to buy a new Richey [*sic*] Mountain Bike. Then it'll only be the beginning.

Clunker Capital of the World

This story, by Richard Steven Street and reprinted here with his permission, first appeared in the July 25–31, 1980, edition of the Pacific Sun.

At unpredictable intervals, determined by whim or the alignment of sun, moon and stars, young men wearing heavy boots and thick leather gloves chug their way up a fire road west of Fairfax, pushing fat-tired hybrid bicycles looking like small motorcycles and variously known as "bombers," "clunkers," "heavy cruisers" and "beach bikes." On the crest where the road meets another fire trail, they rest, set up some stopwatches, prepare a list of those present, and contemplate the race which is about to begin.

Once this is accomplished, someone takes a stopwatch, a duplicate list and slashes his way down the road, a steep descent of 1300 feet of elevation in two miles over gravel, wheel-furrows, rock, deep dust and hair-pin turns flanked by small cliffs.

A few minutes later the first of the riders follows. The rest attack the course at two-minute intervals. Within an hour the entire group has made the descent, racing against the clock, at the mercy of gravity and centrifugal force, often at speeds up to 40 mph, with the best riders—a dozen or so experts who challenge the course as if it were the Olympic downhill, who have memorized every rut and bump and who are willing to pump for more speed when a sane person would apply brakes—negotiating the fire road in about 4½ minutes.

This is the infamous "repack run," discovered about four years ago and so named because when the riders hit the bottom their old brakes—of the Bendix coaster variety—had heated up and evaporated all the grease, a situation requiring bikers to repack the grease before tackling the course again. It is just one of many similar courses, trails, paths and roads which, together with a group of entrepreneurs, experimenters and dare-devil cyclists, makes Marin County the "clunker capital of the world," the center for this unusual sport which uses specially modified bicycles to achieve a two-wheeled form of recreation that combines elements of jogging, skiing, hiking, backpacking and road-racing.

The origins of "mountain riding," as it is called, go back about five years. It began—according to Charles Kelly of Mountain Bikes in San Anselmo—when a collection of Marinites known as "the mountain gang" started trucking vintage balloon-tired bikes to the top of Mt. Tam then riding down via the fire roads. But as the descent became faster and more demanding, the equipment—purchased for a few dollars from Goodwill—quickly broke down. This forced considerable innovation and experimentation, the end result of which was the modern clunker, a peculiarly Marin invention.

The first modification consisted of discarding old coaster brakes in favor of drum brakes, like those used on motorcycles. Secondly, gearing was improved through the addition of a derailleur arrangement borrowed from an old assembly discovered on a tandem bicycle. After that light weight frames were added, followed by a whole series of improvements which cumulatively produced a new breed of bicycle.

What had been a heavy, cheap, familiar, mass-produced, fat-tired, one-speed paper boy's bike became an expensive, light-weight, sophisticated, hand-made, ten-speed, cross-country machine that could go anywhere. Mountain Bike Shop makes the finest such cycles, "the absolute, top of the line, best riding, all-around bike we could come up with after researching it for five to seven years and shattering virtually every part of the bicycle," says Kelly. Price: $1300. ("You can spend up to $2300 for a really specialized model like the Klein road bike," he adds.)

But you don't have to spend that much for a good "clunker." A restored ballooner with 26-inch wheels, special fork, knobby tires, drum brakes and three-speed gearing, goes for between $150 and $400. Schwinn has a $210 model (Spitfire 5), though dealers have a tough time keeping it in stock. Or you can buy an old bike and modify it yourself for considerably less, though the demand for old frames and the shortage of parts may make this difficult.

Why would you want to do this? Because coasting down a long trail on a good clunker is a uniquely exhilarating experience, this owing to the clunker's lack of shock absorbers; the machine tends to chatter and become airborne after confronting a projection along the trail. Hence it is not uncommon to make a 60-foot skid, take a tumble, wrap yourself around a tree, tear up a set of britches or scrape an elbow—all in good fun, of course.

A few enthusiasts have been guilty of flying down Mt. Tam out of control, occasionally wiping out a hiker. As a result, the Marin Municipal Water District, which controls most of the land the clunkers ride, has banned all bikes from Eldridge and Old Railroad Grades and imposed a 15 mph speed limit.

Serious bikers are reluctant to criticize the MMWD, though they are not happy with the ban. "Most of the trouble is these guys coming over from Berkeley with truck loads of kids," says Gary Fisher, another clunker enthusiast. "We are now organizing Marin County Wilderness Wheels (also known as the Fat Tire Fliers), to police ourselves, set certain rules and eliminate the crazies. We recognize Mt. Tam as a special place, politically sensitive territory, and we don't want it abused."

But the clunker craze is not all racing down the fire roads. This is simply the most well-known aspect of the sport. The majority of clunker riders—despite labels such as "The Mad Bomber"—are bike lovers, not racers. They are attracted to the machines more as an adjunct of back-packing and hiking.

"Think of how many fire trails and dirt roads exist in northern California," says Kelly. "There is this huge area to play in. A clunker with up to 18 gears and big tires enables a strong rider to climb about everywhere, traveling three to four times as fast as a backpacker, with much more range, yet in total silence and with far less environmental impact than a horse. In a way it's the poor man's skiing.

"It is hard to describe the connection between the clunker and the backpacker. But you can get some idea of it by riding the Pine Mt. loop, a triangular trail at 1700 feet which meanders between Kent Lake, Alpine Dam and Woodacre. We make that ride every Thanksgiving Day as an 'appetite seminar.'

"I think these bikes are machines whose time has come: sound, sturdy, safe, a good form of local transportation, which is why about half of our customers are using them on the street as well as the hills.

"Right now we're trying to gear up our production operations. We make about 40 bikes a year. But we're aiming at 300 to 400 by 1981.

"Mountain riding is catching on. There are now races up and down the state like the Central Coast Clunker Classic and the 18-mile Tahoe race. There is also a big ride in the Colorado Mountains. And up at Etna, there is this dirt road which is 15 miles long, which goes from 7000 feet altitude to 3000 and has seven continuous miles just like repack. It blows you away."

Inside the Coors Classic

The 1982 Coors Classic was my first exposure to big-time bicycle racing. I had fun, which made me the only person in all that intensity who did. I turned the experience into a magazine article for Bicycling.

The Coors Classic represents differing experiences to different people: to most of the spectators it is the bright-colored, high speed blur of the riders in a criterium accompanied by the unearthly whiff of gears, tires, and moving air. To the promoters it is an endless series of details to attend to, all of which seem to be emergencies. But to the teams, five riders and as many support members each, it is tantamount to a war, and survival is the key to winning it.

I recently had the opportunity to observe the Classic from the inside, while I assisted with the support for the premier American team, G.S. Mengoni, and my perspective on the sport has been altered considerably. For the competitors the event is all-consuming; it is not a game and it does not appear that anyone is doing it for fun. In fact, as the race went on I found myself wondering and even asking the riders: what made them do it? The best answer I could get was something to the effect of, "Well, some people work in banks or stores, and some people ride bikes."

G.S. Mengoni consisted of five riders, Jacques Boyer, AIexi Grewal, David Mayer-Oakes, Wayne Stetina, and Steve Bauer, as well as a support team consisting of coach Mike Neel, mechanic Bill Miller, whose long hours and dedication to his task continually impressed me, Edgar Leano, our Colombian masseur, and his brother Carlos,

who helped with feeding. My function was undefined, since my presence was unofficial, but I acted as an assistant mechanic, ran errands for the coach, washed water bottles, and in general tried to make myself useful enough that my presence was welcome.

A typical race day starts at 6:30 when the support crews get up and put in some work before breakfast. The mechanics prepare bikes, select spare wheels, and pump tires, while the feeders prepare dozens of water bottles with various concoctions according to riders' or coaches' preference.

Rations

During most of the race we stayed in the dorms at the University of Colorado in Boulder, and breakfast was always a noisy affair held in the UMC ballroom. Getting their green meal tickets punched at the door, riders and support crew pile plates full of scrambled eggs, sausage, yogurt, cereal, and fruit. It is amazing to see how much food these skinny riders can put away.

While there is camaraderie across team boundaries, each team eats as a unit. The only subject of conversation heard is bicycles, specifically bicycle racing. Anyone who is into the subject can get more than his fill at the Classic.

After breakfast riders return to the dorms and start suiting up for the race. The mechanics are all on the first floor attending to any last-minute details of bike maintenance, and the hallways are nearly impassable because bikes are parked along every inch of wall. A look inside any mechanic's room reveals greasy rags, cans of lubricants and solvents, a bike on a stand and one or two leaned against beds, and a couple of sweaty guys making an incredible mess of the room while making a bike look like new.

Up in Mike's room, Edgar and Carlos are preparing lunches by spreading cream cheese and honey on rolls, peeling apples and wrapping them in foil, peeling oranges, and trimming bananas to make them easy to peel. Mike makes the tea himself on a camp stove in the dorm room. He loads it with sugar and lemon and pours it into bottles.

"These guys have great support," he says. "What other coach is doing this right now?" He rations out bottles for musettes, for the support van kit, and for the bikes. "All the bikes that have two cages get one tea and one water. One cage, just tea." Each team starts the Classic with dozens of matching, sparkling new water bottles, but as the days pass the collections seem to shrink, get dirtier, and become more diverse as bottles are lost or inadvertently traded.

Battle Plans

As the time approaches for the day's race to begin, the team support personnel load bikes and riders into vans and drive to the start. Along the way strategy is discussed, some traditional, some of it very subtle. "The Czechs don't like the Russians, and they'll work with you against them. The Colombians will only work for themselves, and remember, a Colombian riding on an American team is still a Colombian."

Each team has different goals, and for that reason there are different strategies: some specialize in collecting stage wins, and the easiest way to do this is to win criteriums, which doesn't usually mean much in terms of the overall results, called General Classifi-cation. Riders going for G.C., and this includes the Mengoni team, must be good climbers (because that is where the time is really made or lost) and good time trialists. Hot Spots and primes bring out the sprinters and money men, because primes of over $500 can make the stage win prize money look insignificant. During criteriums much was made by the announcer of Davis Phinney's stabbing an imaginary cash register with his index "phinger" as he collected each of his many primes. On the last day a couple of foreign riders chalked up primes with the same gesture, and I have no doubt that it will spread to Europe, the cycling equivalent of "spiking the ball."

At the start location riders pin on their numbers and start loosening up, riding slowly around the parking lot. The feeders take the van and head for the feed zone, while the support crews put together their spare wheels. Some of the support motorcycles have racks for wheels; otherwise, the mechanics strap together a couple of pairs and hang them across their laps.

The Caravan

Each team is allotted space in the follow vans according to team G.C., the first van carrying representatives from the first three teams, the second with the second three teams, and so on. It was my luck that the Mengoni team was in third place throughout the race, and I rode in the first van with the Russian and Colombian coaches. There was quite a contrast in styles among us regular passengers: we took along a spare bike, four to six wheels, a bag of tools, and a box full of bottles; the Colombian coach took one pair of wheels and a tire; and the Russian coach took nothing, trusting completely to his support motor.

The Russian coach was friendly, although he struggled with the language barrier. On the Golden-to-Vail Pass stage, Eddie B., the U.S. Cycling Director who comes from Poland, drove the van, and the two of them had a lively conversation in Russian. I asked Eddie B. to translate a joke, and he did. "Why are there five Russians in the top ten? Because that's all they brought." The Russian looked pained and replied through Eddie that he thought they could do better, but they weren't used to the altitude.

The Classic is run on a flawless schedule, and the announcer is accurate to the second as he counts down the last ten minutes before a stage begins. Motorcycles, each with a driver and a mechanic, are lined up in two columns behind the starting cyclists in order of team standings, vans behind the motorcycles (the "motors" in race vernacular).

Mike Neel acts as Mengoni team mechanic, not only because it gives him the ultimate responsibility, but also because on the third motor, he is practically part of the pack, and on several occasions this gave him the opportunity to coach our riders. On the Vail Pass stage, Alexi Grewal (in 11th place overall) was dropped at the beginning of a long climb, and when Mike rode up to him on the motor Grewal braced himself for a torrent of exhortations.

Mike was calm, though. "You're riding smooth and you look good. You can catch those guys if you ride your own pace," he said. Alexi put his head down and stayed with it, and just as the pack rolled over the top, he got back on. If he had not joined when he did, he would have lost several minutes on the peloton. As it turned out, he attacked and took third in the stage.

The Gun

The starting gun goes off exactly on the hour and the clicking of cleats snapping into pedals is instantly drowned by the guttural sound of the motors moving out and the clapping and cheering of spectators as we sweep into the street. In the van the CB crackles with reports from the various support vehicles, often delivered tongue-in-cheek. There are so many vehicles that at first everyone just tries to figure out who is who. "Campy Buick, this is Support One. What is your designation, you know, your handle?"

"Support One, this is Campy Buick. Just call us Campy Buick."

The race proceeds smoothly for the first few miles because no one wants to waste energy this early. The Russian coach gazes out the window—he has seen a bike race, but he has never seen Colorado. In a minor stretching of the rules, the Colombians have two people in the van, but they are both so tiny they count for one. The other seats are occupied by the driver, usually John Sipay (a USCF coach who can speak Spanish with the Colombians), one USCF official riding shotgun to watch for rule infractions and list dropped riders, and two or three other people who have enough connections to get aboard for the best box seat view of the race.

The pace picks up at the first Hot Spot, and becomes a contest. No one in the van seems to be watching the pack, but if a rider's hand goes up, everyone sits up to see what jersey he is wearing. There is a flurry of activity when a rider flats; one motor pulls out of line and the mechanic is scrambling off even before it stops. The USCF official writes down the rider's number and gets on the radio with the news, while everyone in the van silently urges on the rider, who is by now back on his bike and chasing through the caravan. Once the rider gains the motors he is back on, because he can pace up to the pack on their collective drafts.

On the Vail Pass stage Jacques suffers two flats, and Mike finds that the dropout spacing on his aluminum Vitus bicycle is different from the other bikes, slowing the changes and demonstrating the advantages of identical team bikes. After the wheel changes he drops back to the van and I hand up replacements along with four or five bottles.

When the inevitable hill starts, the Colombians move to the front and start forcing the pace, and riders start peeling off the back, at first one at a time, then in groups when a gap opens suddenly. Each solitary dropped rider has a desperate look, the knowledge that he is in for a lonely ride.

Farther into the hills the pack splits into two or three groups, and the radio comes alive as the support vehicle drivers try to figure out which one to follow. If there is a breakaway, the appropriate team motors will follow it, so when Mike follows a Mengoni rider off the front, I am the support crew. Fortunately (I felt), I never had to change a wheel.

We follow the break with field glasses until it pulls out of sight, then we get reports every few minutes over the radio from the pace car. Gradually the main pack gets smaller; on the long stages of up to 100 miles it may be no more than 20 riders at the finish.

After the finish exhausted riders collapse at the team van, to be sponged off by the masseur. As soon as they feel like talking, they start discussing the race, asking the coach what they should have done differently or cursing their own tactical mistakes. In Denver, Alexi blew a chance for no worse than third place at the Washington Park Criterium, and was inconsolable.

"I'll never see a chance like that again! I could have moved up three places."

"Come on," Neel says, "you'll get one tomorrow." And in fact he did, getting into the lead break for a fourth place in the Morgul-Bismarck.

After the stage there are formalities to deal with—doping tests, press interviews, autographs, and so on—but at the first opportunity the team heads back to the dorm for showers and massages. At this point everyone is already preparing for the next day's stage. Exhausted bodies and bikes must be repaired in time to do battle again.

Back at the dorm, the mechanics start on the bikes immediately, first washing them with soap and water, then oiling and repairing them, checking all tires and replacing flatted ones, asking the riders whether they had any problems, changing gearing if necessary. This will go on until hours after the riders have eaten and gone to bed.

Meanwhile, Mike Neel and Edgar Leano get started with the massages, a strenuous task that leaves them both bathed in sweat. During the rubdowns the riders are relaxed and receptive to Mike's and their own analyses and projections for the coming racing.

As the days go by, the level of support becomes more and more a factor in the results. Those teams whose riders are better coached, rested, fed, and mechanically supported expend less emotional and physical energy and can recover faster.

The Casualties

Nineteen of the original 75 riders quit or were disqualified, including Steve Bauer of G.S. Mengoni, all for one of two reasons: either they were injured or they couldn't finish inside the 20 percent time limit. Injuries that eliminated riders included broken bones and huge patches of road rash. In Steve's case, he was doing very well on G.C. until he crashed while lapping the field in the Vail Criterium.

Although he got back up and did well on that stage, the damage was done, and for the next week he died by inches, sliding backward on G.C. Because of his abrasions, his sleeping and therefore his recovery were affected, along with his performance. Bronchitis set in, and on the penultimate Morgul-Bismarck stage, which was conducted in a chilling rain, he was close to collapse and barely moving. He quit, however, only when Mike approached him on the motor and told him it was all right.

Over a period of two weeks G.S. Mengoni went from a group of individuals, some of whom had never met, to a team that functioned smoothly as a unit in most aspects. Much of the credit for this must go to Mike, whose personality, experience, and hard work were major factors in the team's good showing. The team was well chosen for this kind of race, and they lived up to most of their expectations although certainly Boyer wouldn't have minded winning the Classic again.

Jacques did well early, winning the Estes Park Criterium, but Alexi became the star of the team, finishing best of any American rider, fourth in G.C. to Jacques' eighth. Jacques had not-so-subtle external pressures because a network camera crew was on hand to record his efforts, and they were obviously expecting him to win.

When Alexi went off the front at Vail Pass and Morgul-Bismarck, Jacques attempted to join him but instead started to tow the field up, and Mike immediately motored up to remind him to ride for his teammate. During the last few days when it was apparent that Boyer was not doing as well as expected, he began referring to the Classic as a "tune-up for the Tour de France."

David Mayer-Oakes rode a team race, and was usually in the main group where he blocked or paced teammates back on after flats. Without making any spectacular moves, he was so consistent in his riding that he finished 14th overall.

Wayne Stetina had a slow start, losing a lot of time in the first mountain stages, but in the last few days he moved up a number of places, and his maturity and experience were steadying factors for every other member of the team.

Bicycle stage racing is the toughest sport there is, and there is simply no comparison to other more traditional sports, all of which end the day they start. At some point about the middle of the race everyone starts looking forward to the time when it is finally over, and the knowledge that it will be is all that keeps some going. The post-race banquet for all the participants is wildly exuberant, because for the first time in two weeks, no one is worrying about tomorrow. But they're all talking about what they'll do different next year.

Flyer Jets to Japan

In 1984 I was invited to the first Japanese national mountain bike championships. I joined Fat Tire Flyer *publisher Denise Caramagno, Tom Ritchey, Dale Stetina, and Dale's wife, Anne. I had no idea what to expect, which was a good thing because I would have been wrong about everything. This article ran in the* Fat Tire Flyer.

During the first week in August, your hardworking *Flyer* staff jammed over to Japan to cover the story on the first mountain bike race to be held anywhere in Asia.

The things we do for our readers. In order to properly research the race we had to have a wonderful time, but that was only a side-effect unrelated to our main purpose. Really.

Denise and I were guests of a Japanese magazine, *Be-Pal*, as were Tom Ritchey, and Dale and Anne Stetina. Our mission, as we understood it, was to help them introduce the concept of mountain bike racing to Japan.

We won't bore you with details of plane flight, being met at the airport by hosts, impressions of Tokyo, our nice hotel, the tea ceremony, big dinner, interview, hot/humid, subway everywhere, spend three days, finally Bullet Train, 150 miles north, mountains, Minakami. There, that sentence saved you three days.

We arrived in Minakami on the afternoon of Friday, August 3. The town is major enough to have the Bullet Train stop there, but it is still a rural area where small farms and truck gardens sprout out of nearly every level or semi-level space. On the steep hillsides there are cleared lanes in the thick forest, where ski lift towers are visible on the steep mountainsides. There is thick, lush grass five feet deep on some slopes, and even though this is a ski area, it is hot and humid. The heat, thick grass, and the gentle singing of one insect in particular that made a chain saw sound like Mozart by comparison, were reminiscent of every jungle movie ever released.

But we digress. We'll skip the accounts of the hot spring baths behind the inn where we stayed or the views from our rooms of the imposing mountains towering over the valley. Our hotel was a mile or so up the hill from town, where the road narrows to one lane and then turns to a path. The inn was a Ryokam, a more traditional kind of lodging than the hotel in Tokyo. Guests parked all their shoes beside the front door, then wore slippers which were stacked near the door, one size fits all (too small).

Saturday morning gave us our first opportunity to really ride our bikes. Dale and I took advantage of our lingering jetlag which had us all jumping out of bed at five and six in the morning, and took off on the trail leading uphill from the inn. It turned into a stairway to a house and we retraced our path, taking instead the paved road toward Minakami. One thing that took getting used to was the concept of riding on the left side of the road; our instincts were to dodge to the right when we met vehicles rounding corners. When the driver steered to the same side, it was just like that car ad, "Oh-oh, oh, oh, what a feeling. . . ([name of Japanese automobile])."

We explored every dirt road we saw leading off the pavement, but each one we tried led to a residence, usually sited between carefully tended truck gardens where there were women working in the last coolness of the day, which was already beginning to heat up. Riding on the main road we used our off-road capability to dodge a couple of dump trucks where were also on the road early. Although most of the vehicles in Japan, including trucks, are smaller than what we are used to, the roads are smaller as well, and we gained a certain amount of respect for the little ladies who pedal their one-speeds slowly around the towns. No wonder mountain bikers in Japan were ready for a race where the only obstacles were natural.

The last road we explored was a service road for a ski lift line, and we pushed our bikes uphill until the trail petered out. Turning around, we found an excellent trail that had been recently maintained and was perfectly groomed for the quick trip down, evidently a ski trail. At the bottom, Dale kept me from becoming a hood ornament by reminding me which side of the road I should be riding on, and sure enough, a car came zooming by seconds after I switched to the proper side. With no shoulder on the road, and lush growth right to the edge of the pavement, there isn't much room to dodge.

Breakfast back at the hotel was not the ham 'n' eggs American style we had been having in Tokyo. Here it was a traditional meal with fish, rice, a raw egg, pickles, and so on. I'll bet you would rather I talked about bikes.

After breakfast we got together with several engineers and designers from the 3Rensho bicycle company, who wanted our opinions on some new and experimental designs they had built. At the same time we were checking out bikes, we were to check out the race course that they were planning to use.

The site was only a half-mile from the inn, on a road Dale and I hadn't tried. When we got there, we asked a few questions about how long the race was, and we were more than a little surprised to find that it was a downhill event only, with a dual slalom afterward. Total distance: less than two miles.

We were asked by our hosts, "How far do you race?" They were surprised to hear that we raced 20 to 30 miles, having heard mostly of our downhill events. Dale in particular is a distance specialist, having won the Coors Classic recently, and one who considers his mountain bike handling ability a shorter suit for him than strength. He was not thrilled by the format, since by this time he was looking for some real exercise, about 50 miles of hard riding.

The bikes we looked at were for the most part not as high-performance as the three Tom Ritchey bikes we had brought. Although there were a number of new ideas, some seemed to be elaborate cures for non-existent problems. A couple of good ones: bash plate under bottom bracket, and a shield to keep the chain from bouncing down between the chainstay and tire. A couple of bad ones: strange structural bracings, weird frame designs.

We tried to be circumspect about our criticisms. After all, these people were our hosts. We took each bike for a ride before making any comments about the equipment, but we had to confess eventually that we liked our reasonably simple bikes, and as the saying goes, "If it ain't broke, don't fix it."

We tested bikes and checked out the downhill course for an hour or so, until the temperature and humidity reached a point where we felt less and less like testing bikes. We adjourned for lunch in

Minakami. Over noodles and fruit in a small restaurant, we decided to spend the afternoon sightseeing in the mountains above the town.

We rode in a van up the hill, on a road that became progressively narrower, winding through lush forests. At an area where a ski tram was running we parked the truck and bought tickets to the top of the mountain, a 20-minute ride in a small car dangling from a cable.

The first thing we saw at the top of the tram was a small group of three mountain bikers riding down a hill to the tram station, and we hailed them when they approached. Through Suzuki, our translator, we introduced ourselves, and at the sound of Tom Ritchey's name their eyes widened. These were some of the riders who would be participating the next day, and they had already seen publicity with our names.

It turned out that the three had found on a topo map what looked to be a passable road from the tramway down to our inn, and they had explored it only to find it washed out and impassable. Now they were folding their bikes into nylon bags to take back down on the tram.

We abandoned the hilltop when it began to rain, and headed back to the inn for another round of baths before the party that was scheduled for that evening.

At this point I had not yet been issued a bike to use in the races, and late that afternoon Tom and I went to the place a mile or so from our inn where most of the cyclists were camped. Arriving at another small inn next to the river, we saw a crowd of mountain bikers that would have done justice to any event in the United States, at least a hundred riders with more arriving. The bike I was to use was on a stand being attended to by no fewer than three mechanics, and as I inspected it, Tom was surrounded by admiring fans.

The mechanics pronounced the bike ready, so I jumped on it for a test spin, and immediately found four or five things that needed adjusting. I returned it with my comments, and once again the mechanics pounced on it. The frame was custom built for SunTour, and the bike was primarily for display purposes. The brakes were the new SunTour/Cunningham power cam, thoroughly adequate to the task, and all the other equipment was first-rate. I missed my Hite-Rite spring though; in only a few months of using it I had become attached. By now Tom was autographing T-shirts, and I even had to do one (fame by association, no doubt).

One thing we noticed at the gathering was the remarkable diversity of bikes; there were more different designs on display than I had ever seen at an off-road event, and it almost looked as though there were no two bikes alike. Although they bore names of manufacturers that were familiar to American riders, many of the bikes were like nothing in the States. Because there is a high proportion of riders with short legs in Japan, they had come up with interesting designs for small bikes; other bikes featured unusual frame bracing or custom treatments.

That night there was a party for all the participants in the MTB Meeting, featuring a Japanese band playing only American hits, and as an extra attraction, the introduction of Five Famous Mountainbikers to the local riders. The band, all wearing cowboy hats and boots, played one last Creedence Clearwater hit, and took a break while we greeted our public. Tom, whose name translates roughly as "To-mu Ritchey-san," was obviously the only name familiar to the crowd, but each of us in turn stepped up and made a brief speech, speaking quickly so that even those in the audience who understood English would not be able to catch the embarrassed mumblings. "Thank-you-very-much, we're very honored, win one for the Gipper, it's not whether you win or lose, it's the thought that counts, do you know me?, this Bud's for you, good night." Wild applause.

The party was still going strong when we left for the short van ride back to the inn and one more dip in the hot spring.

Breakfast was early the next morning because the race began at nine. When we rode up to the race area there were start and finish banners stretched across the road in several places, and more than a hundred riders in a wild variety of fat attire milled about the finish line or trudged up the hill toward the starting line.

A trail had been chopped in the thick grass on the steep hillside above the start area, and like ants or perhaps Sherpas struggling up Everest, dozens of people hiked (with and without bikes) toward a flat area several hundred feet above. We didn't know what was up, but everyone seemed to be headed that way, and we joined them, Tom and I carrying our bikes up. The steep climb and the heat and humidity instantly had our shirts wringing wet. When we reached the plateau we found the reason for the gathering: the pre-race speech was given here by one of our hosts, a Mr. Hiraki, then photos were taken, with our small group pushed into the front row for a long series of shots.

After the photo session everyone who had a bike attempted to ride it down to the starting line, with very few successfully negotiating the steep trail. Near the bottom where it was steepest, riders would now and then disappear with a yell into the tall grass, where a rear wheel would surface briefly like the flukes of a sounding whale.

Because we were expected to win, we had been told that we would not be awarded any prizes. (The trip was a pretty nice prize anyway.) However, in the event one of us killed himself/herself, they wanted everyone to see it, so we started first. Tom Ritchey drew the first shot, and when he took off down the first steep straightaway the starter almost swallowed his whistle. Dale was supposed to go second, but he was still on his way up the hill, so I lined up for the second start, thirty seconds behind Tom.

The starter was still watching Tom though, and then he looked at his clock and said "Go," with no countdown or warning.

"Huh?"

"Five, four, three, ni, ichi . . . go!"

As I took off I knew I wasn't going to match Tom's derring-do, but with the ability we sometimes have to think about two things at once, I remembered that I wasn't wearing a helmet, gloves, long sleeves or pants, and that I wouldn't get a prize anyway.

In spite of not feeling any pressure to perform, I managed to spin out on the first sharp turn, which is a slow way to take the turn but looks great in photos. A couple more sharp turns, a few ruts and rocks, a lashing from the plants overhanging the inside lines on the curves, then a stretch of pavement and . . .wait a minute! Uphill! My mother didn't raise me for this!

The climb was perhaps a quarter of a mile or a little farther. En route to the finish banner I met a truck that filled the little dirt road, then weaved my way between a few hikers before scrambling up the last pitch. At the finish line I collapsed in a sweating, panting heap, and a dozen cameras recorded the results of my poor anaerobic conditioning. In a moment someone procured for me a dry T-shirt, and I used my wet one to wipe clean my face and body of the mud of dust mixed with sweat.

Dale needed three attempts to get off the line, as first one thing then another went wrong with his bike. Finally he got a clean run, and his uphill ability made up for any lack of confidence he might have had in this downhill. Denise came in some two minutes ahead of the next woman.

The dual slalom started while the downhill was still in progress. Two at a time, riders maneuvered through the cones, and after it became known that one side was faster than the other, one line became twice as long as the other.

An announcer gave the times for the downhill over the PA system, and Tom Ritchey was fastest at 4:04. Next was Dale in 4:21, then the first Japanese rider in 4:33. I was sixth, a comfortable half-minute and change back from Tom's mark, and in Slalom I was fifth. By virtue of his convincing time in the downhill and a second in the slalom by only 0.02 second, Ritchey had the crowd chanting, "Ritchey-san, ichiban" (Mr. Ritchey is number one).

There were two events at the MTB meeting that probably won't be found at American mountain bike rallies. One was fire-starting using a wooden friction drill or flint and steel, and the other was a contest for maximum time aloft for handspun propeller toys. The winners of these were presented to the crowd along with the winners of the races, with appropriate fanfare.

Anne, Denise and I decided that we needed to train more, so that afternoon we boarded the train back to Tokyo. Tom and Dale were falling behind on their weekly minimum mileage, so they decided to ride the 150 miles back over two days. They rolled out of the mountains in the sticky heat of the late afternoon, bound for Honjo, 75 miles away.

The next morning at about ten o'clock, Dale and Tom strolled into the hotel at Tokyo. They were forced to take a $40 taxi ride the last 30 miles because even though they rose early and got on the road by 5 a.m., the traffic and the heat on the outskirts of the city made it impossible to continue. Suffice to say we didn't see any recreational cyclists in the city during our stay.

To make a long story only one paragraph longer, imagine if you will in rapid succession: shuttle bus, customs, airport, plane ride (lousy movie), airport, customs, shuttle bus, jetlag. Home sweet deadline!

Giro d'Italia

This is the three-part story on the 1985 Giro d'Italia that I wrote for John Francis.

Giro I

Italy provides a nearly infinite variety of backdrops for its annual Tour, the Giro d'Italia, from Alps to rolling farmlands, from modern, industrial Milan to ancient and beautiful Verona, from the graceful wooden curves of the Vigorelli velodrome to the crumbling marble of an ancient Roman stadium.

The bike race is the jewel, the centerpiece of the Giro, but it's hardly the whole show. The event exists to make money, and to this end 180 men fight a bloody, personal and painful war, which provides gripping drama, while 180 jerseys carry the names of dozens of corporate sponsors, as do the 40 follow cars.

The barriers that hold the crowd off the course, hundreds of meters long, are plastered thickly with advertising. Advertising needs people, and no effort is spared in getting spectators to the roadside for a 30-second look at the race, which comes with a half-hour of advertising. The view may not be great, but what other sport can offer the spectator his choice of thousands of miles of free front row seats?

Two models in jump suits precede the riders, standing through the sunroof of a car; these are the Misses IRGE, the official sexism symbols of the Giro. Their primary mission is to ride ahead of the race and throw out thousands of hats bearing the IRGE company logo along the hundred or more miles. They will be on hand to kiss the winner of the stage while he sprays spumante on the crowd. Then they will kiss the points leader, the mountain leader, and the General Classification leader. Take me to your leader. At no time is any hint given as to what product or service IRGE supplies other than models for kissing racers.

The number of spectators for any road stage is uncountable. For a hundred or more miles there are people lining the roads in the more densely populated areas, although the crowd thins out in the mountains or between villages. Every bike club within 50 miles of the route is in attendance, well turned out in matching jerseys and bicycles. Last year's winner, Francesco Moser, is easily the most popular rider in the race, and his fans go to great lengths to let him know he is appreciated. Signs announce the presence at roadside of Moser clubs, and in the region of the Alps he calls home, his name can often be seen painted on the road in six foot letters.

Although cynics suggested that the course had been designed for Moser, avoiding the long steep climbs where he might lose significant time, the Italian favorite had to settle for second place when all the chips were counted; there would be no repeat of last year's stunning victory on the last stage time trial. Moser kept the leader's pink jersey, the "Maglia Rosa," only through the prologue and the first stage, surrendering it on the second stage to former world champion Giuseppe Saronni. From Saronni it moved to Roberto Visentini before settling on the shoulders of France's superstar, Bernard Hinault.

Nestled in third overall was American Greg LeMond, Hinault's heir apparent. Having a former world champion in a supporting role is a tremendous advantage for Hinault, an example of the depth (and the price tag) of his team, La Vie Claire.

Perhaps most impressive though, were the phenomenal performances by Ron Kiefel and Andy Hampsten of the 7-Eleven team. This was particularly impressive since this was the first showing by an American professional team at this level of racing. By the end of the race, both riders had won stages, and Hampsten finished in the top 20 overall.

Kiefel won on the 15th stage, dropping ex-world champion Gerrie Knetemann and none other than Francesco Moser in the process. Hampsten's solo victory came on the mountainous 20th stage. While no one was painting *their* names on the road, their high placings made a definite impression on both the European teams and the press, since both riders are first-year pros.

While the Americans were getting their first taste of top professional racing, the local villagers enjoyed the spectacle of it all. The race goes through the middle of the small towns along the route. It's the biggest event of the year for these otherwise sleepy villages, and only a hermit could ignore the activity. The schools are emptied for the occasion, and groups of children cheer anything that moves or has advertising on it. On rainy days the children wear identical white raincoats, and when the people come by ahead of the race giving out hats, it's impossible to give just one child in a group a hat, so they all have them. The effect, with the white coats and matching hats, looks like the assembled staff of a midget hospital.

Even though no other type of sporting event has so many immediate spectators, it is unlikely that most who see it can tell what is going on. Actually the Giro can only be adequately followed on television. But if the race is unfathomable from the spectator's standpoint, the heroes are accessible, because the crowd can get close enough to touch their favorites, especially after a finish, when thousands of fans who have waited hours to see a 15-second sprint vault the barriers to ask exhausted riders for autographs. The stars, especially Hinault and Moser, are magnets for people, and if they stop moving, people gravitate to them until they are lost in a swarming crowd. In the hours following a stage finish, fans have the equivalent of an unlimited pit pass, as team mechanics set up shop and clean and repair hundreds of bikes on the streets and in hotel parking lots before an appreciative audience.

The nature of the race makes it difficult for even the working press to get very close to the action, so the journalists who must crank out a couple of thousand words every day use several alternatives to direct observation. Some ride in the caravan or a few miles in front of it with CB radios tuned to the race frequency, keeping track of all the attacks and lead changes without even seeing the peloton. Others ensconce themselves comfortably in hotel rooms and watch the daily live TV coverage filmed from a motorcycle and a helicopter, venturing out after the race in search of interviews.

On a particularly rainy afternoon, the press covering the finish huddles under the reviewing stand and watches the breakaway on television, their backs to the finish line. The lead cars go honking past, but no one turns from the TV; finally, the sprint finish, and still no one turns from the small screen, preferring that view to a wet and crowded glimpse of the real race as it goes by 15 feet away.

Giro II

Today's stage has started, and 7-Eleven coach Mike Neel drives the team's following car also containing mechanic Richard Gilstrap and an unnamed photojournalist. On the roof are four bikes and several pairs of wheels, and inside are more wheels, extra jerseys, raincoats, food, water, beer (for the crew) and most important, a CB radio receiver. This is a good way to see Italy, since the 150 miles will be travelled at bicycle speed, but it isn't much of a way to see a bike race. Because the cars are assigned an order of travel based on the standings of the team's riders, the 7-Eleven car is well back from the peloton, which is invisible ahead of a dozen or more cars.

The CB crackles now and then, when a rider requests assistance, and a car will pull out of line and move up. Those in the car wave back at the crowds, saying "Ciao!" to any pretty girls, until the radio voice says, "7-Eleven avanti." Neel pulls out of line and accelerates between the cars and the police motorcycles, narrowly missing the spectators lining the road. Neel mutters, "It's more dangerous to be a spectator here than a racer," as he misses an especially enthusiastic fan by a few centimeters.

Davis Phinney is riding near the back of the peloton with his hand up, and slows to allow the car to come alongside. "Fifteen cog is skipping," he says, then pulls over while Gilstrap flies out of the car and replaces the wheel. Neel gives Phinney a long running push, and he rejoins the field in a few seconds.

As the car gets rolling, Neel stares at a rider going back down the road in the opposite direction as though he had forgotten something. This is apparently only a demonstration of how slowly things are moving up front, because a few seconds later the same rider casually cruises back toward the pack. During this slow part of the race Neel muses that the Europeans were waiting to see what kind of team would come out of the U.S., and that the team had acquitted itself nobly.

The day wears on, and as the weather changes from rainy to sunny the riders call the car forward one at a time by raising a hand and strip off raincoats, picking up sunglasses, food or water in the process. As Neel hands off a water bottle or musette he instructs the rider to take his hand; he punches the gas and slings the rider right back to the peloton.

"Is that legal?" he is asked.

"Not if the *giuria* sees it, but everyone does it."

Davis Phinney is having a tough day. On a rainy stage the day before his shoes had chafed his feet, and both his big toes are now swollen and inflamed. He tells Neel that every bump in the road is agony, and that he's getting a cramp from favoring the foot that hurts more. Mike takes in the information, then drives next to the car carrying the race doctor, where he holds a spirited discussion in Italian and explains the situation. The doctor moves up next to Phinney and gives him medication for the pain.

As the end of the race approaches, Phinney drifts back again to get his helmet, which he only wears for the sprint. He takes the opportunity to say that the medication is only marginally successful and that he has never been so miserable in a race, but then charges back to the pack. Only half joking, Mike says, "He's not going to let a toe keep him out of this race. We'll amputate it if we have to."

Twenty miles from the finish the pace goes up suddenly to a real racing tempo, and the pack begins to shed riders. Then, a crash. Follow cars suddenly break their neat formation and go all over the road, some trying to get past the pileup, others pulling over to let mechanics in coveralls run to the scene, each carrying a pair of wheels.

A crash is always a crisis. The rider is faced with two alternatives: either get back on the bike no matter how badly he is hurt and try to finish, or quit on the spot. Like the tide, the race waits for no man, but it's hard for a rider to give up on something that has cost him half a year of effort, no matter how much his body tells him to.

Neel and Gilstrap arrive 30 seconds after the crash, but the only rider who hasn't remounted is 7-Eleven's Jeff Bradley, sitting on the street surrounded by spectators and holding a deep gash over his eye. Neel's analysis is rapid, accurate and brutal, qualities that seem to define the Giro. "Get back in the car," he orders. "He's out of the race." An ambulance edges through the crowd, siren wailing, as the follow car moves out again, leaving Bradley by the side of the road to be tended by strangers.

Neel is upset. "He was having a great day, and he was in position to do well on the stage." He curses in two languages. "He had a broken collarbone. We'll have to send him home."

The car overtakes Phinney, riding slowly and holding the bars with one hand, a victim of the same crash. If he was miserable before, he is even more so now, and he is losing a lot of time to the fast-moving peloton.

At the finish line the spectators are excited nearly to hysteria by the sprint, and the excited crowd surges like an angry sea around the reviewing stand where the winner is congratulated, but the story is different at the other end of the field. As stragglers limp in, today's victims of the relentless Giro lick their wounds. In 18 hours they will line up to do it again.

Giro III

The 7-Eleven team will be remembered at the Giro d'Italia as the first American team to participate in that race, but one member of the support crew made as much of an impression as any of the riders. In an event that seems to belong to men only, soigneur Shelley Verses was the only woman working directly with riders. In a race that lasts for three weeks, the support crews are nearly as important as the riders, because without adequate support no rider would last three days. Shelley has earned a reputation among the American riders that made her first choice on the 7-Eleven support crew. By including her on the Giro team, the Americans amazed the European cycling establishment and incidentally received quite a bit of press for that alone. In fact, a female soigneur may have advantages over a male in some situations.

Before taking up race support, Shelley was living in Santa Barbara, California, while studying sports medicine. After becoming involved with bike racing as a masseuse, she worked for the U.S. National Team in 1984. In 1985 she started working for the 7-Eleven team, several of whom she knew from the Olympic team.

"All of a sudden my 'fun' involvement got more serious," she recalls. "I learned all the specialized techniques by watching the other soigneurs. I had what I learned in school, plus what I learned working in the training room, then I learned all the hot stuff especially for cyclists by watching a German soigneur, a Czech or a Pole. I have a combined technique, and I've developed it so it's my own style."

Shelley worked through the Olympics, handling all the road riders, men and women. That's quite a load. "I started at 3 a.m. and I finished at 10 p.m." This year Shelley has worked exclusively with the 7-Eleven team, getting to know the riders and their needs. "They talk to me on a personal level, and they know I can keep things to myself."

Credit the riders with getting Shelley to the Giro. She was not scheduled for the trip until a week before the race started, but the riders pressed for her inclusion, and at the last minute she got the call. "I was nervous," she says. "I didn't know whether I would be accepted by the other massage people who were working with us, and I didn't know whether I would be harassed or whether the team would be embarrassed, so when I got here I was really quiet and careful. People thought I was somebody's girlfriend or wife or something. But after the news started going around they figured out what I was doing."

Shelley wasted no time getting involved with the Giro. "At the prologue I was cleaning up Davis [Phinney] when Moser came over. He said, 'You work for the team?' I said 'Yeah,' and he asked me to rub his legs. I said 'No,' and he said, 'Yeah.'

"And Davis said, 'Moser wants you to rub his legs. Do it.'

"I said, 'Okay,' and started to rub his legs, and immediately all the cameras started coming over."

Shelley's massage must have been effective. Minutes later, Moser won the prologue time trial.

Canol Road

This is the story of a mountain bike tour in the most remote location I have ever visited, Canada's Northwest Territories, close to the Arctic Circle. The story was published in Cyclist *magazine in 1986.*

Having read of the adventures of people conquering remote goals such as the Himalayas, Kilimanjaro, and Mont Blanc via mountain bike, I have always felt a twinge of jealousy for those who embark on these historic firsts, since the riding in our civilized part of the world seems so tame by comparison. This year however I finally had my chance to put my tire tracks where no bicycle had ever been when six of us cycled Canada's Canol Road just 200 miles south of the Arctic Circle in the rugged tundra and mountains of the Far North.

First the thanks and credits. CP Air supplied the round trip from San Francisco to Whitehorse, and several suppliers were kind enough to outfit me for the trip: Bruce Gordon and Blackburn racks, Needle Works and Kangaroo panniers, and Plumline clothing. Also, thanks to Tony Carson at Tourism Yukon for abundant services rendered.

The Canol Road was built at enormous expense and hardship during World War II to supply oil from Norman Wells, which was at the time the northernmost producing oilfield, to Whitehorse some 600 miles away. By the time the construction was completed, the strategic elements that caused it to be built had changed, and it was abandoned only a few months after the first barrel of oil arrived in Whitehorse. While the part of the road that lies within the Yukon Territory is maintained, the 200 miles that lie within the wild and rugged Northwest Territories have now been unmaintained for four decades and are impassible to motor traffic. It sounded perfect for mountain bikes.

The last outpost that can be reached by vehicle from Whitehorse is Oldsquaw Lodge, a summer observation post on the tundra for naturalists studying the unique flora and fauna of the region. In August the birds have shed their brilliant mating plumage and the wildflowers have bloomed, so the operators of Oldsquaw, Nancy Eagleson and Sam Miller, decided to experiment with a mountain bike tour on the Canol. Accordingly three men and three women pushed off on a brilliantly clear day, bikes loaded with gear, for the first ever mountain bike ride in the road's 40-year history. Our crew consisted of Americans Wendy Lippman, Al Farrell and myself, plus Canadians Anne Mullens and Tony Carson, guided by Nancy Eagleson, who was born in the U.S. but is now a resident of Canada.

Only a mile or so from the lodge the road was washed out so badly that no four-wheel vehicle could cross. As we struggled across the gap, our guide Nancy mentioned that no hunters could penetrate past this point in trucks, so game would be plentiful from here on. The evidence of game was everywhere, because the Canol makes a perfect game trail and all the large animals use it. Tracks, and what the locals politely refer to as "sign" of grizzly bear, moose, caribou and wolf, were everywhere. To these we added our own distinctive marks, fat tire tracks.

Low willows grow thickly along the sides of the road, a natural habitat for bears. Sam had told us, "These are wild grizzlies, not park bears. They're not used to people, and they aren't nearly as fierce as people think they are. If they hear you coming mostly they'll just run away. But if you come around a corner fast and run into one, or scare a cub, you're in trouble." Accordingly, we held our pace to a very reasonable speed, and whistled and sang with enthusiasm to give Mr. or Ms. Bear time to amble off the trail.

Riding down a valley, we came on one of the old work camps left from the time when the road was built. The officers' quarters have been turned into a makeshift stable for the pack trains that use the road, and the walls are marked with many scribbled names and dates. In front is a line of trucks that were once parked in a neat row, but have been moved around by the action of the permafrost and the salvagers who long ago retrieved the tires and wheels. A few dozen barrels are stacked as they have been for forty years, and the unhealed scars of a shallow quarry which supplied the gravel road surface attests to the length of time it takes for the tundra to recover from the insult. On a cliff high above the camp a pair of golden eagles observed us from their nest.

Descending to the first creek crossing we encountered another form of northern wildlife, one that seems in little danger of extinction. Canada has 130 species of biting insects and the national bird is the mosquito. These creatures hardly qualify as insects.

At this first crossing some of us carefully took off our shoes and socks before wading across, the last time anyone took such precautions. With water blocking our route every mile or so, we got used to striding into the cold, hip-deep water in jeans and boots. Cold and wet feet are a fact of life in this country, and since everyone has them, it's no use complaining.

As we sat eating lunch on the road we heard the unmistakable sound of a tiny engine, truly a surprise. Presently a tiny trail motorbike appeared, a Honda 70 loaded down with an inflatable rubber raft, a rifle, tent and sleeping bag, food, camera gear, and under all that, a rider who was as surprised at seeing us as were to see him. He introduced himself as Archie Knill, and he told us that he had started the previous summer from Norman Wells at the end of the Canol. Caught in August by inclement weather, he had stored his bike at a hunting camp and flown out, returning nearly a year later to retrieve his bike and complete his trip. He told us of a harrowing river crossing the year before, when his raft had capsized and dumped all his gear and motorcycle. After fishing it all out, he had to disassemble and clean his motor on the bank before continuing.

Archie told us about what we would be facing the next day when we followed the Ekwi River. "I had to cross it seven times," he told us, "but you can carry your bikes, so you shouldn't have any trouble except the last one, where it's pretty deep." We assured him that he had nothing that difficult ahead of him. Archie also gave us a couple of what we were beginning to realize were in everyone's repertoire here, the "I've been chased by bears" story. Grizzlies are more numerous than people here, so people living in the area are bound to run across them once in a while or even more often. No one who told such a story had actually been eaten by a bear, and in fact recorded instances of such behavior on the part of bears are extremely rare in the NWT, but everyone had apparently escaped the Canadian version of "Jaws" by the merest of margins. It seems to be a tradition in the north to regale travelers with bear stories before letting them venture into bear territory.

Our first night's camp was at a tiny cabin Sam had built from the telephone poles that had once stood by the road but had fallen years before from the action of the permafrost. Other materials came from the remains of washed-out bridges, since there were no trees of any kind in the valley. Before we could enter the cabin we had to remove the bear boards: nail-studded, iron-bound boards that were bolted over the door and window to keep out curious grizzlies. One corner of the cabin had been clawed by a bear seeking entry, and Sam had told us that it was because it had smelled the chainsaw oil inside. "They seem to love petroleum products," he said. "They'll drink motor oil if they can find it."

Sam had laboriously delivered a food supply and some firewood to the cabin a few days before, and a bush pilot named Bud Hall had flown a cache out to our next camp. Accordingly we ate very well with Nancy putting together excellent dinners, and breakfasts of bannock, a staple of the north. Bannock is comprised of flour, water and salt, fried in oil and washed down with camp coffee, which is made by dumping grounds into boiling water and drinking the result. There are two schools of drinking such coffee. Some strain the grounds through teeth or moustache, while others chew them thoughtfully while expounding on what fun they are having.

The next day was as clear and warm as the one previous, and it seemed hard to believe that this country lies under ice and snow most of the year. As we followed the valley of the Ekwi, the road deteriorated, until we found ourselves struggling down a canyon with sheer sides and no trace of the road. Ironically, the track of Archie's Honda assured us that we were headed the right direction. Now we started river crossing in earnest. The slippery rocks and the deep, cold, rushing water made it quite a chore to carry a bike loaded with touring gear across, but removing panniers and ferrying everything across in several loads would have taken far too much time considering how many times we would need to cross. Since the women couldn't lift their bikes high enough to keep gear out of the stream, each of the men first carried his bike across and then returned for one of the women's, not out of any displaced chivalry, but for reasons of efficiency.

As we struggled down the canyon, a grizzly perhaps a quarter mile away on the other side of the valley ran into the brush and disappeared. High above on the barren ridge, a lone bull caribou profiled his magnificent antlers against the sky.

It took until late in the day to cover the 35 miles to our next camp, but during the Arctic summer the sun is up nearly all day. Finally we spotted the small landing strip and hunting outfitter's cabin where our food was stashed. Sure enough, next to the strip was our padlocked barrel, so we loaded our panniers with enough supplies for dinner and breakfast, leaving the rest to be retrieved later.

We spent the next day exploring, hiking and fishing in the area, and we were surprised to meet several more people. Although there aren't many in the region, those who are here concentrate their activities around what's left of the Canol. The first to run across our camp were a German couple, hiking their way to Oldsquaw from Norman Wells. The news they brought us of a river too deep and wide for us to cross meant that we had gone as far as we could get without a raft, so we cancelled our plan to strike farther up the road.

A little later a helicopter followed the road past our camp, and the pilot circled and settled in for a landing a few hundred feet from us. The visit was strictly social, and we gave the three men from the chopper coffee. The pilot asked if some of us would like a quick flight, and we jumped at the chance. An aerial touring service, in the middle of nowhere!

Our thrilling ride lasted only a few minutes, but covered more territory than we could have in a week on bicycles as we swooped over rugged peaks whose heights rarely if ever see humans. Then suddenly we were back on the ground saying goodbye. In half an hour the helicopter would be at Oldsquaw, two cycling days away.

When we turned back on our path for the return trip we found the going much easier because we knew what to expect. Still, it took until late in the day to reach our first campsite at Caribou Pass.

As we stopped for lunch next to the river, we were surprised by the sight of a bull caribou running unsteadily down the middle of the stream. A large and recent wound on his neck showed that he had only moments before escaped a hungry predator, probably a wolf. We theorized that the long-legged animal had eluded pursuit by running down the stream, which would have been more difficult for a shorter-legged wolf.

We spent another day exploring the Caribou Pass area, and we had a few anxious moments when two of our party were long overdue on a hike. It turned out that they had encountered a bear, and had taken a much longer route than originally planned in order to avoid him. From our camp we could see Dall sheep on the high ridges, and tracks in our camp indicated that a parade of fauna had passed in the night, including moose, wolf and wolverine.

The weather held until our last day of riding, when skies turned leaden and a cold wind whistled down the valley. Accordingly, we didn't waste any time getting back to Oldsquaw. There is an amazing difference between wet feet on a warm day and wet feet on a cold day. The sauna at the lodge was a magnet.

By late afternoon we were all back at the lodge, clean, warm, well fed, beers in hand, and ready to match bear stories with any local citizen. The next day we would begin the three-day trip back to our civilized haunts.

Universal Bike Review

This was a piece I penned for the March/April 1986 issue of the Fat Tire Flyer. *Reading it will save you the trouble of buying all those monthly magazines in order to find out which bike to buy.*

Everyone wants to see bike reviews in bike magazines, but after reading a few dozen of them one begins to realize that they are all the same review with only a few elements changed, such as the name of the bike and the specific angles of the geometry. As a public service we are printing the Universal Bike Review, which has several uses. First, by plugging in all the right information, you can find out as much about any bike as most magazine reviews will tell you. Second, by filling in your name and address at the top of the Universal Bike Review and sending it to a mainstream bicycle publication, you will become a published writer and forever afterward acknowledged as a Bicycle Expert. (Before submitting the Universal Bike Review to a magazine for publication, be sure to type it onto a fresh sheet of paper and fill in all the correct names, numbers, and adjectives.)

At Last, the Universal Bike Review

No doubt about it, when the engineers at Interplanetary Conglomerates designed the You-Name-It All Planet Bike (APB), they meant business. The first glance reveals a pair of wheels and sundry other parts attached to a sturdy diamond frame, with an excellent paint job and attractive decals. Looking closer, we observed that one of the decals on our test bike was slightly off-center, but this was the only flaw in the finish work, and later tests revealed that the asymmetry didn't affect handling.

The frame is (*choose one*) **brazed**, **lugged**, **T.I.G.-welded**, **M.I.G.-welded**, **heli-arced**, **glued together**, which is by far the strongest method of construction, good for years of reliable service. Tubing is (*choose one*) **Reynolds**, **Tange**, **Columbus**, **True Temper**, **aircraft aluminum**, which has a reputation for excellence unmatched by any other type of tubing. Because of its unique construction, the You-Name-It frame is light enough to race, yet heavy enough to take the abuse of long-distance touring.

You-Name-It frame geometry is the most advanced in the bicycle industry, reflecting years of development. The numbers are (*choose number between* **67** *and* **74**) degree head angle, (*choose number between* **65** *and* **74**) degree seat angle, (*choose number from* **11** *to* **14**)-inch bottom bracket, and (*choose number from* **16** *to* **21**)-inch chainstay. These dimensions and angles are radical enough to provide high performance for racing, but conservative enough for comfortable recreational riding.

The fork offset of (*choose number from* **1** *to* **3**) inches, coupled with the conservatively radical head angle (see above), gives (*choose two adjectives*) **solid**, **predictable**, **brisk**, **positive**, **nimble**, **lively**, **responsive** steering, without sacrificing (*choose two*) **comfort**, **stability**, **performance**, **handling**, **traction** or **high-speed tracking**. Our testers took this bike over the toughest ground they could find, and the bike came back asking for more.

When it comes to really riding the bike, the You-Name-It has performance to burn; the only word that describes it adequately is (*choose one*) **interesting**, **amazing**, **radical**, **indescribable**. The fine balance of aggressive yet conservative geometry and componentry challenges the novice rider to give his best but won't get him in trouble, while at the same time it is advanced enough for the expert without holding him back. The geometry gives excellent traction for hard climbing out of the saddle on uncertain surfaces, and provides stable handling for those insane downhills that should only be attempted under controlled conditions by experts wearing helmets.

The component group is the well-known and nearly universally respected Sumbichi gruppo, which like many of the finest bicycle components in the world, is imported. The shifting was crisp and positive, the brakes worked, the cranks didn't break or fall off, while the seatpost and saddle held us up admirably and the handlebars appeared to steer the bike perfectly. The pedals, hubs, bottom bracket, and headset were well-lubricated, and had (*choose only one*) **sealed cartridge bearings requiring no maintenance**, **conventional loose-ball bearings which permit easy maintenance**.

To be sure, the bike isn't perfect, and in addition to the misaligned decal we thought the end plugs on the handlebars were an icky color. But this is nit-picking, and these can certainly be replaced easily enough.

When Interplanetary decided to build this bike, they were serious about the project, and the bike shows it. When the going gets tough, the tough will get You-Name-It!

(For more information about this and other fine Interplanetary Conglomerates products, please see the four-page full color ad that Interplanetary Conglomerates took in this issue.)

Fun in the Sun

This story appeared in the Fat Tire Flyer *in 1987.*

"You're coming to Puerto Rico," Robert Leith, the race organizer announced rather than asked every time we spoke either on the phone or at several bicycle shows. The last time he told me was shortly before the race was scheduled to take place.

"No way, man. Can not do. Too far, can't spare the time, the sun gets in my eyes, I got a lunch date, blah, blah blah."

A week later, I was getting off the plane in San Juan, and Robert was waiting near the baggage claim area. "I told you that you were coming to Puerto Rico," he beamed. Also getting off the plane was Kimberly Caledonia, winner of the 1986 Chequamegon classic, with her brand new American Breezer.

As usual, my luggage had not arrived with me, the third time in my last five flights that has happened. We piled into Robert's van and took off through San Juan, stopping by Por Fuera, Robert's bike shop, and also stopping to pick up a couple of his friends and a large dog named Jonas before heading across the island for Humacao, where the race would be held. Robert mentioned that some of the top pros from the States were already here, including the Marin Bike team of Joe Murray, George Theobald and Gary Summers, plus Max Jones (Ritchey USA) and Ron Andrews (Fat Chance). Trials Champ Kevin Norton and otherwise observed ace Dave Arbogast completed the gringo invasion, with an assist from the Specialized race support

"team" consisting of Tom Hillard, a few bikes, many huge Specialized banners, and a stopwatch.

Robert drove so casually through the red lights that we concluded that the color either meant something different here, or that they were only for tourists. Pulling up to the automatic toll-taker on the turnpike, he announced to the machine, "Three Puerto Ricans, two gringos, and a dog," before tossing his 35 cents into the hopper.

After about an hour of driving, we arrived in Humacao at the Palmas hotel, one of the most plush resorts in Puerto Rico. Somewhat in contrast to the poorer sections of the island, the Palmas features a perfect tropical climate, deeply blue water and beautiful sweeping beaches. The resort was one of the sponsors of the race, and the staging area was on the vast grounds near the sailing and wind-surfing center.

Jetlagged out, I got up late the next morning, and started looking around for the time trial that was scheduled. I couldn't find anyone, because as it turned out they were already out there racing. Finally, I saw Gary Summers of the Marin team riding through the parking lot and he directed me to the start-finish area, where I arrived just in time to see the last rider cross the line.

Ultimate bummer. It turned out that Kimberly Caledonia in her enthusiasm had crashed her new bike badly, and by the time I got out of bed she was already in the hospital with a broken wrist, a concussion and facial injuries. Later I was shown the ditch where she crashed, and I can only note that it was indeed treacherous, although no more hazardous than obstacles commonly found in other races. The object lesson here is that it is unwise to go all-out on unfamiliar courses until all hazards are identified.

The Observed Trials were scheduled to take place that afternoon near the stables about two miles from the staging area. I borrowed a far-too-small Rockhopper from Tom and headed out there. On the way I spotted a local citizen riding along, and I asked him where the stables were. His eyes widened. "You're going to ride all the way out there?" In spite of the vast distances involved, I was, and in ten minutes I was there.

Kevin Norton and Dave Arbogast didn't compete in the trials, because the course was set up for the local riders who had no experience in trials and these two could have cleaned it easily, but they couldn't resist putting on a show. (In the pro ranks riding in the trials for stage race purposes, Max Jones, Joe Murray and Ron Andrews finished in a three-way tie with one point apiece.) After the crowd was warmed up by watching all their friends attempt the sections, Kevin and Dave rode the course backwards, on one wheel, blindfolded, and with both hands tied behind their backs. In spite of this exaggeration, they still made it look easy.

After the trials, most riders and spectators retired back to the staging area, where local freestyle riders tortured a few bikes for everyone's amusement, accompanied by the consumption of vast quantities of beer on the part of the spectators.

Day two featured the distance race starting at two in the afternoon. It was originally scheduled for three laps of the 13 mile circuit, but at the last merciful minute it was shortened to two laps at the request of the pro element. The afternoon start gave the crowd plenty of time to set up the biggest tailgate party ever seen at a bike race. By race time the number of spectators was in the thousands, anywhere from 2,000 to 4,000 depending on whose estimate is accurate. One measure of the crowd is the fact that the local Budweiser distributor was one of the sponsors, and still the beer booth ran dry. One spectator asked me whether this was like a race in the States.

"Not really. Usually we have the race first, then the party."

By race time everyone was plenty ready. Joe Murray and Max Jones warmed up by taking a wind-surfing lesson within sight of the starting line. Dave Arbogast did the obligatory automotive assault, riding over a beached GM whale, pausing to do a little two-wheel slam dancing on the top.

The crowd went wild. Next he pounded a picnic table into submission. Then he had to stop and sign autographs, either on baseball hats, T-shirts, or the small Specialized flags stuck in the ground to delineate the starting zone, which were all immediately torn out of the ground and presented for a signature.

Just before the race started I got on the too-small and completely hammered Rockhopper and headed out to take pix. The nature of the course allowed me to intersect the riders at several points on each lap by cutting across, so I caught the action in a couple of locations near the start, then headed out for the more remote trails that wound through the densely overgrown hills above a beautiful cove.

The Rockhopper was becoming a liability, since the headset was completely shot, the 17-inch frame was six inches smaller than my bike, and the bottom bracket creaked like a haunted house. Finally, I abandoned it, stashing it in the bushes and hoofing it up the road a few hundred yards. While I did this, I remembered that I had been warned repeatedly by the locals not to leave anything around that I wanted to keep, but the only people in this remote area were those in the bike race, right? I took the chance. Because the course markings were designed to be read by riders going the other direction, I wandered off course for a few minutes, an error that turned out to be significant.

So now you are thinking, "I'll bet I know what comes next." Wrong.

The pro race leaders came by on their second lap, led by George Theobald with Joe Murray in second place about a minute back. I took my photos, and headed back to the bike. To my relief I saw it where I had left it in the bushes. I waved to the sweep vehicle which passed me as I approached it. Then I saw to my horror that the front tire was off the rim! The tube was wrapped around the handlebars! Sabotage! I whistled and screamed at the sweep vehicle rolling down the road, but the occupants had the windows up and the air conditioning on, and the CB was crackling. They disappeared around the corner.

I surveyed the situation. No pump. The tire wasn't even a Ground Control any more. It looked as though someone had switched wheels on me. I took a deep breath. The situation wasn't really life-threatening, unless I found the guy who did it. No need to panic.

There was a need for considerable profanity, however. I accompanied this with a few well directed kicks to the machinery.

Limited options. I decided to ride the bare rim until the bike stopped, then I would kick it the rest of the way. I pulled the tire the rest of the way off the rim and wrapped it in a figure-eight around my shoulders.

If the bike was uncomfortable before, with the too-small frame and the hammered headset, riding with the bare rim just about squared my displeasure. This might not really have been a problem, but I was also toting a few hundred pounds of cameras, which is all it takes to get one good shot.

My slow pace on the alternately rough and sandy surface gave me plenty of time to ponder the situation and plan my revenge when I found the thief. Suddenly, the sound of an engine, and the sweep vehicle reappeared coming back up the road! Saved!

The driver told me that the rider who had taken my bicycle had sent them back for me. I corrected him as we loaded the bike in the back. "He just took the wheel."

"No, he took the bike. Look again."

I looked, and on closer inspection it was true, it was another Rockhopper, same size and color and also with a hammered headset, but it was not the same bike.

As I pieced the amazing story together later, a rider in the race who was mounted on another of Tom Hillard's Specialized loaners had been trudging through the heat for half an hour with a flat tire, when to his utter and complete amazement, he came across an identical bicycle in working condition and no one around. (The only reason he had not seen me was that I had missed the trail marker and for a few minutes had gone up a side road.)

Being a religious sort, the man could conclude only one thing; his prayers had been miraculously answered.

Without questioning the source, whose ways after all are too mysterious for mere mortals, he humbly accepted the heavenly gift, and continued on his way. Of course he realized that the bike had not exactly dropped from heaven, because God would have at least tightened the headset, so he informed the sweep driver as soon as he made contact.

When I arrived at the start-finish, the news of the escapade had already gone out over the CB network. At this point, I still didn't have all the details though. I unloaded the bike, and when I saw Tom on the other side of the parking lot, I threw it as far as I could in his direction. He and Kevin Norton sat and smirked as it bounced past them.

They filled me in, and a little later the actual rider came and offered apologies so abject that I had to tell him to stop. For most of the participants, this was the best story to come out of the race.

Meanwhile, back at the race, George Theobald had won handily, followed in order by Murray, Summers, Andrews and Jones. The first of the local riders was not far behind. Wico Colom works for sponsor Por Fuera, and had practiced on the course for four months hoping to give the pros a surprise, but even out of their element, they were too tough this time. Wico put in a strong ride, and he was encouraged enough by his performance to announce that he was going to follow these guys back to the States and challenge them at a few races on their own turf.

Although the terrain was reasonably challenging, the heat was a major factor in the race, even among the locals who were used to it. The temperature was particularly hard on riders like Max Jones, who had come directly from the Sierra Nevada, where he runs a cross-country ski area. Riders who didn't tote enough water found themselves severely dehydrated and were for the most part reduced to trudging up the last few hills, slopes that they could have ridden easily had they been more refreshed.

Iditabike, 1987

As the editor of the Fat Tire Flyer, *I received an announcement of the formation of a club called Mountain Bikers of Alaska. A note at the end mentioned that the club planned to put together a mountain bike race on the Iditarod Trail.*

I included that news in the magazine, which inspired several of my readers to fly to Anchorage to join the Alaskans for the first event in 1987. The club had never dreamed of the event going national, but with out-of-state riders and coverage in bicycle magazines, it did.

The Captain's voice came smoothly over the loudspeaker. "Ladies and gentlemen, as some of you may be aware, we've had a little problem, but it's under control now."

I looked out the window to see which wing had fallen off or which engine was on fire. But all it turned out to be was an attempted hijack, the old finger-in-the-pocket, would-you-believe-I-have-a-gun? routine that went out with "Get Smart." Talk about clichés—the guy wanted to go to Cuba, but the plane was going to Alaska. Now he's going to jail, but his baggage probably went to Argentina.

But the hijack attempt and the ensuing SWAT, FBI, and National Guard invasion of the plane when it landed in Anchorage faded into soft focus next to the more clearly etched events that took place over the next few days on the Iditarod Trail. The hijack turned out to be just the icing on the wing.

At the airport I got quite a reception, although the hijacker got a bigger one. Laurel Bull and Janet Niichel picked me up and whisked me to the local REI where I spent a bundle making sure I would stay warm. It turned out that I was a modest celebrity among the Iditabikers. All right, maybe I wasn't so modest, but I was still a minor celebrity. The reason for this was that the only notice outside Alaska of the race had appeared in the *Fat Tire Flyer*, and those few paragraphs had resulted in riders from five other states showing up, turning the race from local challenge to a nationally covered event.

From REI we went back to Laurel and Dan Bull's house, the unofficial HQ for the Iditabike, where the floor of the spare bedroom was littered with gear belonging to the other Californians, Howard Drew and Janet Niichel.

How cold was it? It was so cold . . . it was so cold . . . well, it wasn't that cold, down to about zero Fahrenheit, T-shirt weather in Alaska. But it must get pretty cold, because the ice on the lakes is a couple of feet thick.

We got moving long before dawn on race day; the first item on the agenda was the pancake breakfast at the VFW hall. As the riders chowed down, they offered pessimistic predictions as to what might happen out on the trail, such as a foot of new snow or temperatures 40 below zero. The general consensus was that the tougher it was, the better, and one rider even insisted that the six-hour mandatory rest stop was for wimps only. He had reason to eat these words later, when the course turned out to be tougher than even he was ready for.

Everyone had a secret weapon, ranging from the chemical heaters that permitted riders to travel with lighter camping gear, up to sled systems that allowed the rider to tote a huge pile of supplies sufficient for 40-below nights and 60-knot winds. Mandatory equipment for riders included a sleeping bag, tent or bivvy sack, stove, and flares. You can't just go out and buy a sled for a bicycle; they aren't made commercially. So each sled-toting rider dreamed up his or her own, attaching at either the chainstay, the seat cluster or to a touring rack. Because the pannier loads were lighter and also because the trail conditions never got extreme, the traditional touring setup turned out to be faster, although it provided less margin for extra equipment. For future races, organizers plan to examine each rider's equipment carefully to make sure no one cuts the safety margin by travelling too light.

The starting line was on a frozen lake at Knik, a one-saloon town known as one of the hotbeds (coldbeds?) of sled-dog racing; that should give you some idea of the climate. The majority of the people at the starting line were in the race, and the rest were either related to someone in the race, officiating, or exploiting the event journalistically. There was a rumor that a spectator was going to show up, but he must have gotten lost.

Enough preamble. After a couple of aborted countdowns, someone finally said "go" and with the traditional whooping in unison from the riders and the others gathered at the line, the pack shoved off.

The front end of the race immediately turned into a duel between two "lower 48ers," Dave Zink of Minnesota and Mike Kloser of Colorado, while the sled-toters moved to the far back of the rapidly stretching pack. The dynamic duo cranked through the 41-mile Big Su checkpoint together a little over three hours into the race, and Mark Frise of Wisconsin pulled in 20 minutes later followed closely by Alaskans Les Matz and Mark Corson. From here the going got

tougher as the riders hit deep snow on the trail, churned up by the thousand dogs and sixty-plus dogsleds that had preceded them, and kept soft by relatively warm temperatures around the freezing mark. The next 30 miles took them over six hours, and the two leaders pulled into Rabbit Lake a minute apart before leaving together.

The trudging on the trail took more of a toll on Frise, who was by himself, having left Big Su about 20 minutes before Matz and Corson, and when he reached Rabbit Lake he trailed the leaders by over two hours.

Meanwhile, back at the starting line, I was getting all this news over the shortwave, because the plane that was supposed to fly me to Rabbit Lake broke part of its ski landing gear and couldn't set down on the frozen lake. Because the dogsled race was going on at the same time, the planes in the area that might have been available for charter were already in use, and the airspace over the Iditarod Trail was so crowded with small planes that most of the pilots not already out there didn't want to go.

Finally the race organizers found a Cessna 180 four-seater for me and two other journalists, but we could only go to the halfway point at Skwentna because this plane didn't have skis and needed a real runway, if the snow-surfaced strip at Skwentna qualifies anywhere but Alaska as a runway.

In the lower 48, when you get in a small plane, the pilot goes through a checklist of about thirty items to make sure the plane is going to work when he turns the key. In Alaska, where every fourth adult has a pilot's license, he gets in, turns the key, and asks you where you want to go as you taxi down the runway. If you give the pilot a compass heading he says, "Don't give me that crap. Just point." Flight plan? Surely you jest.

We didn't know which way to point, so we just told the guy to fly us over the Iditarod trail to Skwentna. In return, he asked whether any of us had problems with airsickness. I don't, but I was a minority among the three passengers. The other two guys confessed to having a touch of the green face, and the pilot got a big grin.

Even following the trail visually from the start, we had a hard time keeping track of it in the maze of snowmobile trails. Finally we spotted a biker, obviously Nels Johnson of La Crosse, Wisconsin, from his distinctive yellow North Face outfit. Having identified the proper trail, each of us kept one eye on the ground and the other on the sky for other planes in the immediate vicinity, which came along every couple of minutes.

At one point we spotted a biker and asked the pilot if he could come around so we could shoot a few photos. "No problem," and the next thing we knew he stood it on one wing and turned it around in the same radius a Volkswagen turns in. The stall warning buzzer went off, which didn't bother me until I asked later what it meant, and the other two guys turned green. They don't have a ride like that at Disneyland.

Skwentna is a town of 150, but on this day, since it was the first major stop for the sledders, it was the most crowded it ever gets with people checking out the Iditarod. There were about two dozen planes parked next to the snow runway, and a bunch of ski-equipped planes on the frozen Yentna River close by where several of the dog teams were resting.

As we got out of the plane, a teenager on a snowmobile offered to run us around the area for a few dollars, and since we were far ahead of the bikers at this point, we took a ride to the river and spent the afternoon hanging around the mushers.

Concerning the bikers, there was no news except for a shortwave report of the first three to drop out. After exhausting the possibilities of beer drinking and story-telling, we crashed on the floor of the one-room schoolhouse.

Middle of the night. "Wake up. They're here."

"What the hell time is it?"

"Quarter to four."

We rolled out of the sack, and stumbled into the kitchen, where Kloser and Zink were chowing down on moose stew. "I can't believe I just pushed my bike seventy miles," Kloser said. It had taken them nearly 14 hours to cover the 66 miles from Big Su, and then they had wasted another hour by getting lost within a mile of the checkpoint and wandering around on snowmobile trails in the dark.

There was another guy at the checkpoint with a bicycle, a hard-core type named Roman Dial who did a good job of embodying the Alaska spirit. Not having the money to enter the race, he had started with the racers but turned off the trail and by taking an easier route had beaten them to Skwentna by four hours.

Zink and Kloser were hating life. Kloser took off his shoes and inspected a bandaged toe. "I froze this one skiing once, so it's real sensitive. Looks like I'm going to lose the nail. I'll live."

The prospect of returning through the miles of mush was depressing for them, so we held a hasty strategy session between the four journalists, the race official, and Roman Dial. Dial offered to lead them back on the Yentna River route he had taken, and both riders embraced the suggestion.

A little more than an hour after Kloser and Zink showed up, three Alaskans cruised in, Les Matz, Carl Tobin and Mark Corson. Mark Frise had wrestled with indecision about continuing, quitting the race for a while, then deciding to go on. In doing so he had dropped hours behind, taking an entire day to cover the 66 miles from Big Su to Skwentna. In addition to the news of trail conditions we were getting from the riders, the radio and phone reports were that half the entrants had already dropped out. The race was rapidly turning into an all-time classic, if that is spelled o-r-d-e-a-l.

A little over five hours behind the leaders, Martha Kennedy pulled into Skwentna after riding alone through the night. Of all the remarkable stories of endurance that came from the event, hers was the most impressive, since she had none of the emotional support of those traveling in groups.

After resting and eating, and with the news that the return route was much faster, a much-refreshed pair of leaders pulled out into the bright morning sun along with guide Roman Dial. From this point on they had smooth sailing, and made excellent time. But now a new problem arose. Kloser and Zink had become close buddies as they had endured hardship together, and in some respects were not really racing against each other, since when one stopped to adjust clothing or even to admire the scenery, the other waited. But someone had to win this thing, and both felt that an agreed-upon tie wouldn't be appropriate. They decided to sprint the last hundred yards or so across Knik Lake to the finish.

By the time they reached the finish they were ahead of even the more optimistic estimates of their arrival, and it was almost a surprise for those waiting when the two appeared on the far side of the lake in the long northern twilight. Both came out of the saddle to the sound of excited cheering from a dozen people at the finish line, and as they crossed, Zink was the winner by about two bike lengths.

Relaxing afterward over beers and mooseburgers in the Knik bar, both riders allowed that for most of the distance it had been a team effort more than a competition between them, and although Zink was willing to call it a draw, Kloser wouldn't let him. "No way. You won."

The next rider, Carl Tobin, finished nearly three hours later, having moved up a couple of places when Matz and Corson, who were ahead of him, went off the trail by mistakenly following the tracks of some of the riders who had quit the race. First woman Martha Kennedy, like Zink a resident of St. Paul, Minnesota (the two had trained together for the race), took an astonishing sixth place overall, arriving at 4:30 a.m. having once again pushed through the night alone.

Nels Johnson was the only real casualty. Although he is an experienced cold-weather rider, Nels checked the condition of his feet only because the checkpoint official suggested it. He was shocked to find one of them blackened and frostbitten, the result of wearing too many pairs of socks which cut off the circulation. Nels was flown to an Anchorage hospital for treatment, where prompt attention saved his toes; Nels says he will be back next year.

In all, thirteen riders finished, the last taking over two days to cover the distance. Using the lessons learned, the Mountain Bikers of

Alaska plan to make next year's race even better, and actually started the planning as soon as the last rider (organizer Dan Bull) finished.

There is no doubt in my mind that after an inaugural event that had a few rough edges, the Iditabike will in future years become a classic event of the sort that defines the human and mechanical possibilities of mountain biking far better than any number of lap races around parking lots for points. It may not be the national championship, but winning the Iditabike takes more strength, heart and soul on the part of the rider than any other fat tire event. And aside from winning, just finishing is a victory.

Nice Guys Finish Last

By Don "Captain Dondo" Cuerdon

(From August 1988 Mountain Bike for the Adventure*)*
Used by permission of the author.

It takes a special person to cover 200 miles of frozen tundra on a mountain bike in a day and a half; it takes a real mutant to stay out there for three days. With all due respect to the top Idita finishers, I believe the most heart-rending heroics occurred at the back of the pack.

As in any war story, these were ordinary people thrust into extraordinary circumstances. . . .

"I hate this, I hate this, I hate this. But I'm here so I might as well keep going," said Alan Schreiver, pounding his fist into his thigh. He had limped into the warming tent at Big Su Station slightly ahead of me but in a similar condition: wet, tired, and riding a grossly overloaded bike. But there was something inside urging him on.

I knew what I had left. That's what an experienced racer learns through trial and error. I knew it would take more luck and determination than I could muster to make it around the 210-mile loop. But ignorance is bliss in the case of the neophyte. What he doesn't know won't hurt him . . . until it hurts him.

This was the first race of any type for Schreiver, a U.S. Air Force crew chief based in Dover, Delaware. About 6 o'clock Sunday evening, I watched him stumble into the darkness with Jim "Nanook"

Hutto across the Big Su River. They began an odyssey only one of them would complete. Nanook's race ended at the halfway point in Skwentna. Schreiver wouldn't cross the Knik Lake finish line until 10:30 Wednesday morning.

But our hero didn't cross the line alone. He teamed up with Mike Chard and Bob Woolsey somewhere on the tundra. They amused each other by taking photos of their hallucinations. The best was a shot of snow blown against a tree in the likeness of a dinosaur. It was an understandable bit of confusion when you consider these guys sometimes humped for 24 hours straight to make it to the finish before the Wednesday noon cutoff.

At 11:15 Wednesday morning, Curt Eury rolled across the line as the last official finisher, with 45 minutes to spare. He'd traveled most of the distance with Alan's group. He had to—his hands had become so numb with handlebar palsy that he couldn't open his panniers to get food or clothing. He'd tried bear-hugging the bag and pulling the zipper with his teeth, but it wouldn't budge.

When he met Alan's group, he begged them not to leave him in such dire straits. But there was no need to beg. As Charlie Kelly said last year, this is a "brotherhood of pain." Nobody dies trying if someone else can come to his aid.

I didn't know Alan Schreiver well, but I sensed a significant change in his life. Before the race he was like Clark Kent, mild-mannered, unobtrusive, a little goofy. But this caterpillar who entered the cocoon of Iditabike changed from one of life's spectators, to a participant, to a winner in 73½ hours. All the nice things about him are still there, but now he carries himself like Paul Bunyan.

Sitting next to me at the awards banquet, he'd occasionally break into a huge grin and say, "I made it around, didn't I?" more as an affirmation than a question. Yes, my friend, you certainly did.

Gizmo: How to Take All the Fun out of Cycling Without Spending Too Much

At first I tried to sell this story to Bicycling *magazine because, well, they were paying me to write stuff. I attended an "Editorial Breakfast" where we were supposed to pitch our ideas. When I got my turn, I said, "I have this story about a guy who's so anal about his riding that he knows how far and exactly how fast he has ridden every inch of the year, so he never has any fun."*

Every head turned toward a particular editor who fit the description, and the story idea died with the look on his face. When the magazine fired me a while later, this is the guy who got to pull the trigger.

I remember the day Al got his new bike computer. How could anyone know that it was the beginning of a new era in bike riding?

I got over to Al's house on a sunny morning, just as he was unwrapping the little gizmo and inspecting the fragile-looking wires and the gizmo itself and its little handlebar attachment.

"What's that?" I asked, innocently.

"Don't you read the bike publications? These new computers are all the rage. All the top racers use them."

"When I was a kid, all the top geeks used them," I said.

"Those were old mechanical speedometers. They weren't very accurate. Plus, they only told you speed."

"Yeah, I remember Eddie Fallon's speedometer said he was going 60 miles an hour all the time, even when his bike was parked."

"After I calibrate this baby, I'll know within an accuracy of plus-or-minus 0.00062 how fast I'm going, plus I'll know my average speed, elapsed time, and distance."

"What about your IQ?"

"Very funny."

"You wanna go on a ride?"

"I'm going to hang around here and get this thing installed and calibrated," Al said. "Go ahead without me."

The next day I went over to his house again, and he had everything installed and checked out. "Ready to ride?" I asked.

"Yep. And for the first time we'll know how far and how fast we really go."

We took off on a favorite trail. We grunted our way to the top of the ridge, and stopped to catch our breath and enjoy the view. It was an exceptionally clear day, and I said, "Just check that out."

"Yeah, we only averaged six miles an hour all the way up here. We could have run up here faster than that."

"No, I meant the view."

"The bright sunlight reflects off the glass and makes this computer hard to read sometimes," he replied. I wasn't sure what that had to do with the view, but I let it pass.

"Which way do you want to go down?" I asked. "The Old Swede Trail is right over there, or we could go along the ridge and back on the road."

"Let's go on the ridge. I always wanted to see how fast you could go through those big rolling downhills. And if we finish by going back on the paved road, we might raise our average speed for the ride to over ten miles an hour."

I wasn't sure why it was important to raise our average speed to that figure, but I let it pass. We got back on our bikes, and Al punched a button on his computer. "This thing has a Time Out for stops. Wouldn't want it calculating rest time into Average Speed, would we now?"

"I guess not."

We started up the road, blasting through a steep set of rollers where the road is wide open. Al got a little ahead of me, and as we slowed down, he yelled something over his shoulder that I didn't hear. Finally I caught up to him. "What was that?"

"I said, we only got going twenty-eight point four-two-three miles an hour. Do you call that fast?"

"It seemed like we were going pretty fast. I got a little scared."

"Well, we weren't going that fast. We were only going twenty-eight point four-two-three miles an hour. Actually, you were probably even slower than that, because you were behind me."

I wasn't sure why that was important, but I let it pass.

"That's a great downhill, anyway," I said.

"It's not as fast as you thought it was." Al punched his computer button again and took off down the paved road. He yelled something over his shoulder again that I didn't hear, and I didn't catch him again until we were back in town.

"What was that you were saying as you took off?" I asked, although by now I figured it had something to do with average speed or distance or time.

"I was saying that after I push the Time Out when we stop for a rest, I shouldn't start it again until we get back up to speed, because that affects our average speed."

"The difference must be microscopic whichever way you do it," I said.

"Yeah, but we fell just two-thousandths of a mile-per-hour short of averaging ten miles an hour for that whole ride."

"So what?" I asked.

"Well, you know . . . It would have been nice to break the ten-mile-an-hour barrier." I didn't understand why ten miles an hour was a barrier, but I let it pass.

Al and I rode together fairly often, but after he got his computer, the character of the rides changed. He announced average speed goals before rides and after the rides he deflated egos by declaring how short the ride had actually been or how slow we had been going. Because he didn't count rest time as average speed, he started riding in a series of short bursts, racing from stopping point to stopping point, at each one punching the button on his computer for the Time Out while he flopped and gasped and prepared for the next mad sprint. I would usually arrive a few minutes later, just as Al got his breath back.

He would always greet me with the result of whatever arithmetic he had been working on with his pocket calculator. "If I can maintain an average of sixteen-point-two miles per hour the rest of the way back, I'll average fifteen miles per hour for the whole ride."

Al hardly saw scenery any more. If you talked about the view, he kind of stared at you and responded with more numbers. The purpose of each ride became the generation of statistics, which he began cataloging and charting on a personal computer when he got home. He started carrying gridlike forms which he filled with numbers at each stop, to be entered later into his computer spreadsheet.

Considering all this, Al was almost too weird for anyone to ride with, including me. We rode less and less, as each ride became an attempt to edge his record average speed upward by a hundredth of a mile per hour. When I saw him around town, he would immediately start spouting the numbers, as though anyone but himself cared. He had pie charts, line graphs, column graphs and spreadsheets in a file folder that he carried with him, and if he could buttonhole you for more than a minute, he would start showing them to you. By now he had added a pulse meter, and he was charting body fat, weight, caloric input, and projecting his miles per year. In his struggle to keep all the lines on all the charts riding, he was beginning to look a little haggard. Actually he was beginning to look a lot haggard.

Even though I wasn't riding much with Al any more, one morning I found myself riding past his house and I stopped in. Al's wife told me that he had already gone on a ride, and she told me which trail he had planned on using. "If you hurry, you might catch him."

I didn't figure I could catch him, but I took the same trail anyway, and after riding a short distance I was surprised to see Al sitting beside the trail next to his bike. As I approached I could see that his knee and elbow were bleeding; he had apparently fallen very hard.

"Hey buddy, are you all right?" I asked as I rode up.

"Yeah, I'm okay, but I broke my speedometer."

"Gee, that's too bad," I said, while thinking just the opposite.

"At least everything else works, so I can get home." He spun a wheel to check for straightness. "It's a nice day to be sitting out here anyway."

"What about your average speed?" I couldn't resist a little dig.

"My what? Oh yeah. Well, I won't be able to figure it out anyway, and my knee hurts, so I guess I'll take it easy for the rest of the way."

"You want to go back?"

"We're already out here, and I can keep up if you want to take it easy. Let's finish the ride."

We rode along casually, and for the first time in a while, Al looked at more than his handlebars and the road directly ahead. "Look at that big tree that fell over."

"Al, that tree went down six months ago. Haven't you been out here since then?"

"Plenty of times. But I hadn't noticed it."

Al was in a talkative mood. He mentioned the fine weather, then he noticed a set of deer tracks and stopped to speculate on where the deer might have been going. When he stopped to inspect the tracks, he stabbed reflexively at the place where his computer should have been on his handlebars, then looked around sheepishly to see whether I had noticed. After a while he picked a flower and put it into his empty clamp.

Finally we arrived back at Al's house. In spite of his skinned elbow and aching knee, Al was in a great mood as he put his bike away in the garage. "Hey, that was a good ride. Do you want to go out again tomorrow?"

"Sure. Uh, do you think you'll have your computer fixed by then?"

Al was already taking the remains of the clamp off his handlebar. "No, I don't think so." He put the parts into the original box, and placed the box on the highest shelf above his workbench. "Let's just go out and have a good time."

Bob Weir MTB Interview

I wrote this for Dirt Rag *around 1992.*

I got the call from my deep-cover mole in the Cannondale bicycle factory. "The Grateful Dead just bought 10 new mountain bikes. This might be a story; do you think you can check it out?"

Since I live in Marin County, California, which is also where the Dead have their headquarters, it wasn't too difficult to get the unlisted number of the Dead office. When you call this number, a woman picks up the phone and says, "Hello," and after some interrogation, admits that this might be the Dead office, who wants to know? "I just heard that you people bought 10 mountain bikes. Is that true?"

"Gee, I don't know anything about that. Let me put you in touch with the publicist."

She gave me the number. "Hi. I'm working on an article for a cycling magazine, and I heard that some of the Dead bought mountain bikes. Can you tell me anything about that?"

"I don't know anything about bikes. Look; I've got a new album coming out, and a video, and I'm working full time on those. I can't help you with bicycles."

Having exhausted the official channels, I went for what the Reagan administration referred to as a "second channel." I called my friend Howard Danchik, who works for UltraSound, the Dead's sound company. "Howard. I just got word that you guys ordered 10 mountain bikes. What's the story?"

"True."

"Are the Grateful Dead really mountain bikers?"

"Not really. Most of the bikes are for the sound crew, but one of them is for Bob Weir."

"Bob's a mountain biker?"

"Yeah, he's pretty far into it. In fact, he broke his shoulder riding his mountain bike."

Now we're getting somewhere. A little further questioning revealed that the reason for the 10-bike purchase (the order was increased to 15 later) was so UltraSound could take out a dealership and get the bikes wholesale. Howard also told me that most of the sound crew and Bob already owned fancy Fisher mountain bikes and wanted the Cannondales as number two bikes for taking on the road or for distribution among wives and offspring.

The fact that Bob Weir was a mountain biker seemed like a good story idea, and I decided to see if he wanted to do an interview about his mountain biking. Once again, this meant getting past the bureaucracy surrounding the Dead. Bob is well-protected, so I sent the message to him through several channels: his personal management, Howard from the UltraSound crew, and mountain bike mogul Gary Fisher, who was my roommate for four years before he was who he is.

Progress. I called Gary, and he said, "I talked to Bob yesterday, and he said some guy wants to interview him about bikes. He wanted to go on a ride with me and talk bikes so he didn't embarrass himself."

A couple more calls to Bob's personal management, and I was told that Bob had agreed to do the interview. After swearing me to secrecy, they gave me his home phone number. Bob lives in a semi-remote location near a network of mountain bike trails. The best way to conduct the interview seemed to be taking a ride together, so we made arrangements to meet at his house. Bob said, "Let's go in the afternoon. I want time to go out and get a helmet before I get my picture taken on a bike."

Bob met me on his deck, shirtless, wearing gym shorts and high-tops, and looking remarkably fit for a musician. Three mountain bikes waited patiently on the deck, where Bob was giving instruction on their use to a pretty blonde woman. I did my best to present a non-intimidating image of a regular guy who didn't want to bug him about the band or blow him away with my riding; as part of this attempt I showed up wearing jeans and a T-shirt rather than full-on cycling togs.

Bob allowed as to how he didn't really understand why bike riders would care for his thoughts on cycling, but he was game to talk. "I'm no expert on bikes, but I have some pretty firm opinions on them." In return, I admitted that the deeper I got into this the less of an idea I had as to what direction this interview was headed, that I didn't come prepared with a single question, and that all I brought was my camera and tape recorder.

"Great. Let's ride and talk."

A few minutes later, Gary showed up and the four of us prepared to ride. For Bob this meant replacing a few small parts on his bike, cleaning and lubricating the chain, and fastening a small tape recorder just like mine to the handlebars. "Is the tape recorder to keep me honest?" I asked.

"Not at all. I get a lot of ideas when I'm out riding, and this is really a convenient way for me to take notes."

We started up the road into the hills. Bob's lady friend was new at this and didn't care to join us on a hard-core ride, so Bob gave her a map and instructions that would take her on a short but pleasant round trip. Bob, Gary and I headed uphill, and I waved my recorder near him while I asked a series of dumb questions, punctuated on the tape by heavy breathing from both of us.

I wanted to know how Bob got turned on to cycling.

"I had a bike when I was a kid; I don't even know what kind it was. I dropped bikes when I was 13 or 14. About my middle to late 20s I took up running for exercise; I was a distance runner in high school. In the late seventies, running was starting to happen, and it got my attention. I ran pretty much daily for about 10 years. I got as high as 70 miles a week, although I averaged more like 30.

"Last year about this time I was on tour in Colorado with King-fish. It was a really short tour and we ended it up in Vail. Between this friend in Vail, and Howard from UltraSound, they dragged me out. Howard had been promising to get me on a bicycle because he knew I was a runner, and he thought I wouldn't have any problems getting into bicycles. He knows that I have an appreciation for 'tech.'"

If there is any passion the Dead and their immediate associates share besides the music, it is an appreciation for things that are well made and work right.

"Howard figured I was a natural for mountain biking, and he was right. He got me on a mountain bike in Vail, and the first time I tried it we got to about 12,000 feet. And I had to do it again the next day. The next day I came home and I called Gary [Fisher]."

Gary Fisher is well known in the cycling community as one of the principals of the mountain bike movement, and produces his own bicycle line. In 1966 he met the Dead when he was a junior bicycle racer, and the Dead, along with Quicksilver Messenger Service, were hired to play a post-race dance at a bicycle race. Gary, who is now bald but who sported nearly waist-length hair during the early seventies, became one of the unofficial "Party Krew."

"I didn't even know who Gary was, but Howard said he had a friend who made bikes, so I called him. I guess Gary remembered who I was" [interviewer laughs] "but I'd never known him by his real name; we always called him Spidey."

It must have been some time since you two had run across each other.

"Yeah, but it didn't take me long to recognize him."

Tell me about breaking your shoulder.

"The second day I had my bike, for want of anything better to do, I rode all the way to the top of the mountain, and that was wonderful, just ducky. I got all pumped with endorphins going up there, and then we came down. I was with a friend who was also more or less a novice, so we were making up the rules as we went along. We were pumped with endorphins, and by the time we got halfway down, adrenalin as well. I was perhaps less cautious than might have been prudent. I hit a particularly pernicious crag in the road, and did what I understand is called a 'Polish Wheelie.'

"I landed in a driveway, right at this guy's feet, and fortunately he turned out to be a doctor. Well, he was an eye doctor, but at least he was a doctor. My shoulder wasn't working right, and my arm wasn't working right, and I couldn't figure out why. I had a bump in my shoulder; I figured it was dislocated. Anyway, it was broken, and I was laid up for about a month."

Did that screw up any band business?

"Yeah."

So you got the hot looks from some of the guys?

"Garcia, fortunately or unfortunately, was also laid up at the time, so it didn't mess up too much. So having seen the pavement, I'm not really anxious to do anything like that again."

That just gets you your membership, though. Once you've done that, nobody can look at you and say, Well, he's not real.

At this point I shut off my recorder and concentrated on keeping up with Bob, with mixed results as nearly an hour later he and Gary finished the main climb a hundred yards ahead. Apparently my non-intimidation plan was working. Shortly after that we hiked another quarter-mile to a mountain top, where we surveyed the Bay Area.

Why don't you expound philosophically on why bikes are the coolest invention since the guitar?

"They're almost as good for meeting girls."

Would you say you meet a different class of girls?

"Yeah, but without variety you can't have a horse race, everybody knows that. But aside from that, I've heard . . . that the bicycle is the most efficient machine ever devised by man in terms of calories expended for work done. Philosophically, I like that a lot. It's Technology, Servant of Man, in its very finest form."

How about a comment on the fact that a lot of people in your immediate social circles have taken up mountain biking?

"It's a really pleasurable form of exercise, which appeals to all the guys I know. I was into running, and I was a real tough guy. I thought bicycles were for yuppies initially, and anyone who wanted a real workout could put on their running shoes and go out the door and get a real workout.

"All the time I was thinking that, Howard Danchik . . . was saying that sooner or later he was going to get me on a bicycle and I would be hooked. And he did and I was. Now I get every bit as good a workout on a bicycle as I did running, and I have more fun."

A lot of runners get more and more into their sport until they reach a point where their bodies start to rebel. Did you ever have any problems like that?

"I was fortunate and I worked through a lot of that. If you get maniacal, you can hurt yourself with anything. I realized that and I took it slow and easy. Bicycling too; I've hurt myself bicycling, and I didn't waste any time. You can hurt yourself doing anything; you could drink a lethal dose of water. There's a toxic or lethal dose of just about anything, and I found the toxic dose with both running and biking, but I realized that and was able to cut back to well within my limits.

"Whatever you do, if you intend to do it for any length of time, you want to adjust your way of doing it, your schedule or whatever, to make sure you allow for fun, or you'll start inventing reasons why you can't do it. And I need the exercise. I also need the fun."

Just so I have it on tape, you said that Bill [Kreutzman] was the only other bike rider in the band.

"And he not much, but that may all change."
Does he own a bike?
"No. If he did he probably would [ride]. He's into running. I'm not pushing him, but I think sooner or later he'll discover bicycles himself. From what I can see, anyone who's into running can get into biking, although there have to be a few people who prefer running to bicycles."
I could never appreciate the pounding on my body.
"You don't do it smoothly enough then."
I have fragile ankles, and I worry about getting hurt running.
Bob laughs, interviewer rationalizes.
All right. What you're risking in injury on a bike is a completely different thing.
"The risk factor is not really in the same neighborhood. It's your approach; in both cases, if your approach is right, it's not going to get you, and if it's wrong, it's going to get you. If you're a little bit careless by nature on a bicycle, sooner or later that'll get you. But if you're a little bit careless by nature at running, sooner or later that will get you in terms of a long-term injury like tendinitis. [By comparison], bicycling got me real quick."

Several nights later, the same group of Bob, Gary and I took a more adventurous ride, a full-moon excursion to the same mountain top, starting at 1 a.m. from Bob's house. As on the previous ride, the pace up the hill was brisk, and conversation was sparse and punctuated by heavy breathing. Arriving at the top about 2 a.m., we watched while the lights of the Bay Area were slowly obscured by fog.

"This is Technology, Servant of Man, this is what it gives us. You were talking about stuff that works right; we made it up here in not much more than an hour.

"I've got a hurdle that I'm just about past, if I can train my way past it, that would put me up here pretty easily under an hour. On certain inclines I've just got to sustain a spin, or one gear that I'm not quite [using]. All I have to do is just get mad."

Bob consults his wristwatch, which he has laid on a rock. "Seventy-one-point-one degrees.

"If there's a fixation that I hold on stuff that works right, this is why. [The bikes] got us here quickly, quietly and pleasurably. Nothing more need be said. For the Gentle Reader, we're sitting on top of a mountain, surrounded by moonlit clouds maybe five hundred feet below us in all directions, with a couple of holes, through which we can see the lights of civilization, peeking and winking at us. All is quiet."

I'll say. Except for that damn cricket.

"A couple of years ago I was in Cabo San Lucas [Baja California]. One of the friends I was visiting had a boat and we went out fishing; I got bored with that. We found ourselves in the middle of a big school of dolphins, I mean acres. I had fins and a mask and a snorkel, and I lost my little mind and dove in and just started swimming along with them. At first they wouldn't pay any attention to me; it's not like they were running away, they just wouldn't pay attention to me. I was sort of chasing them, and I didn't notice how far away from the boat I was getting. I got somewhere between a quarter- and a half-mile away from the boat before I looked back and saw it way off.

"Suddenly I was surrounded by those guys, and they'd come up to me and check me out and swim around. They were curious. They made squeaking and clicking sounds. As far down as I could see, about a hundred feet, and as far around me in any direction as far as I could see, there were these six- to ten-foot dolphins swimming around. Really beautiful; it was just another world. I lost all sense of time and any consideration other than the desire to communicate with these guys. And they were trying to communicate with me, and I was trying to communicate with them, and I don't know that we didn't get something across, because we were all trying.

"God knows what level they communicate on; I don't think they see time like we do. Or much of anything else for that matter."

It would be pretty hard to have any common concepts.

"All we really had was just eyeball to eyeball. I got pretty close [to a whale] on a surfboard once. I was going out to play with a pup where they were breaching. I headed out to play with the pup, and up popped mama. I tried to go around her one way, and she moved a little bit forward, and I tried to go around her the other way and she moved a little bit back, presenting an insurmountable obstacle. They don't like stuff that's hard, apparently, and she could hear the waves against my board.

Gary: "The fog is moving in."

"It's going to be thick when we go down there. I'm going to have to go slow. I'd piss a lot of people off if I got myself hurt right now.

"Why don't more people do stuff like this?"

Everyone wants adventure, but they want it to be safe.

"Or just fun. 'I want to be a real cowboy for two weeks I'm not talking about no Frontierland, I want to be a real cowboy.'"

There are a lot of people who have never done anything remotely as physical as this. . . .

"They could be here too, rather easily, in a few weeks time, if they took it easy, a little bit at a time. It isn't like they would be sacrificing themselves; it would be enjoyable for them, and they just don't know it yet. But they will; I have a lot of confidence in people."

You put the tape recorder on your bike because you said you get inspiration while you're riding. Does the rhythmic activity of bike riding give you musical ideas?

"As often as not I get lyrical ideas; the lyrics come with a melody and the whole thing [is] in a complete package."

Gary: "Riding a bike is one of the few places you can go any more and not be interrupted."

That's true; a lot of people want Bob's attention. In this instance I can get it because I'm willing to jump on a bike and follow you around.

"You get an entirely different side of me, almost necessarily, than the people who get me between the hours of ten and six on the telephone. I'm a fairly busy fellow, and the number you have, only the people I want to talk to have. Even so, during the hours when we would normally talk . . . well, you know what it's like; I've got a billion projects.

"I do it, and I don't mind it so much that I'm thinking pretty fast. My manner of speech and my delivery must be a little bit different when you get me during those hours. I use different language; it's just that I'm in a different world. When I'm up here . . . we went for

10, 15 minutes at a time without saying anything during the ride up here, and I was never under the fear that the conversation would be over and the phone would be down, and that you'd be unreachable on the phone."

Gary: "Haven't you played telephone tag, where you call and the guy is on another line, and he calls back and you're on another line."

"Charlie and I have already done that."

That's right. I talked with [you] yesterday, and [you] got three calls while we were having a one-minute conversation. Bob, your gig is creativity, but that kind of activity denies it to you . . .

"No, that's not true, because I get flying when I'm thinking and talking that fast. I have times of day when [I deal with] mundane matters, like taking care of my gate, my garden, the mechanics of keeping my business rolling . . . I do [this] in late morning. In the early afternoon I get in touch with people with whom I have projects going, and we go through mechanics. By early mid-afternoon most of what I'm doing is going into the meat of whatever projects we're talking [about]. That's followed by a bike ride on a good day, if this is a well-orchestrated day. Then I get back, have a couple of capper conversations on stuff that I've been working on, and it starts turning into evening.

"There are times of day when certain stuff works best. Often I'm not going to be at my creative best when I'm fresh out of bed, but I can think nuts and bolts pretty well."

You say you don't do all your creating on a bike, but you must do some.

"Oh yeah. I don't generally get on my bike until after I've had a few good flings at something fairly creative, and then I get to pack that off on my ride."

You kind of chew on the stuff before you ride, then digest it while you're riding.

"It works out really well that way. On a ride, I'll put the headphones on and remove myself from everything entirely, going uphill. I don't wear headphones going downhill because I consider that to be dangerous. Uphill, I figure if I stay to the right, I'm not going to get hit by anything behind me, and I can see ahead, and I'm not going fast enough to present much of a danger to anything. What are the current modes on that, do you know?"

It's illegal to wear headphones on the streets of California while you're riding a bike. It's illegal in a car for that matter. But I've seen plenty of people wearing headphones and I've never seen anyone cited for it. Current thinking is that you can get away with it.

"For training, it's great; it's just like music in the dentist's chair. You get a better workout.

"When the song ends, I can click the tape off, and what I've pushed aside when I clicked the tape on comes flooding back, and it'll all be different."

So you get your subconscious working on the problem while you devote your higher brain to riding.

"I don't even need the headphones to do it. I can get myself far enough away from what I've been thinking of just by pushing myself to the point where I'm starting to deal with things like pain and . . . my aerobic limit."

I like to think that I get a lot of ideas on my bike.

"It isn't a particularly new way of thinking. Socrates used to teach his classes at a brisk walk. He was a firm believer in the notion that aerobic exercise produced higher thought."

Gary: "Do you do some type of thinking when you're playing your music?"

"Yes . . . it's thought, but I'm not thinking in English. It's just a different language. I really like it, needless to say.

"When I'm on a bike and I'm listening to music, I often bring tapes that I might not normally listen to and might not normally expect to appreciate. But when the endorphins kick in, and I get to that aerobic high stage, I'm a little more open, I can accept things a little more easily, and I appreciate things a little more readily. I'm a big fan of a lot of kinds of music now that I never thought I'd be. It's opened me up, and as a musician that's nothing but good for me. These days I'm really big on Shostakovich.

"For the Gentle Reader's information, the fog has completely surrounded us, and there are no lights peeking through. We are an island at this point, in the bright moonlight."

What's the smallest place the Dead have played in the last few years?

"Maybe the Beacon Theater in New York. It's about 2500 [capacity].

"People think when we play a little room it's a big treat, that it's intimate. We can't play those little rooms. We hear the sound back from the back wall and it scares us. We're into the Big Reach; we're starting to get the hang of playing stadiums."

CODA

It was said by Michael Treacy, former professor of management at the Sloan School of Management at the Massachusetts Institute of Technology, that "every innovation starts as a joke, then it becomes a threat, then it becomes obvious."

Today the mountain bike is obvious—a major component of the two-wheel scene. Online there are scores of people claiming that, hey, they cobbled together something like a mountain bike way back when but never quite got around to doing anything with it. Probably because they knew that their backyard invention would be treated as a joke.

That is where Charlie Kelly and Gary Fisher were different. They had the passion to take the clunker—subsequently renamed the mountain bike—from a joke into a game-changer that over three decades helped revive a dying cycling industry, create new niche industries, and start a new sport with Olympic status.

But when we met in 1977 they were still at the joke stage of innovation—to outward appearances just a pair of escapist northern California hippies who'd assembled some junkyard bikes, having fun with their friends racing these outlandish contraptions down the local Marin hills.

Then they suggested I ride one. After two hours hurtling down fire roads, I was sold. It was the most fun I had ever had on a bike. Did I want one? Gary had devised some 20 clunkers out of cannibalized old Schwinn Excelsior frames. Go on, he said—take one back to England. Just $275. Two days later I collected my very own clunker. I was a convert.

Riding off road was a revolutionary idea. So were comfortable tires. It was infinitely preferable to the then-ailing cycling industry's products—uncomfortable devices that had to compete with cars for road space.

Even then Gary and Charlie knew they were on to something. They were the freewheeling alchemists of a very '60s-style dream. And though they didn't know it, they possessed all the attributes that business schools nowadays define as being necessary for great innovators of technology start-ups.

They had a unique idea, vision, creativity, unbridled passion and drive, total acceptance of uncertainty, a tolerance of failure, teamwork, curiosity, adaptability, and a nose for marketing.

Not that any of this was immediately apparent. Their HQ and Gary's home in Fairfax was a rundown one-room shack in a back alley behind the town bar. Its desperately thin wooden walls were decorated with beat-up cycle frames and bike race posters. Its only table was a sheet of plywood supported by empty six-packs. Every few minutes, or so it seemed, a newcomer, his jeans and T-shirt covered in sweat and dust from some particularly hair-raising off-road ride, would pile into the tiny room—bike and all—and discuss how to fix some part on his clunker or improve its performance.

Gary, a cyclocross competitor then making ends meet as a bike-shop mechanic, was the inventor and a test rider. He knew just what a threat his creation presented and the heresy he was promoting. Charlie, roadie for a local band with a determination never to wear a tie after his army service, was the other test rider, constantly suggesting improvements, tracking down components, then using them until they broke. He was also the chronicler.

Early on, when only a handful of friends rode together, Charlie was noting down and recording their feats. He'd sit for hours crafting the articles, sending them to outdoor magazines, only to have them rejected. Egged on by Gary, he'd rewrite and resubmit. Slowly he got published. Around Fairfax, Gary and Charlie turned several hundred on to mountain bikes. The first custom bikes were appearing.

Word was spreading. Charlie started the *Fat Tire Flyer*, a newsletter-cum-fanzine that would in time metamorphose into a fully fledged magazine. Its style was Charlie's—underground, wry, dry, and irreverent, detached from commercial hype and deeply attached to the off-road freedom the mountain bike delivered. The *Flyer*, and Charlie writing as SeeKay, was the authentic voice of a bicycle revolution in the making.

Not everyone loved the *Flyer*. Manufacturers, who were slowly realizing that they were going to have to climb aboard the mountain bike bandwagon, were never comfortable with it. Few supported it. The *Flyer* and Charlie kept the record straight, refused to hand out plaudits just because of the size of an advertising budget, and were never afraid to call a bike unworthy of the name "mountain bike" if it was really just a cheap, useless klutz being sold as a "low-end, budget-conscious machine."

Conflict with the bicycle business was never far away. It was not that the mountain bike was disliked by the smug, closed, clubby world that in the pre–mountain bike era called itself the cycling business. It was positively loathed.

The joke was starting to become a threat. It represented to hardcore traditionalists and cycle companies a rejection of every one of the basic premises that underpinned bicycling. It stood on its head the very basis of modern cycling—the assumption that the only place to ride was the road. This concept, in turn, made nonsense of the notion that the lighter the bike and the skinnier its wheels, the better the ride. Kelly and Fisher's solid-as-a-rock mountain bike with its chunky tires and heavy-duty parts was a throwback, a contradiction.

It was a hostility I experienced firsthand on my return to the UK. On my first clunker outing I accidentally chipped the chainring. A visit to the local bike-repair shop proved instructive. As I wheeled the clunker in, the bike-shop owner's judgment was brief and brutal: "You can take that thing out of here immediately. If it ever catches on, it will destroy the bicycle trade."

Fortunately, for the millions who enjoy riding mountain bikes in places once accessible only by foot or horseback, Gary and Charlie didn't give a damn about such entrenched attitudes.

They went into business together to build the first commercial mountain bikes. At the 1981 New York Bicycle Show, Japanese manufacturers, less inhibited about what was "correct" and ever quick to spot a trend, flocked enthusiastically around one of their first production prototypes. The Japanese liked what they saw, measured up, and went home and cloned mountain bikes. Senior Japanese bike executives started arriving in Marin, demanding to be taken on off-road excursions.

Europe, the home of road racing and traditional bikes, was not as easy to conquer. Thanks to Charlie, I had become interested in California's other fast-growing sport, BMX, and cofounded the UK's first BMX magazine. This led to meeting Richard Ballantine, author of the eponymous best-selling *Richard's Bicycle Book* and publisher of the UK's main cycling magazine. Richard was intrigued by the clunker and its possibilities. But making the breakthrough in the UK required some creative pump priming. Where the U.S. could boast wilderness, the UK offered just countryside. It required something more to capture the imagination.

Then in 1982 two young Australian lawyers, Tim Gartside and Peter Murphy, approached Richard with a scheme to ride across the Sahara on roadsters and write an account for his magazine. Richard suggested they ride mountain bikes instead, and our two magazines teamed up to import two of Gary and Charlie's first Japanese-manufactured mountain bikes designed by Tom Ritchey. The bikes arrived in pieces and needed to be assembled. Richard Ballantine enlisted a somewhat bemused Gary Smith of the London shop F. W. Evans Cycles, best known for its wheel-building expertise, to prepare the bikes.

Tim Gartside and Peter Murphy's 3,410-mile north-south crossing of the Sahara in early 1983 was a landmark adventure. On their return they were so fired up by the mountain bike that Tim organized the Fat Tyre Five, the UK's first mountain bike events, while Peter Murphy went on to edit *Bicycle Action*, the UK's first mountain bike magazine. And F. W. Evans became one of the first UK stores to sell its own brand of mountain bikes.

In the UK, the mountain bike was starting to become obvious.

—Richard Grant

ACKNOWLEDGMENTS

There are many people to thank for their contributions to this effort, none more than Joe and Connie Breeze. In 1977 and 1978, Joe built 10 bicycles for me and a few others. These bicycles represented a watershed in cycling: the first all-new bikes designed and built for an emerging sport. More recently, he spent nearly as much time studying this manuscript as I spent writing it, checking my factual accuracy and working overtime to provide representative images. Connie read every word and applied her copyediting skills for the final polish, always moving me in the direction of precision. Any remaining errors are mine and crept in around the edges of that process.

Without Gary Fisher's collection of old one-speeds, I might never have taken a bike off-road, and I remain in awe of his knowledge of bicycles and bicycling. Tom Ritchey's phenomenal design and fabrication skills made it possible for two unlikely candidates in a rented garage to change the world. Wende and Larry Cragg captured a brief but golden era with their photography. Alan Bonds, who shared a house with Gary and me, won the first Repack and took the art and science of clunker assembly to peak expression. Pete Barrett created the images that defined us.

Old friends Dean Bradley, Don Cuerdon, Richard Grant, and Darryl Skrabak were kind enough to provide additional material that helps describe the adventure I was fortunate to have.

The membership of Velo-Club Tamalpais inspired me to ride bikes, and the original Repack crew inspired me to ride them fast downhill. The members of the Morrow Dirt Club of Cupertino were years ahead of Marin County in clunker technology and showed us the next step in off-road bikes. The Larkspur Canyon Gang and the Berkeley Trailers Union joined us at Repack at the very beginning, helping to create modern mountain bike culture.

Ted Costantino at VeloPress took my copy and a lot of images and made them into something better than I could have imagined. Finally, I would like to thank my agent, Robert Wilson, for getting me this opportunity.

CREDITS

The publisher would like to express sincere thanks to the artists and photographers who contributed so generously to this work. Every effort has been made to identify the owners of the images. In the event of error, we will gratefully acknowledge any rightful copyright owners in all future editions of this book if we are made aware of their identities.

INDEX

REPACK RACE RESULTS

Site: East face of Pine Mtn., 5 miles northwest of Mount Tam, near Fairfax, California.
Length/Drop: 2.1 miles/1,300' **Format:** Individual Time Trial at 2 min. intervals.

RACE #1   Thursday, October 21, 1976
1) Alan Bonds	San Anselmo	5:12 (the only one who didn't fall)
2) ?	—	—
3) ?	—	—
4) ?	—	—
5) ?	—	—

[This page missing from Charlie Kelly's Repack logbooks.]

RACE #2   Tuesday, October 26, 1976
1) Bob Burrowes	San Anselmo	4:50
2) Fred Wolf	Fairfax	5:19
2) Alan Bonds	San Anselmo	5:19
4) Wende Cragg	Fairfax	5:43
5) Bob Peterson	Fairfax	6:24

*Racers: 9 **Notes:** Fastest dog: Ariel (7:30)*

RACE #3   Saturday, October 30, 1976
1) Joe Breeze	Mill Valley	4:56
2) Fred Wolf	Fairfax	5:08
2) Bob Burrowes	San Anselmo	5:08
4) George Newman	Larkspur	5:17
5) Alan Bonds	San Anselmo	5:34

*Racers: 11 **Notes:** Joe Breeze's and George Newman's first Repack*

RACE #4   Saturday, November 13, 1976
1) Joe Breeze	Mill Valley	4:44
2) George Newman	Larkspur	4:46
3) Fred Wolf	Fairfax	4:55
4) Jerry Riboli	Corte Madera	4:59 (Personal Best)
5) Otis Guy	San Anselmo	5:09

*Racers: 13 **Notes:** Otis Guy's first Repack*

RACE #5   Saturday, November 20, 1976
1) George Newman	Larkspur	4:47.51
2) Joe Breeze	Mill Valley	4:49.58
3) Gary Fisher	Fairfax	4:50.36
4) Otis Guy	San Anselmo	4:50.44
5) Fred Wolf	Fairfax	4:50.95

*Racers: 21 **Notes:** Gary Fisher's first Repack*

RACE #6   Sunday, November 28, 1976
1) Joe Breeze	Mill Valley	4:32.17
2) Fred Wolf	Fairfax	4:37.66
3) George Newman	Larkspur	4:44.58 (Personal Best)
4) Alan Bonds	San Anselmo	5:05.74
5) Eric Fletcher	San Anselmo	5:10.52

*Racers: 15 **Notes:** First out-of-county riders, Berkeley Trailers Union*

RACE #7   Sunday, December 5, 1976
1) Gary Fisher	Fairfax	4:22.14 (Personal Best)
2) Joe Breeze	Mill Valley	4:33.81
3) Fred Wolf	Fairfax	4:40.65
4) Otis Guy	San Anselmo	4:43.59
5) Alan Bonds	San Anselmo	4:56.46

*Racers: 14 **Notes:** Only race Charlie Kelly did not time*

RACE #8   Sunday, December 12, 1976
1) Otis Guy	San Anselmo	4:25.68 (Personal Best)
2) Joe Breeze	Mill Valley	4:27.71
3) Charlie Kelly	San Anselmo	4:57.82
4) Alan Bonds	San Anselmo	4:59.50
5) Les Degan	Fairfax	5:06.46

*Racers: 19 **Notes:** First racer from out of Bay Area, Craig Smith, Sacramento*

RACE #9   Sunday, December 19, 1976
1) Joe Breeze	Mill Valley	4:24.07 (Personal Best)
2) Otis Guy	San Anselmo	4:40
3) Fred Wolf	Fairfax	4:42
4) Alan Bonds	San Anselmo	4:46
5) George Newman	Larkspur	4:47

*Racers: 18 **Notes:** Fast rides, but time to take a break for a few months.*

RACE #10   Sunday, April 3, 1977
1) Alan Bonds	San Anselmo	4:50
2) Benny Neinricks	Berkeley (?)	5:03
3) Charlie Kelly	San Anselmo	5:04
4) Bob Burrowes	San Anselmo	5:06
5) Ron Brookman	Berkeley (?)	5:07

Racers: 9

RACE #11   Sunday, April 10, 1977
1) Bob Burrowes	San Anselmo	4:39
1) Alan Bonds	San Anselmo	4:39 (Personal Best)
3) Joe Breeze	Mill Valley	4:40
4) Fred Wolf	Fairfax	4:49
5) Ron Brookman	Berkeley (?)	4:52 (Personal Best)

*Racers: 16 **Notes:** JB hit a tree. "Breeze Tree" named.*

RACE #12   Monday, July 4, 1977
1) Fred Wolf	Fairfax	4:28.83*
2) Bob Burrowes	San Anselmo	5:01.82*
3) Alan Bonds	San Anselmo	5:03.43*
4) Tim DuPertuis (?)	Mill Valley	5:04.23*

*Racers: N/A **Notes:** *Times listed are not official. Racer's crash aborted race. "Vendetti's Face" named.*

RACE #13   September 17 or 18, 1977 (as last leg of Alan Bonds's cross-country "Enduro")
1) Alan Bonds	San Anselmo	4:27.61*
2) Joe Breeze	Mill Valley	4:52.66*
3) Rob Stuart	Larkspur	5:01.97*
4) Roy Rivers	Larkspur	5:07.57*
5) Craig Mitchell	Fairfax	5:08.39*

*Racers: 16 **Notes:** *Times listed are not official.*

RACE #14   Sunday, October 2, 1977
1) Joe Breeze	Mill Valley	4:34.58
2) Fred Wolf	Fairfax	4:40.95
3) Bob Burrowes	San Anselmo	4:41.69
4) Alan Bonds	San Anselmo	4:42.36
5) Charlie Kelly	San Anselmo	4:58.99

*Racers: 16 **Notes:** First Repack for Kent Bostick, future Nat. Road T.T. Champ.*